In memory of Edward Finn
A role model for complete players now through eternity

Contents

Introduction

· ·

Congratulations. You've already taken a first step toward becoming a better tennis player. Just by picking up this book, you show that you have a desire to become a complete tennis player. And that's where your success starts—with your desire.

Chances are you have amazing potential that you haven't developed yet. Most players do. What holds them back? Often they lack an understanding of the game. I'm not talking about the rules or generally accepted strategies of the game, but the game's inner fiber. There's a rhythm to tennis, like a dance. It's something you can learn mentally with work, and eventually it gets inside you allowing you to *know* that you have to get to the net and put this point away. Somehow you begin to know that it is time to go for the winning shot. This may sound crazy, but for the complete player, it is all part of the dance.

The game of tennis has changed a great deal in the last 15 years. Keeping up with these changes hasn't been easy. While there has been a wealth of new information circulating around the game via television, magazines, and tennis instructors, it's been more difficult to find this information organized into easy-to-understand progressions of how to learn and apply these newer skills.

All of my career, I have questioned tennis specialists, coaches, players, doctors, managers, and therapists, asking them about the services they provide and how they enhance the skills of the players they are working with. Their responses, most of which are represented in this book, have not only been fascinating, but could be categorized into four main skill groups:

1. Stroking skills, including groundstrokes, volleys, overheads, and approach shots (see chapters 1 through 5)

2. Preparatory skills, including equipment selection, physical conditioning, sleep, etc. (see chapters 6 and 7)

3. Mental strengthening skills, such as learning to deal with pressure effectively and handle stress (see chapters 8 and 9)

4. Playing strategies and tactics, such as analyzing your opposition, adjusting to your environmental and match conditions, preparing for matches, etc. (see chapters 10 through 13)

A second thing that holds some people back from their best tennis is wasted effort. They may say they don't have the time to train properly for tennis, but the fact is they are wasting the time they're already putting into the game by working on stages of skills that are not applicable to their stage of tennis development for that skill.

You don't become a star player overnight. It takes time to develop your skills and the other elements of expert play. For some drills and techniques, I've divided the complete player's development into three stages: the *core*, the *mileage*, and the *fine tuning*. No matter what your present level is, you can make crucial improvements in your game. But it's important to know your level for that skill, so you can work on the right stuff. It doesn't make sense to try to fine-tune skills that you don't really have yet. Nor should you keep drilling your core skills when you're ready to fine tune them. I have worked with professional players before whose stroking and playing skills were in the fine-tuning stage, but they hadn't been introduced to core mental skills. Even professional players need to return to the core stage every so often, reviewing the basics of adjusting, rotation, swing, and so forth.

When you have honed your core skills in a certain skill area, you're ready to expand your abilities in the *mileage stage.* Mileage-stage drills lock the core skills into your muscle memory through efficient practice methods so that proper execution becomes a habit. While the core stage centers on the practice court, the mileage stage revolves around actual matches. Consistency, placement, and court positioning are still emphasized, but you'll also learn to polish your unique strengths into court weapons that can win for you.

The *fine tuning stage* is for those who are ready to go the distance. At this point, it's not just about using tennis skills, but being confident in them. It's not about winning this point or that match, but rather making the strong commitment necessary to be a consistent winner. Players at this stage are willing to pay the price, mentally, physically, and emotionally. This requires determination and discipline, on the court and off.

At the fine tuning stage, your mental skills take on greater importance. We assume that your core skills are learned and habitual by now, but that's true of your opponents now, too. What makes the difference? What puts you over the top? Your awareness of what is happening on and around the court, your selection and execution of tactics, and the effective deployment of your unique winning weapons. You must develop focus, concentration, and commitment to win at the fine tuning stage.

Do you know what else holds people back? Unbalanced lives. Another aspect of fine-tuning your game involves sharpening your ability to maintain balance among the skill groups and keep tennis in perspective with the big picture (see chapter 14). Whether you're a pro or a player who plays a match every other weekend, or a high school tennis player you are more than just a tennis player; you have a life. You're a friend, citizen, a son or daughter, perhaps and spouse or parent. Perhaps a student or employee. If tennis becomes your whole life, it will ruin other parts of your life and ironically that will distract you from achieving success in tennis. The complete player strives to be the best tennis player he or she can be as part of being the best person he or she can be. Have fun, but be serious about it. Keep your life in balance and your mind in focus. This book will help you get started—the rest is up to you.

Acknowledgments

Special thanks to my family: Stan Williams, Tessa Williams, and my sister, Tanya Williams. And to all my tennis families: the Daniels family, (Charlie, Markeata, Gordon, and Elliot); the Hill family, (Gregg, Sr., Marsha, Gregg, Lauren, Brittany, Gray, and Drew); the Haas family, (Peter, Bridgit, Sabine, Tommy, and Karin); the Venison family, (Peter, Diana, and Jon); David Harris; the Finn family, (Ute, Andrew, and Eric); the Vargas family, (Franz, Helga, and Susi); Wolfgang Kosheks; Martina Unrein; Jim Thomas; and the Meyer Woldon family, (Sandy and Agi).

Special thanks also to Martin Barnard, Julie Rhoda, Randy Petersen, Thomas Excler, the late Ed Finn, the late Hans Jurgen Montag, Connie Bernhard, Dr. Simon Small, Karsten Schultz, Dr. James Loehr, Bob Brett, Joe Brandi, Tom Seifert, Pat Etcheberry, Bobby Banck, Peter Haas, Rafael Font De Mora, Mitch Adler, Galen Treble, Alexander Raschke, Charlie and Marabel Morgan, Renee Gonez, Tom Parry, Ed Wilson, Mike Meringoff, Phil Irish, Gunter Bresnick, and Uli Kuehnel.

Playing With Tennis SMARTS

Stance. Grip. Backswing. Point of contact. Follow-through. If you've taken tennis lessons, this is what you've learned. Eighty percent of tennis instruction focuses on these elements. And it's all good stuff; you can't play tennis well without mastering these skills.

But take another look at that list. Four-fifths of it—grip, backswing, point of contact, and follow-through—is all about your swing. Yet the swing is only part of the complete game of tennis. It's a crucial part—no question about it—but there's so much more. Every weekend, tennis courts around the world are crammed with people who may have great swings but nothing else. They're partial players, not complete players.

The SMARTS system, detailed here and throughout this book, is designed to round out the process of tennis instruction, to emphasize the swing *within the total context of the game*. If you master the six fundamental skills of the SMARTS system—**S**eeing, **M**ovement, **A**djusting, **R**otation, **T**ransfer, and **S**wing—you'll be playing tennis at your highest level and will understand your game in a whole new way.

> **S**eeing. You need to know what to look for in your game and to *see* what's going on around the court, where your opponent is, what he or she is doing with the ball, where you are in the court in relation to your opponent, and the type of shot you are receiving and sending.

Movement. *Movement* skills include the first step, accelerating steps (pivot sprint, crossover shuffle, and carioca step), movements around the ball, and recovery movements. Many tennis instructors let students figure these moves out for themselves, but proper movement is a prerequisite to hitting a successful shot. Whether you're moving to hit a shot or recovering to hit another shot, the quicker you move into position to hit the ball, the more time you'll have to vary your shot. Great tennis players are like dancers; they have to learn the steps to dance on the tennis court.

Adjusting. *Adjusting* comes naturally to the best players, but anyone can learn this skill. As the ball approaches, you need to make a number of minor movements with your head, eyes, feet, legs, arms, and hands to position yourself to hit the best shot possible.

Rotation. Now it is time to start dealing with the swing itself. The first element of a tennis swing is *rotation*. To get maximum power in your swing, you need to rotate your body in such a way that you store power in your large muscle groups that you can then unleash into the ball. Certain shots require more rotation than others, and you also can use rotation to disguise your intention from your opponent.

Transfer. *Transfer* means putting your body weight behind your swing. Along with the rotation of your body, this adds power to your shot. You want a clean transfer, without wasted effort.

Swing. Swing-stance, grip, backswing, point of contact, and follow-through are presented here with an emphasis on strike zone preference and points of contact for varying phases of play. The differing strengths and weaknesses of varying grips, swing speeds, rhythm, and timing are discussed as well.

By breaking your game down and drilling each aspect of the SMARTS system within your game, you will become the best player you can be.

Seeing

Some players seem to know exactly where the ball is going to be. Others constantly guess in the wrong direction. What separates the anticipators from the chasers? Quite simply, it is knowing what to look for and how to look for it. The complete player—whom all of us serious tennis players strive to be—has that skill.

We see the same thing in other sports, too. In basketball, for instance, the players have to be aware of their positions on the court, where their opponents are, their opponents' tendencies, where their teammates are, and where the ball is in relation to the hoop. In soccer, hockey, and even football, players need to develop similar awareness skills. It's a matter of using soft focus, that is, using your peripheral vision to take in information along with focusing on the ball—observing the whole playing area. By surveying the whole game with this soft focus, players are able to create opportunities to break their opponent's serve, hold their own serve, and ultimately win more games.

Developing Your Soft Focus

Soft focus allows you to read your opponent's intent on each shot, correctly identify the playing cues, and approach the ball characteristics that your opponent is sending to you in order to give you a sense of where you are on the court. Using your peripheral vision with soft focus requires you to train your eyes and brain to take in and process as much information as possible and make sense of it. Here are a few exercises you can practice to develop this skill:

Juggle. Begin with three small beanbags of the same size and eventually progress to three old tennis balls. Taking two of the beanbags, alternate tossing both bags in the air using the same hand. Now with three bags, imagine a box directly in front of you with the numbers 1 and 2 at the upper corners of the box and 3 and 4 at the lower corners. Toss the bag in your left hand (point 3) to point 2 and the bag in your right hand (point 4) to point 1. Start trying to keep all three bags going at once. Juggling is a great way to develop soft focus.

Short-court rally. Start a rally in the short court (service boxes). Rally one ball and then add another. Slowly back up to the baseline. A more advanced version involves performing the same exercise with volleys.

Colors. Practice with different-colored balls. Assign a certain kind of shot with a certain color of ball (e.g., hit all orange balls with a forehand, yellow balls with a backhand, etc.). Have a friend or coach feed you easy balls that bounce around the service-line area. Depending on the color of the ball, vary your shot selection according to what shot you assigned to that color of ball.

Numbers. Mark four numbers on four tennis balls and have a friend randomly throw you different balls. You must then call out the number that is on the approaching ball as you catch it.

These exercises require you to respond quickly to what you see, but they keep your attention broad, so you don't lock in and focus hard on one element. Rather, you are aware of what's happening around you, but you're focused on your game, your next move. You may invent other exercise variations on this theme.

What You See Is What You Get

It may be painfully obvious, but to observe everything happening on the court, you need to see it. One of your most important tennis skills is one you probably take for granted, your vision. On the tennis court, what you see is what you get.

If your eyes are naturally weak, you'll need corrective lenses, like Martina Navratilova (glasses), or Mary Pierce or Mark Philippoussis (contacts). A thorough eye exam will tell you not only about the strength of your eyes, but also about your depth perception and how well your eyes function together.

Most of us have one eye that's slightly dominant. Research shows that the dominant eye's connection with the brain is *10 to 13 times faster* than that of the other eye. Seventy to 80 percent of people are same-sided—that is, right-handed with the right eye dominant or left-handed with the left eye dominant. The rest of us are cross-dominant.

While I strongly recommend a professional eye exam to check vision and determine eye dominance, you can conduct a simple test at home to discover whether one eye is dominant:

1. Roll up a piece of paper to make a tube.
2. Hold the tube in front of your eyes, at arm's length away from your face. Look through it with both eyes and choose a particular spot you see about 30 feet away.

3. Now close your left eye. If you still see the same spot through the tube, then you have a dominant right eye (like Ivan Lendl). Close your right eye; if you still can see the spot with your left eye, then you have a dominant left eye (like Andre Agassi). Some people (like John McEnroe) have central dominance, with neither eye dominant, or only a slight difference.

Adapted from *Inside Tennis* ©1989 by Jacek Rayski.

Once you know which of your eyes is dominant, you can learn to position your head and eyes more effectively. Say you're a right-hander preparing for a forehand ground stroke. As you line up your body for the shot, the ball is approaching on your left so it is closer to your left eye than to your right. But chances are, that's your weaker eye, so your brain isn't getting this visual information as quickly as it could. By keeping the head straight and seeing the ball with both eyes until the last possible moment, you give your brain the most accurate information as quickly as possible. Your anticipation will be better, your shots cleaner and your errors fewer.

What to Look For

On the tennis court, every split second counts. The sooner you recognize the ball's direction or your opponent's strategy, the sooner you can anticipate the ball's arrival. Timing is crucial, and you can get more time for yourself by looking for certain details.

There are four types of visual cues that can help you if you learn to look for them and adjust your play accordingly. First, before stepping on the court, *check out the playing conditions* and how they will affect you. These include the weather (wind, rain, sun), your surroundings (indoor, outdoor, size of crowd), the playing surface (grass, clay, hard, synthetic grass, carpet), the kind of ball you're using, and your opponent's equipment.

Second, look at *your opponent* and learn as much as you can about his or her techniques, preferences, geometry, tactics, style of play, and body type. Even if you've never played this person before, you can observe things during your warm-up and early in the match that will help you plan your strategies. Watch him closely when you're hitting balls to him—notice how he hits back to you. Does he hit short balls away for winners or does he end up hitting a short ball himself? Is he in position, lined up with his hands and feet displaying good body control and balance, or is he off-balance and flailing?

Third, as the adage says, *keep your eye on the ball.* Not just where it is, but what it's doing. Watch to see just what type of shot your opponent is trying to send to you. Is she slicing the ball, putting underspin on it, or varying the height and depth, speed, direction, and placement of her shots?

Finally, *be aware of positioning*—where you're standing on the court when you're lining up to hit your opponent's shot and where your opponent is on the opposite side of the net. If you're deep in the court, you must hit the ball higher over the net. If you're moving in on a floating ball, you need to get ready to attack.

Most of these visual cues become second nature to the experienced player, but you must never stop observing. Tennis success starts with seeing these cues. When you master and maintain this skill, you're well on your way to becoming a complete tennis player.

Visual Acuity

To see properly on the court, you must keep your head still. To do this, you must maintain proper balance. Most errors on the tennis court are caused by poor balance, usually brought about by lack of body control. Body control is the effortless suspension of the *center of mass*—located just below the belly button for men and slightly lower for women—during your best performance. On the tennis court you should carry your center of mass as if you were carrying a ball of jelly in your stomach. Too many uneven, jerky movements cause that ball to roll from side to side, creating a loss of balance. Similarly, compare playing with rounded shoulders and hips back, lunging for balls, maintaining a tall posture by keeping your chest out and carrying the jelly ball. By maintaining this posture, you will appear to move effortlessly across the court as if your center of mass were suspended.

Think of this area as the hub of a wheel. All the spokes radiate outward from this hub to support the tire and allow it to rotate smoothly. The hub in tennis players is the stomach and lower back, with the head, arms, legs, and upper body as the "spokes." If you have control over the hub, then you can move quickly over more of the tennis court and remain in good balance. Your balance improves, as does the positioning of your head for maximum visual acuity.

Stand up and read this paragraph over again while jogging in place, bouncing your head up and down, and swinging your arms wildly. Then imagine how tough it would be to hit a fast-approaching tennis ball with your head and body out of control. Keep your head still and you'll be able to play the best tennis of your life.

Richard Krajicek demonstrating body control while quickly approaching the net.

Movement

The casual observer might assume that tennis is all about swinging, but it's more about footwork. You see Pete Sampras deliver a perfect smash, and you think it's the power of his arms that won the point for him. But the credit should go more to his feet and legs for getting him to the right spot to make that great shot. You can have the best swings in the world, but if you're not in the right place at the right time, forget about it.

Speed is important in tennis, but foot speed is only one part of a total package. You have precious few seconds between the time your opponent hits the ball and the time you need to be in place to return it. We can divide that total response time into *reaction time* and *movement time*. Reaction time starts when you see the ball approaching and ends with your first step. Movement time includes all the other steps you take until you hit the ball.

Many sports involve intricate eye-hand coordination. But if you want to play this great game to the max, you'll need to develop *eye-foot* coordination. As you learn to see everything on the court clearly, you need to translate that information into instructions for your feet. Where will you move? How? Footwork is crucial. The other SMARTS skills of adjusting, rotation, transfer, and swing will follow, but they're all greatly affected by your ability to move quickly and accurately.

Imagine yourself in the middle of a compass. The ball may come to any point on that compass. You'll need different footwork depending on the direction and the distance to the ball. So the first step (literally) of good court movement is the decision of how and where to move. Then comes the actual movement that gets you lined up, with one or both feet behind the incoming ball, to hit it with maximum control and power.

Commit yourself to moving every time you step on the tennis court. Bjorn Borg once said that if you want to improve your first step and anticipation, try to get to every ball within two bounces. Even if you don't think you can get a ball on the first bounce, keep going after it. Eventually, with determination, your anticipation and first step to difficult balls will improve and you will start to reach balls that you previously didn't think you could get.

Getting Started

As long as the ball is in play, as a player you are constantly moving. You're always recovering from the last shot or setting up for the next one. Your opponent is about to hit the ball. How do you start?

The Athletic Stance

Get in the habit of adopting a ready position after each shot and before the next one. Stand with your feet shoulder-width apart and your racquet comfortably in front of you. Slightly bend your ankles and knees and relax your arms. This stance, used by athletes in all sports, puts you in a good position to see your opponent's shot and allows you to start movement quickly in just about any direction.

Split and Hit —1-2-3-4

The best players tend to use a series of small steps after they hit the ball; however, the split step helps you assume an athletic stance, placing you on the balls of your feet, so you can quickly push off and move to the approaching ball. In fact, some of the best movers on the court take two, three, sometimes four steps in place after hitting the ball. They're committed to staying on the move, always ready to go to the right spot on the court at a moment's notice. Granted, if these two to four steps in place are overdone, it is a waste of energy. But, done in a relaxed way, this is a good habit to develop for staying in motion on the balls of your feet.

First Step

As the ball approaches, you don't have any time to waste. You want your first step to be explosive and cover as much court as possible, especially if you have to run a long distance. If the ball is closer to you, try to get the foot closest to the ball lined up where you perceive the ball will bounce. For example, if the ball is coming to your right, move your right foot first. If it's on your left, move your left foot first. It may not feel like the most natural movement, but taking a quick first step, even a half-step, with the foot closest to the ball allows you to create an early foundation from which to rotate, transfer weight, and swing with time permitting.

Moving on the Court

Once you've taken that all-important first step, what then? We can divide the rest of your tennis movement into the following three stages:

- **Initiation**—accelerating movements you use to get your body moving to the ball
- **Control**—decelerating and adjusting movements to put you in proper striking position
- **Recovery**—getting back into position to see and react to the next ball

You want to travel across the court (initiation), obviously, but you also need to prepare to hit the ball when you get to the right place (control) and then move back into position, ready for the next ball (recovery). Good court movement progresses smoothly from one stage to the next. Top professionals blend all three stages of movement when hitting their shots. The following sections present some of the moves that you can learn to do in order to help you flow around the court.

The Unit Turn

After taking your split step when your opponent has made contact with the ball, you are now in an athletic stance ready to move in any direction. The unit getting your body in position to strike the ball, turn is one of the most basic movements in tennis. Beginners often just move their racquet arm back, but the body and racquet need to move as a unit as you rotate your hips, legs, back, torso, and arms into place. You can move your arm and racquet as a unit by pivoting on the balls of your feet. Now if you have to hit the ball quickly, the racquet is already in position.

The Unit Turn Sprint

The maximum distance you'll ever have to move on a tennis court is about 46 feet, and for most shots you'll only need to travel 6 to 18 feet. Within this range, use the unit turn sprint. Do the unit turn first to get your body prepared for your stroke, and then sprint to the ball. When sprinting, remember to stay low and work your arms, keeping your racquet out in front of your body.

Shuffle Steps

If you don't have to cross the entire court, shuffle steps will help you. These short, quick movements allow you to cover an area of two to six feet in any direction.

There are several types of shuffle steps you can drill and use in your match:

- *Lateral shuffles* (side to side, while facing the net) help you to change directions quickly. This is useful if your opponent plays balls behind you.
- *Fore/aft shuffles* help you to stay sideways while moving forward or backward to your shots.
- *Crossover shuffles* help you to quickly cover distances of four to six feet by using an explosive crossover step followed by shuffle steps. For instance, if you're recovering after hitting a wide forehand, let your right foot move across your left, going into shuffles to get back into position.
- *Diagonal shuffles* help you to get back into position after a shot. These require a stronger amount of rotation of the hips and torso.
- *Airborne shuffles* are more difficult, but they can help you to reach high balls. They're similar to the basic shuffle step, except you're springing off the ground and landing on the foot that's closest to the net.

When shuffling, step out explosively with the foot closest to the ball while simultaneously pushing off the other foot. Don't let your heels click together and keep your feet shoulder-width apart to maintain a good base to push off.

Areas of Action

In the initiation phase of your movement, you may need to move right or left, forward or backward. We can narrow down your basic travel paths to four: along the baseline, toward the net, along the net, and back toward the baseline. Different types of footwork will get you there and prepare you for the proper shot.

Table 1.1—Advantages of Open and Closed Stances	
Open stance	**Closed stance**
Forehand topspin	One-handed backhand (slice or topspin)
Forehand topspin lob	Swinging volley (forehand/backhand)
Approach shot (backhand/forehand)	Half volley (forehand/backhand)
Two-handed backhand	Drop shot (forehand/backhand)
When returning a hard flat or slice serve	Slice lob (forehand/backhand)
In a fast-paced exchange of forehand ground strokes	Passing shot (if time allows)
	Serving
	Attacking a second serve

a.   *b.*

Figure 1.1—Arantxa Sanchez Vicario demonstrates the (a) open stance; (b) closed stance.

Footwork Along the Baseline

As long as you're staying at the baseline, you'll need a unit turn with some shuffle steps, or maybe a unit turn sprint, to get you into position. But what position? You can choose an open stance or a closed stance, depending on the situation. In the open stance, your hips are facing the net (figure 1.1a). In a closed stance, your nonracquet shoulder is closest to the net (figure 1.1b). The open stance is easier to get into, but the closed stance allows you to use the skills of rotation and transfer to a greater degree (see table 1.1).

Recovering on the Baseline

It's crucial to quickly get back to your ready position after a shot. This is especially challenging when you've just had to run to make a shot. The proper footwork can save you a few steps and speed your recovery. If you don't have far to go, a few shuffle steps should do the job, however, the crossover step is an easy way to accelerate and cover a lot of court. If you don't have much time, you'll need a unit turn sprint to get back into place. This is a common scenario if you're hitting short and your opponent is running you side to side.

Footwork Going to the Net

If you can get to the net while keeping your opponent deep in the court, you have a strategic advantage. But getting there can be a challenge. At the novice and intermediate levels the move to the net often happens by accident when your opponent hits the ball short into your court; this is why I encourage beginners to set up inside the baseline. But it also can be an effective ploy to hit short, drawing your opponent forward, and then lob the next shot over his head. As your opponent hurries back to get your lob, you can move forward to the net. Just make sure your lob is well over your opponent's head before you sneak up to the net, or you might get a felt sandwich.

It's also a good idea to anticipate moving forward when you hit an angled shot or drive that takes your opponent beyond the sidelines. Look for cues to see that your opponent is in trouble such as taking a large step, lunging, or swinging wildly at the ball and missing the shot by a great deal. If you decide to go to the net and you see that your opponent is outside the singles sideline, be sure to cover the down-the-line passing shot. And you may just get up the nerve to sneak toward the net in the course of normal ground-stroke play by hitting a high, deep ball up the middle of the court and sneaking in behind it. At the strong intermediate level, players will approach the net immediately after serving, volleying the return in the air with a quick volley. Or you could take advantage of a weaker second serve with a *chip and charge*—chipping, slicing, or hitting the ball deep in your opponent's court and following your shot to the net.

When you move toward the net, remember the following crucial points:

1. Move toward the net quickly and smoothly, attempting not to jar your head.

2. If you're trying to gain good position on the net, get through the area from the baseline to the service line as quickly as possible. After your split step, your first step toward the ball should cover as much court as possible but not to the point of being uncomfortable.

3. Stay low as you move. Since you're moving forward in the court, you're likely to catch the ball on a short hop or a low volley. You can adjust upward if the ball comes high.

4. Keep your racquet up in front of you to be ready for the volley.

There are a variety of ways to get from the baseline to the service line as quickly as possible—and still be able to line up for a midcourt shot follow:

Sprint. Run! Especially if you're following your own shot toward the net or racing crosscourt for a drop shot, just *get there* as quickly as you can.

Shuffle. If you're just moving forward two to four feet to reach a short shot, make your unit turn and use a sideways shuffle to get in place for a forehand shot. Or, for a ball that is farther away, you might sprint to the area and then shuffle into position.

Power step. The power step is an open stance that usually follows a sprint transition. Run for the ball, plant your foot closest to the ball, keeping your body open to the net. The power step is a good way to hit the ball and keep moving toward the net.

Carioca. Upon approaching a backhand, if you are right-handed you plant your right foot and step behind it with your left, essentially turning your back on the net, your chin resting on your right shoulder. This gives your body the rotation you need for a strong backhand. On the shot, step on the right again. Right, left, right. Cha cha cha. If the ball is just a few feet in front of you on the backhand side, you can just step into the carioca. Or you may need to sprint a bit first, ending with a strong right step—right, left, right.

Footwork at the Net

Once you're at the net, you have a strategic advantage, but you still have to hit the ball. You usually don't have a lot of time to react. At the net, your seeing and reacting skills are especially important.

Ready position. Once at the net, adopt a ready position as usual, but keep your hands a bit farther from your body and your racquet head up. This way, you can move your hands and racquet into position more rapidly when the ball comes.

Split step. As soon as your opponent makes contact, hop into that split step. Like a cat on a hot tin roof, land softly on the balls of your feet, ready to pounce anywhere.

Unit turn. Hips, torso, shoulders, and racquet are one unit as you turn to forehand or backhand. At the net, however, you may not be making a full 90-degree turn. You may only have time to turn 45 or 60 degrees, but your body still moves as a unit. Remember to stay low in your turn, ready to move up into your shot as needed.

Step out. At the net, with reduced reaction time, that first step is especially important. Step out with the foot that is closest to the ball. Cross over with the other foot if you have to cover more ground.

Shuffle. Most of your net play will involve only short distances, a few steps right or left. Shuffle steps should be enough to get you into place.

Lineup. As with any shot, you need to line up your feet and hands on the incoming ball, but your movements at the net will be shorter and more concise.

Hit and step. For years tennis pros have encouraged players to "step and hit." While that's necessary on low and wide balls, sometimes there's just not enough time at the net to step first and hit high or medium-height balls. Instead, you can hit the ball first and take your step as a recovery. This will feel more natural but still allow you to transfer your weight into the shot.

Punching shot. The whole nature of your swing is different when you're at the net. You don't need as much rotation here, so the full rotation of a ground stroke isn't necessary. Instead, use an abbreviated swing using your opponent's pace in creating a punching shot. Step into the swing and punch it.

Square up. Immediately after stepping into your volley, square up with your other foot to return to a ready position. Most intermediate players step *back* into a ready position, but that gives up valuable territory. Follow the shot—that puts you one step closer to the net.

In addition to those basic movement guidelines, there are a few special steps you might use during net play:

Balance step. This is a stabilizing move for low volleys, used frequently on first volleys in which the ball has dipped down toward your feet. Step forward transferring weight onto your lead foot just before you hit the ball. Get as low as you can (like a lunge, but be sure to keep your back straight). Players often will drag the trailing foot on its side in order to get low enough and still continue toward the net.

Run and through. This is a "cowabunga" move, requiring total commitment. When you see your opponent has hit an easy floater, run to the ball with your racquet high in front of you. Try to catch your opponent's return high and put it away.

Recovering Lobs Over Your Head

Of course sometimes you rush the net and your opponent sends you right back by lobbing a ball over your head. You need to change direction quickly, cover some ground, and also get in position for a good return. Here are some movements that can help you:

Unit turn with jab step. The jab step (as Dennis Van Der Meer calls it) actually moves you *toward* the net with short, sharp intensity, like a boxer throwing a jab. This stores energy in your front leg on which you then push off, changing direction and going into a shuffle, crossover, crossover shuffle, or sprint (see figure 1.2).

Unit turn shuffle. For lobs that require you to move only three to four feet in either direction, this combination works well. The key here is to start your unit turn as soon as your opponent puts up the lob.

Jab-unit turn-crossover-shuffle. Say you are closing in on the net quickly, and your opponent sees your approach and puts up a lob. After taking a jab step toward the net, push off your front leg with a strong crossover step to get your momentum going backward.

Unit turn crossover. Some players prefer crossing over moving backward.

Unit turn with bicycle smash or scissors kick. If the lob is very deep but not quite over you—you can jump off your back foot and reach it with your racquet—this move will give you height and maintain balance. As you jump off your back foot, scissor your legs landing on the same foot with which you took off. It's like taking a stride (or pedaling a bicycle) in the air. This move requires precise timing and athleticism.

Hang-time smash. This is something like a volleyball smash. Push off the ground, leaping into the air with both feet.

Backhand smash or runaround. You need to make a quick decision here based on how much time you think you have. If the lob goes over your nonracquet shoulder and catches you by surprise, then you need to make a unit turn to your backhand side. You will be lined for a backhand smash. If you think you have enough time, then sprint back in a semicircle that puts the lob on your forehand side.

Between-the-legs smash. This showy shot will impress your friends, but it's a low-percentage play. To learn the shot, have a friend hit short lobs over your head. Keeping a loose wrist, run directly at the ball as it bounces in your court. Think of jumping onto a horse. With

Figure 1.2—The jab step.

your legs spread wide, hop over the ball as it's descending and snap your racquet on the back underside of the ball while looking over your shoulder to see where your approaching opponent is. That's all. Just be sure to practice carefully.

Adjusting

Picture this. You're in a match and your opponent hits a ball wide to your forehand. You pivot sprint, staying low, taking large strides and working your arms in front of you, moving faster and faster until you get to the ball—but now it's bouncing toward you. You can't stop in time and you end up running right into the ball. Or maybe you're playing the dreaded moonballer, and you prepare to hit the high-bouncing ball—but it springs right over you and you miss it altogether. Your ability to adjust to a variety of different situations will ultimately determine your success on the tennis court. The skill of adjusting helps you to get lined up on the approaching balls quickly.

Previous SMARTS sections discussed what to look for on the court and how to move to the ball. You're seeing the ball as it arrives, and you've moved toward it. Now it's time to adjust your hands, feet, and torso to the proper height and placement of the ball, setting up your rotation, transfer, and swing. Obviously, adjusting involves movement, too, but the minor movements are more important. This section discusses movements around the ball, decelerating movements such as the stutter step, movements away from the ball, and sliding movements. In addition there are flexion movements from the ankles and knees that, when executed on a solid base with rotation added, create tremendous power. Adjusting is the skill of coordinating major and minor movements to get into optimum striking position.

Adjusting is especially important when you play opponents who hit high ground strokes or those who slice their shots. If you have to sprint for wide balls, you'll need to make adjusting movements once you get there, but you'll also have to adjust for a ball headed right at your body. Whenever the ball skids or thuds or dances in a way you don't expect, your skill of adjusting needs to take over. Some players panic in these situations. Or they stick to what they think is the good form they learned, but they end up standing too tall for a low slice or running too high for a wide ball and never getting the racquet in the proper place.

Scoping Out the Situation

Seeing skills continue to be important to recognize what kind of ball you're receiving and to anticipate what it will do. Think of a scope on a rifle, but you control the crosshairs. The horizontal line is set mostly by your hands and by the bending of your legs and ankles. Set the vertical by lining up on the approaching ball with your feet at a proper distance from the ball. When you've lined up the vertical and horizontal elements with the precise position of the ball, let it rip.

Adjusting Steps

Let's say a ball bounces with medium pace in the center of the court. What route does the player take to reach it? Most novice and intermediate players run straight to the ball and then make their adjustments to hit it. But better players take a more rounded approach to the ball. They anticipate the ball's flight path and then circle around to intercept it. That way they can already be lined up when they reach the ball.

Boris Becker moving around the ball to get into optimum striking position.

Around the Ball

Movements around the ball are necessary when a ball comes straight at you. This might happen while you're at the net, returning a serve, or if you decide to run around your backhand to use your forehand as a weapon.

Say your opponent launches a second serve into the center of the box. You have a choice of hitting a forehand or backhand. I encourage players to run around second serves whenever possible and use the forehand. With the forehand you can have a much later point of contact and still hit a successful shot. The backhand has much more margin for error.

When moving around second serves or trying to run around any backhand to hit your big forehand, think of the letter C. Running in a C-pattern ensures proper distance to strike the ball. You also can use a C-pattern when approaching the net. When you're on the net and a ball is coming low or high at your body, you might try a backward C to help you get your hips and shoulders turned to counterattack the ball.

Next time you are on the court, try the C-dance to work on this movement. Have a friend volley directly over the center line while you practice moving around the approaching ball, getting your feet to one side of the center line and then the other, transferring your weight forward into the volley.

Another time to use a C-pattern is when you come to the net and your opponent lobs you. If you pivot and run straight back, the ball hits you in the back of the head. I encourage right-handed players to pivot to their left and run a backward C-pattern, which helps them circle around to hit a forehand.

Stutter Steps

Stutter steps are smaller steps used for deceleration after moving quickly toward the ball. They can be used to adjust your distance to the ball or to stop you after running through a high volley.

Backward Steps

Often when the ball comes too close, like on a deep ground stroke or in returning a kick serve, to get proper distance you need to move backward away from the ball. If, let's say, you're rushing the net when your opponent lobs you, you need to change direction quickly and push off, going backward, moving away from the ball using a scissors kick to maintain your balance.

Sliding

Use sliding movements when you come to the net and you don't have time to get around the ball. Slide in one direction, deflecting the ball in the other direction.

Transition Shots

Approach shots or transition shots (as they are now called) fall into two categories, depending on your intent with the shot:

1. To hit an outright winner; or,
2. To hit the shot and gain position on the net for a winning volley.

Transition movements blend different adjusting movements that you can try the next time you are on the court:

Around and set, load and explode. Do this the next time you receive an easy ball in the middle of the court. Move around the ball using a C-pattern, or backward C if you are left-handed. Create a good base with your feet on which you can rotate and then explode, uncoiling into the ball.

Around and through. This is a transitional combination helpful on low balls in which you need to approach the net gaining position. Move *around* the ball and step *through* the shot with your trailing leg then continue to the net. Often on low balls or wide balls the trailing leg helps recover balance. High volleys also require an around and through move.

Low and slide. This is important if you're moving diagonally toward the net and the ball comes directly at you. Stay low and adjust the position of your hands to meet the ball. Don't lift up your body; you don't have time to set up a solid base. Slide across in the direction you're already moving and deflect the ball the opposite way.

Rotation

Every swinging shot—serves, ground strokes, overheads, and angles—you hit on the court involves rotation. Proper rotation requires good timing and an awareness of the proper amount of rotation to use. Most intermediate players have to be encouraged to rotate their bodies, since it's not natural to rotate away from the oncoming ball.

Powerful strokes on a tennis court are actually a series of well-timed rotations working together. Remember that the center of mass is like the hub on a wheel; your hips, shoulders, legs, arms, and eventually your racquet rotate around this hub. For this reason, it's important the hub remain vertical when you hit tennis balls. Any slight deviation in the axis of this hub affects your shot. When a top is spinning fast, it stays on its base; but when it loses momentum, it starts to wobble and falls to one side. Powerful rotation requires a properly aligned center.

Coiling

Did you ever play with one of those balsa-wood airplanes, the kind with a propeller you wind up with a rubber band? The twisting of the rubber band actually stored energy. When it untwisted, energy was released: the propeller spun and the plane flew. That's what happens in the rotation process of tennis. Coiling stores energy that is powerfully released with the uncoiling.

Start from a solid base. For most players, the legs serve as the base, not just the feet. Sometimes you'll see professional players set up their base of support with their feet, flexing their legs and coiling up on this base, then exploding off the ground as they hit the ball. If you can do that consistently, great, but most people can't. So let your legs anchor you, and let your upper body do the coiling.

Now let's take a look at different areas in which we can use the elasticity of our muscles to generate more power. Take the forehand, for instance. If you're a right-hander, your right hand draws the racquet back and your left hand extends in front of you or slightly to your right side, depending on how you prefer to line up. As your racquet arm starts to go back, it stretches the chest muscles. As the coiling continues, you feel the stretch in the legs, gluteal muscles, hips, torso, shoulders, arms, and even hands. When all those large muscles are stretched, they are primed and ready to be let loose. The sensation of elasticity can really be felt in the backhand. During a one-handed backhand, the body coils in the opposite direction. For right-handed players during the coiling, the left hand is on the throat of the racquet, pulling it back and stretching the muscles in the back of the shoulder. The energy is stored through the muscles in the back of the shoulder, the torso, gluteus, legs, and arms. The back of the shoulder actually points to the ball, with the chin resting on the right shoulder, giving the back a good stretch. As this energy is released, the right arm moves forward and the left arm counters to keep the shoulders balanced and aid the acceleration of the swing.

When should you start to coil? There are two schools of thought on this. Some players such as Venus and Serena Williams coil immediately before the approaching ball crosses the net. Others—clay-court players and those with excellent timing and whip-like strokes—coil when the ball bounces.

Each method of coiling has advantages and disadvantages. An advantage to coiling before the ball crosses the net is if you want to transfer weight into your shot by moving toward it, then your racquet is already in position before the ball bounces. You also can hide your shot from your opponent, holding the backswing and delaying the racquet arm from coming through until the last possible second. This can help

Notice how Boris Becker is setting up his base of support, flexing his legs, and coiling.

you to come up with a passing shot and your opponent already has achieved a good position on the net.

A disadvantage to the early rotation is that you might not feel comfortable having the racquet back so soon. It may even feel less powerful if your hips are not synchronized when uncoiling with the shortened backswing.

Later coiling can result in more power, since the racquet is actually still completing the backswing when the hips and shoulders start uncoiling. But the timing is more difficult; if you don't get fully uncoiled in time, it will drastically affect your shot. Players who take the racquet back with the bounce can get into trouble if the ball comes deep or fast.

Control and Uncoiling

In tennis, many movements are balanced by counter movements. For example, on a one-handed backhand, the free arm moves back toward the fence as the racquet arm swings forward. On a scissors smash, your body moves backward, reaching up for the smash, and your legs counter by going forward and scissoring. In the control phase of your rotation you have some muscle groups pulling and others pushing to balance one another. For a moment, your body is cocked, wound up, ready to spring—but in perfect balance, awaiting the right moment to uncoil, releasing all that stored muscle elasticity into an effective swing.

As you uncoil, you need to stay in balance. As the kinetic energy flows through your unwinding body, you'll release some muscles and flex others. Think of a whip motion—the tail of the whip holds back until the last possible moment, and then it snaps with the power of the whole whip behind it. So it is with your energy flow, as you release your hips, torso, back, shoulder, elbow, and wrist.

In this process, you don't want to waste any energy, so keep your head still and your shoulders level. Let the uncoiling proceed evenly. Some experts speak of locking in the wrist and elbow, such that they each assume an angle of 70 to 90 degrees as you coil. *Keep them at that angle* until the last possible moment to ensure the whiplike motion of your racquet.

Sometimes releasing the angle of the wrist helps you get the ball back into the court when in a defensive position. The term "educated wrists" refers to a player's ability to use his or her wrist when necessary.

When you uncoil properly, you will feel a rhythm to your swing. The even flow of energy will feel right to you. As you practice, you'll develop the rhythm of your entire gain—seeing, moving, adjusting, coiling, releasing, and squaring up again. When you watch the great players, it seems effortless because it *is* effortless. Sure, a lot of work goes into a game, but there's no wasted energy. The complete player trains and learns to move from one shot to another with economy and grace, letting the energy flow.

Transfer

Transfer and rotation can generate power. Sometimes they work together, but often you may choose one or the other. When you transfer weight into a shot, the mass you have moving behind the ball creates extra force, and therefore, more speed or pace on the ball. So, if you're stepping strongly into a shot (transferring your weight), compensate by shortening your backswing. Otherwise, the combined power of rotation and transfer might send the ball into the next county. Or if you do combine rotation and transfer, taking a full swing while transferring weight into the shot, try increasing the spin on the ball. You'll be gaining control of these two powerful energy resources by imparting spin on the ball.

With a complete weight transfer, your weight moves from one foot to another, but not always from the back foot to the front. On ground strokes it's not uncommon for right-handed players hitting an open-stance stroke to rotate on their base, transferring weight from the right foot to the left (or on a backhand open stance from the left to the right). Some players jump off the left foot for a smash and land on the right, actually springing backward.

Timing

The key factor determining your ability to transfer weight is *time.* Will you have the time to set up a weight transfer? Obviously, the farther you have to go for the ball, the less time you have to transfer your weight. Or if a ball is coming toward you at a high speed, you only have time for minimal rotation. But if the incoming ball is close enough, with an angle and pace that give you a second or two to spare, then get ready to shift your weight into the ball. On a ground stroke, for example, you already may be rotating forward, using your hips, shoulders, and torso, but try getting extra force by transferring your body mass into the shot, moving from your right foot to your left. Or you can transfer weight by a shuffle step, a shuffle set, or a carioca-spring step. Getting this extra force into the shot gives your stroke more pace.

Foot Alignment

Proper foot alignment is crucial for transfer also. If your feet are not properly supported or in alignment, they still may be moving *inside your shoes* even when you think you've stopped. Foot alignment also affects your balance and therefore the accuracy of your shot. For instance, I know some players who have very nice supports in their shoes, but when they perspire their feet start to slide inside their shoes, causing their toes to jam forward. The same thing occurs when players double up their socks, trying to cut down on the shock of playing on a hard court.

It's always impressive to see the power generated by young tennis players such as Anna Kournikova when they step into their shots. They transfer their weight—even though they may not weigh much—and hit the ball powerfully over the net.

Swing

Everything we've learned so far leads up to the swing, but it's hard to swing effectively without seeing your opponent's cues of the approaching ball and anticipating your location, movement, and necessary adjustments. Rotation stores energy in the stretched muscles of the hips, shoulders, chest, arms, forearms, wrists, gluteals, legs, and ankles and releases that energy by uncoiling. Transfer then gives power and pace to your shot as you put your weight behind it. Now it's time to rip with your swing.

Points of Contact

We can identify the swing's three basic points of contact. They are attack, rally, and defensive contact points. Each point of contact will vary depending on your grip and where you like to take the ball. That is to say that a semi-western grip will be capable of meeting the ball further in front of the body than a continental grip given that the shoulders are facing the net at impact.

Attack, Challenge, and Counterattack

The attack contact point is in front of you, allowing you to get more of your mass behind the shot. As you watch players who really attack the ball, notice that their

Anke Huber attacking and taking the ball on the rise.

bodies tend to lean into their shots and they extend their arms into it, whether they're going for an outright winner or just on their way to the net. This forward transfer of body movement happens best when the point of contact is farther forward.

Players who use the attack contact point enjoy taking balls on the rise. Balls hit in front of the body tend to have power and give your opponent less time. This is especially helpful when you're hitting passing shots. Hitting balls in front of the body doesn't allow for a lot of spin, but it's enough to keep the ball in the court.

Rally

The rally contact point is parallel with the hips or slightly in front. Usually the ball is struck at the peak of its bounce. With this level positioning, it's easy to apply topspin, slice the ball, or hit it flat. The player may use an open or closed stance and slightly lean in the upper body.

Defensive

The defensive contact point is behind the hip line, with the player making contact later. This contact point is clearly not meant for attacking—it's for playing defensively and keeping the ball in play.

With this positioning, the ball is hit as it drops from its apex, so the contact point is usually lower and closer to the player's body. Players use a more radical swing path, going low to high or high to low, giving the ball lift and spin. If the player is backed up behind the baseline and on defense, then typically a more open stance is assumed, with the body being more upright.

Thomas Muster, on defense, is scrambling to get the ball back. Notice the extreme upward swing of his racquet giving the ball lift and spin.

Strike Zone

A rendezvous is going to happen between your racquet and the ball, but where on the racquet? The point of contact gives us a forward-backward coordinate for this meeting; your strike zone determines the up-down coordinate. Strike zones can be high (shoulder height or higher), medium (shoulders to knees), or low (below the knee). What's the best strike zone for you? It depends on your grip, body type, the court surface you're playing on, how well you're playing, and the type of shot you're trying to execute. When you properly anticipate where the ball is going and when it will get there, you can put yourself in the proper place to meet the ball in your preferred strike zone, at your preferred point of contact. There are always surprises, especially on kick serves and high bounces, and you may need to swing higher or lower than you had planned.

The term *strike zone* comes to us from baseball, and we can learn a few things from that game. Baseball's strike zone is similar to the medium strike zone in tennis, precisely because that's where most batters meet the ball best. However, some batters have different preferences—just like some tennis players. There are high-ball hitters and low-ball hitters in both sports.

Strike-zone preferences also help you scout out your opponent. In baseball, opposing pitchers and catchers know where the batter likes to meet the ball, and they stay away from that area if they can. In the same way, you can read your opponent's preferences and stay away. For instance, if you see the other player using a continental grip, you know she will have problems if she allows the ball to get high.

Swing Path

What path does your racquet take through the air when you swing? How is the path for your ground strokes different from the path for your volleys?

Players choose from a variety of swing paths. Vic Braden used to paint the various swing paths on the fences. To put topspin on the ball, swing low to high. You can do this most dramatically with a looped backswing, which looks like a sideways question mark. A semiloop is less flashy, but often just as effective; take your unit turn with the racquet higher than usual, then drop the racquet as you start your swing. You also can produce some topspin with a straight backswing—straight back with the racquet head under the ball and then up and outward in the desired direction. Studies have shown that the ball picks up six to eight miles per hour for every foot the racquet drops in the swing path. Choose the one that works best for you.

To put backspin on the ball, try a high-to-low swing path. Make your unit turn with the racquet six inches higher than usual. Then swing down and across the ball, being sure to follow through. This is an easy swing to learn, but it's like candy—fun to try, but not always good for you. Backspin requires less swing speed, so you can get away with sloppy footwork. It also slows down the ball and, therefore, the game. Older players have a lot of fun with backspin, but I try to keep younger players away from it. It's a consistent and effective shot for changing pace, and a nice addition to an advanced player's game, but it teaches beginners bad habits.

You also can try various swing paths on your serve. For a flat serve the racquet follows the flight of the ball after contact, but for a slice serve the racquet veers off a bit to the right—and even more for a kick serve! Obviously the swing path affects the way the racquet strikes the ball, resulting in different spin, direction, and power.

Racquet Face

Your racquet face may need to be open, closed, or straight, depending on what you intend to do with the ball (see figure 1.3). Open the face if you're receiving low balls, if you want backspin, or if you're playing on grass. An open racquet face gives the ball lift, making it a good idea under certain weather conditions—if it's cold or if the balls are heavy because they're dirty or wet. If the ball is high or if you want topspin, close the face slightly (but this is not my favorite method for topspin because it can lead to a wristy stroke if used excessively). When making contact for a driving forehand, a straight racquet face is your best bet.

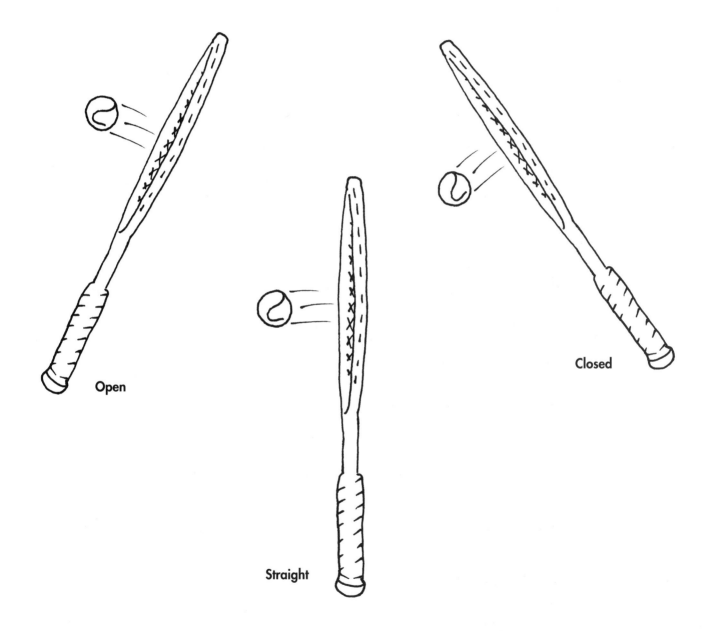

Open

Straight

Closed

Figure 1.3—Diagrams of racquet face positions.

Getting a Grip

Novice players typically give the racquet a death grip that offers control but also muscle fatigue and loss of power. The better players have a moderate grip, though they may tighten or loosen their grip in specific game situations.

Coaches often encourage players to choke up on their racquets. This gives them more racquet control, but it sacrifices power. That might make sense for a beginner the first few times out on the court, but I urge players to grip their racquets lower to give the wrist increased flexibility, allowing a greater range of movement and more power. It also helps you disguise your shots.

How tightly do you grip your racquet? For instruction purposes, I've defined three different grip intensities:

Tight to fight. The hand has a death grip on the racquet that only a hammer and chisel could loosen. Too many muscles are contracted, resulting in a rigid swing and early fatigue. Novice players often use this grip, and even intermediates will tighten for a killer ace, a shot they're aiming for under pressure or an out-of-position shot they're trying to muscle over the net.

Just right. The racquet can be pulled out of the hand but with resistance. Here the ideal blend of power, fluidity, and control is established by contracting the muscles just enough to hit the ball. It's actually not a constant level of pressure on the racquet but one that flows tighter or looser depending on the shot required. As you get into the rhythm of the game, you'll feel the right times to tighten and loosen your grip.

Loose as a goose. The racquet can be pulled out of your hand easily with little or no effort. Many players prefer to grip their racquets this way before they serve and some coaches will encourage their students to practice the entire service motion just holding on to the racquet with two or three fingers. This works wonderfully until contact is made in which the player then has to contract the muscles a little more to regain control and hold on to the racquet. Still, this grip can be helpful on drop shots, drop volleys, and anytime you want to reduce the pace of the ball.

Now that we've discussed the tightness of your grip, let's learn about the various types of grips. Each grip has areas and shots where it works well and others where it doesn't. For instance, if you have a full western grip, you're probably comfortable taking high balls or executing a swinging volley. With a continental grip you'll be more comfortable with lower balls, and you'll have some trouble with balls above shoulder level because your hand is in a weaker position—it's more on top of the grip instead of behind it. The position of your hand helps some shots and hurt others. You'll want to make your grip choices to go along with your strike zone and contact point preferences. Tables 1.2 through 1.4 present the advantages and disadvantages of various grips.

Swing Speed

You don't always have to swing as hard as possible to win a match. Just as a good baseball pitcher uses change-ups and breaking balls to set up a blazing fastball, you can vary the speed of your swing and keep your opponent guessing. If you vary speeds in your practice time, starting slow and building up speed, you'll develop a wide repertoire of speeds to use in a match.

Table 1.2—Forehand Grips

	Continental	Australian forehand	Eastern forehand	Semiwestern	Western
Best contact point	Rally	Rally	Rally	Attack	Attack
Most difficult contact point	Attack	Attack	Defensive	Defensive	Defensive
Best strike zone	Medium	Medium	Medium	Medium	Medium
Most difficult strike zone	High	High	Low	Low	Low
Advantages	Good for all strokes. Requires some wrist on the forehand side. Saves time, no grip change. Serve, volleys (the open face imparts backspin on the ball naturally). Overheads, backhand slice. Low and wide balls for the two-handed player.	Good for most strokes. Requires less wrist on the forehand side. Serve, volleys (especially high on the forehand volley). Overheads, backhand slice.	Strong all-around grip. Good for hitting flat or topspin, lobs, and high forehand volleys. Saves time if used also for a two-handed backhand—no grip change.	Best contact is in front of the body, allowing for optimal weight transfer. Also a strong grip for hitting the ball flat or with heavy spin. Strong wrist position. Topspin lobs.	Contact also can be in front of the body. Can generate a lot of spin and is excellent for the topspin lob.
Disadvantages	High-bouncing balls with heavy spin. High strike zone or attack contact point. Wide balls require more wrist to return.	High balls on the backhand (difficult to generate topspin on the backhand side with this grip). Attack, contact point, and backhand in the high strike zone.	Hard to meet ball at the defensive contact point and get away with it. Low balls. Balls in low strike zone require the racquet face to be opened up for net clearance.	Hitting low sliced balls, half volley, and low volleys (low strike zone). Easy to spray balls from the defensive contact point or hit short.	Hitting low sliced balls, half volley, and low volleys. If you must hit in the low strike zone or defensive contact point, your shots may land short due to heavy spin.

Table 1.3—One-Handed Backhand Grips		
	Eastern backhand	**Western backhand**
Best contact point	Rally	Attack
Most difficult contact point	Defensive	Defensive
Best strike zone	Medium	High
Most difficult strike zone	Low	Low
Advantages	Good for the one-handed backhand, serve, smash, backhand volley, two-handed backhand. Nice grip for hitting spin (slice, topspin, or flat).	This is a great grip for one-handed backhand players who play on clay and like hitting with extreme topspin, or players who use the same face of the racquet to hit both forehand and backhand. Alberto Berasategui uses this with a two-handed backhand.
Disadvantages	On low balls, the wrist must be fanned downwards to open the racquet face for net clearance.	Watch the rolling over of the wrist on passing shots and high balls. This is not a good volley grip.

For example, preparing for a tournament, Boris Becker starts the first two or three mornings just hitting high balls in the middle of the court, getting into a groove. I call this a *groove session*—a way to enhance your feel and tune up your basic skills. In such a session, you're just lining up to the ball, adjusting your hands and feet to a good stance at a proper distance to the ball, and taking a flowing, accelerating swing. Get a partner to send center ground strokes to you at a slow, steady pace. At this speed, you can concentrate on your SMARTS and develop your blend of skills.

As the week progresses, you would increase intensity to 50 to 70 percent and begin running for balls and adjusting to different shots. Keep raising the power of your swing until you're hitting consistently at 90 percent or better the day before the tournament, and you're trying 100 percent for a few sustained periods. By the time you reach the match, you've rehearsed varying swing speeds and can execute them all. Bobby Banck, coach of Mary Joe Fernandez, adds that swing speeds vary more with players who like to hit the ball flat. Players who hit with heavy topspin tend to swing consistently at the same speed.

In a match don't try shots that you have not practiced. It's the same thing with swing speeds. Building swing speeds into your *practices* will yield great results in your competitive play.

Sharpening Your SMARTS

The SMARTS skills give you a framework for understanding and working on your game. You may have a great swing but poor vision. You may move across the court quickly but not adjust well when you near the ball. You may have a smooth rotation on your ground stroke but an awkward weight transfer on your volleys. The SMARTS system can help you troubleshoot your game and work on your weak areas. Chapter 2 helps you take this general information and apply it more specifically to the shots of your game.

Table 1.4—Forehand and Backhand Grip Combinations				
Combination grips	Eastern backhand / eastern forehand (both hands in a position of strength)	Eastern backhand / continental	Eastern backhand / semiwestern to western (backswing tends to be more like a batter's windup)	Right-hand continental, eastern forehand or semiwestern with left-hand continental, eastern forehand, semiwestern, or full western
Best contact point	All	Rally or defensive	Attack	Defensive
Most difficult contact point	None	Attack	Defensive	Attack
Best strike zone	High	Medium	High	Medium
Most difficult strike zone	Low	High	Low	High
Advantages	Disguise, control, power. Ball can be met and stabilized effectively in all contact points. Works well for service returns, lobs, and passing shots.	The strength of this grip is that the right hand in the eastern backhand grip controls the stroke so the left hand can be released for slice volleys or balls out wide.	Good for high balls and heavy topspin.	The left hand (for a righty) is the dominant hand in these varying combinations, because the left hand is behind the grip. This puts a lot of wrist in the shot and aids disguise. It's great for a flat return because there is no grip change.
Disadvantages	Low, angled balls are very difficult. Very high balls or wide balls also can cause problems. It's not easy to hit two-handed slice or volleys when the ball comes directly at the body.	High balls or very low volleys on the backhand side in which the wrist must be turned downward.	Low balls are difficult to recover.	Not particularly strong for volleys. Sometimes the depth of the ground strokes suffers because the left hand dominates the shot causing a rolling, with the right elbow getting buried into the side of the stomach. Because of the forehand grip, it is difficult to hit a solid one-handed backhand. The left hand drives the stroke, so if the ball is low or high you need to muscle the ball. The two-handed slice also is challenging.

Note: The more the dominant hand moves in front of the grip, the greater the role of the wrist on both hands.

Dominating Serves and Returns

The SMARTS system outlines basic stroking skills. Every shot you make on the court involves seeing, movement, adjusting, rotation, transfer, and swing, whether it's your forehand, backhand, volley, lob, or serve. As you're drilling your shots, you can now work on them with the SMARTS system to troubleshoot your weakest shots. I divide all shots into three categories:

Swinging shots. Power comes primarily from rotation and swing (and when possible from transfer, depending on how much time you have and on your level of play). These shots include serves and returns (covered in this chapter) and forehands, backhands, smashes, swinging volleys, lobs, angles, and drop shots (covered in chapter 3).

Punching shots. Power comes from transfer and rotation (the power from your swing differs with each type of shot). Punching shots include volleys, drop volleys, angle volleys, and half volleys (chapter 4).

Transition shots. These require a blending of rotation, transfer, and swing. Included here are approach shots, high volleys, and second service returns (chapter 4).

My descriptions of the various shots are necessarily detailed to properly focus on your technique. Later chapters deal with intention and strategy. But never forget that tennis is a dance. As you work on these moves, you may feel as if you have two left feet, but ultimately you'll be gliding around the court with precision, power, economy, and control.

Let us start off with the swinging shots. I have prioritized the two most important swinging shots as the serve and the return. Fifty percent of all points we play in a competitive match start with either a serve or a return.

Serves

Along with drilling each SMARTS objective as you improve your swinging shots, it helps to develop handy phrases that will remind you of proper technique as you play. I've provided cues for each skill, but feel free to create your own cues that work for you. Just be sure to *use them!*

Andre Agassi's stance at serve.

Seeing

When you get to the court, observe the environmental conditions. Is there sun or wind that might affect your ability to see or place your toss? Prepare yourself with a few practice tosses from both sides of the court to get a feel for your best positioning.

Next line up with your dominant eye closest to the ball to help you make a quicker, more accurate connection with it. Say you're cross-dominant (i.e., right-handed and left-eye dominant): choose a more closed stance for your serve (like Agassi). If you are same-sided (i.e., left-handed and left-eye dominant), try a more open stance. Of course other factors also will affect your choice of stance for the serve—such as lower back flexibility, timing, and your most effective legwork—but don't ignore your eyes. Get yourself in the best position to see.

Before serving, look to see your opponent's starting location and grip (forehand or backhand). Based on this information, think of your options and choose a spot to hit, but don't look directly at it. You want to keep your opponent guessing.

Movement

Any movement needs to start from somewhere. Strong movement starts from a solid base. For singles play, set up within five feet of the center hash mark. Use a balanced stance from which you can counter-rotate (twist) and then push off, moving upward and outward toward the ball. While you're drilling this movement, keep your weight evenly distributed or slightly toward the back foot. As you become more accustomed to the movement, work on shifting your weight forward to back to forward. You can build the following movement factors off a good base:

Toss. You will vary your toss according to the type of serve you're hitting, but be consistent at getting the toss where you want it. This takes practice. Find a fence post and try to toss the ball 10 times up the post without variation or spin. Then try it again while flexing your legs as if you're going to serve. During play, many players try to line up their tosses with the net post. Others prefer to rotate their hips and shoulders more, so they line up the toss with the inside of their leg. See what works best for you.

Footwork. As you push off the ground, you can do several things with your feet. They can remain apart as you push off the ground, or you can slide your back foot up next to your front foot creating a platform to push off upward to your toss. Some players like to scissor their legs in the air; others land on the foot closest to the net, or on both feet.

Trophy pose. Look closely at a tennis trophy and memorize that position. Or videotape professional tennis players and freeze-frame the tape at the point of your favorite player's serve. Copy that pose: tossing the ball up with your arm; other arm pulled back with the racquet poised for attack; legs flexed; and body stretched tight like an archer's bow.

Trophy pose.

From this position, if the base is solid and your toss is good, the rest is easy. Now you're just pulling the trigger. The trophy pose gets your hips and shoulders coiled, with a thorough stretching of your chest, shoulder, back, and oblique muscles. Now you just release those stretches in a chain reaction—hips, torso, shoulder, elbow, wrist—creating an explosion of kinetic energy. Your racquet is directed upward to the toss like a whip. The acceleration of your arm and racquet toward the ball carries you into the court.

Adjusting

Some players seem to be serving machines. Every toss is perfect and their form is always flawless. But most of us mere mortals aren't like that. Not only do we struggle with our own errant tosses and occasional bad form, but we also contend with gusts of wind or sun in our eyes. Or perhaps, as the toss is going up, your opponent takes a step to the spot where you were planning to ace him. The realities of tennis force us to make certain adjustments, even in midserve.

You have several options for adjusting on a serve:

- **Adjust your position** along the baseline to serve to your opponent's weaknesses. For example, if you're serving to the outside of the court to force your opponent's weak backhand, you might position yourself farther away from the center of the baseline. Then you can take advantage of the lowest part of the net and get a better angle on the serve.

- **Adjust your toss.** There are different tosses for kick serves, slices, and flat serves. With a kick serve, you toss the ball more above your head. A flat serve is more in front of you, and the slice serve is more to the side. You also can toss into the wind or away from the sun to compensate for adverse conditions.

- **Adjust your swing path** on the spur of the moment, especially if the toss is imperfect or windblown. Obviously, you need to meet the ball where it *is*, not where you expect it to be. If you change strategies, preferring a kick serve to a flat serve, your swing path will need to change accordingly.

- **Adjust the racquet head** at contact to vary direction, height, spin, pace, and depth. The head of the racquet should be up on the backswing, but it may meet the ball at different angles on a kick serve or slice. You also might decide to pause in the trophy pose (a la Steffi Graf) or have a continuous racquet motion (like Greg Rusedski).

- **Adjust your grip.** For the most part, you'll want a relaxed grip that tightens at some point during the swing. This is a matter of personal preference, and you can experiment with different grips and tightness to see the effect on your serve.

- **Adjust the bending of your legs.** You should have some flexion as the toss goes up, but you can experiment with different amounts, depending on your flexibility and personal strength. Stay balanced and relaxed when going into the trophy position and you'll be able to adjust quickly.

Rotation

Rotation on the serve will vary, depending on the player's stance, flexibility (especially of the lower back), swing path, and service intentions. I've already discussed the trophy pose and how it coils the body upon a solid base. The legs are balanced and flexed, and perhaps rotated a bit forward, while the upper body is counter-rotated back. In addition, the left shoulder is up and the right shoulder is slightly lower in the trophy position.

As the coiled energy begins to be released, the flexed legs extend and the counter-rotated trophy pose starts to uncoil, starting with the hips, the torso, and then the upper body. It's hard to keep this uncoiling action on a stable axis, so imagine your left arm pulling you up to the point of contact. The racquet stays back, like the end of a whip. Only after the chest muscles release, sending a chain reaction through the arm, does the racquet rip through to meet the ball. As the right arm whips forward, the left arm acts as a decelerator by coming to the side near the hip or across the body and stopping there. It's like a jackknifed tractor-trailer. The tractor slams on the brakes but slings the trailer forward. Your racquet arm is that trailer.

The last rotation is that of the racquet hand and forearm. The forearm rotates outward (pronates) and then the wrist and racquet snap through to meet the ball.

> **Cues**
> Extend, reach, pull
> left arm up
> Load and explode

Transfer

Transferring weight into your serve requires rhythm and timing. Start with your weight on both feet, followed by one step into the court if your swing is that forceful. To start transferring more weight into your serve, start with your weight on your back foot before going into your service motion. Or, if it feels more comfortable, start with your weight forward, then rock back onto your back foot before going forward into your serve. As the ball is tossed, the weight of the body naturally transfers forward to the front foot. The transfer of weight continues up and out to the toss while the legs forcefully push off the ground. This transfer continues as the ball is struck and the body moves into the court.

There are several ways to complete the weight transfer. Some players like to step into the court with the back foot, while others prefer the front foot. Choose the best way for you, considering your starting stance, amount of rotation, swing, and intention.

Many good players angle their hips into the court as they serve. Their feet, of course, stay back, avoiding a foot fault, but they bend their hip out over the baseline, creating even more of a body stretch, and transfer their weight forward. On the serve, then, their bodies follow their hips into the court as the weight is transferred forward, adding power.

Creating sharp angles with your various body parts (see photo on page 31) is a key to developing a powerful serve.

> **Cues**
> Hips forward
> Trophy pose

Swing

As we saw in chapter 1, your swing has many factors—grip, swing path, strike zone, and point of contact being the major ones. Consider these as you work on your serve. But you also can choose what type of serve to hit. You have three basic options:

1. A **flat serve** is the most direct, straight and strong, like a baseball pitcher's fastball.

2. A **slice** is a curveball, curving left from a right-handed server. When it hits it often skids and stays low.

3. A **kick serve** is more difficult, but it often has a dramatic effect, diving sharply and kicking to the left of the returning player. It's something like a pitcher's screwball.

Boris Becker demonstrates a kick serve.

As we'll see, different parts of your swing will vary according to which type of serve you've selected.

Grip

The continental grip is the most popular choice for normal slice and flat serves. But for kick serves a backhand grip actually works best. I'd suggest the eastern backhand. This allows you to impart more spin when meeting the ball above your head. Keep a relaxed grip on the racquet until just before you meet the ball. Then your tightening grip will help transfer kinetic energy into the racquet and to the ball.

Swing Path

Rhythm is crucial as you begin your backswing. Start slowly, pulling your racquet back and moving into your trophy pose, then quickly crack the whip. Slow, slow, *quick*. Get the feel of this rhythm.

Here's the normal swing path for a serve:

1. **The backswing.** Point your racquet at the net post, then draw it back past your right hip. Your upper body is beginning to coil. On the backswing, some players like to drop the racquet head, like a pendulum on a clock, so it's almost pointing to the ground. Others like to lift the racquet straight up into the trophy pose. That's your choice.

2. **The toss and trophy pose.** You may toss the ball from your fingertips or from a flat palm, but keep it relaxed. Don't hinge at the wrist; keep your whole arm extended. The ball should go high (a few feet beyond the height of your extended racquet) and a foot or two in front of you. Imagine the face of a clock: toss the ball at 11 o'clock for a kick serve, 12 o'clock for a flat serve, and 1 o'clock for a slice. After the toss, your left arm extends straight up, as if you're reaching up to grab a rung of a ladder. Your right shoulder stays low, your right arm extended behind you, with the racquet head up. Some players pause at this point, others move continuously into the whip motion. You can figure out which style gives you the best rhythm and power.

3. **The drop.** As the legs straighten, the racquet drops to its lowest point down the back.

4. **The whip.** The racquet speeds upward to the ball. The coiled energy is unfurled with fury through hips, back, chest, shoulder, arm, and wrist. Depending on your type of serve, the wrist and forearm will rotate some before impact.

5. **Impact.** The body is fully extended. The coiled energy is released into the ball.

6. **Follow-through.** The racquet continues outward across the body for slice and flat serves, but more to the side for a kick serve. The whip motion will cause you to bend at the waist. Your weight transfer and follow-through drive you a step or two into the court.

> ## Cues
>
> Slow, then quick
>
> Pretend you're throwing your racquet at the ball
>
> Serve like you're throwing a baseball
>
> Spaghetti arm
>
> Check your watch as you serve (pronation for slice)
>
> Serve with spin
>
> Elbow up (follow-through)

Strike Zone, Point of Contact

Virtually all serves are struck in the high strike zone. (Underhanded serves are legal but rare.) But points of contact vary for the kick, flat, and slice serves. For a flat serve, hit the ball straight on, but for a slice you'll meet it on the ball's right side. For a kick serve you're tossing lower but more directly above your head, and the racquet meets the ball low—around a 7 o'clock position—brushing up toward 2 o'clock. That's what gives it such a nasty spin.

Racquet Speed

Bob Brett

Coach who has worked with Boris Becker, Goran Ivanisevic, Nicolas Kiefer, Andrei Medeudeu, and many others

Racquet speed is hand and arm speed. But how do you get your arm moving quickly? Many beginners try to muscle the ball, tightening their arms to generate more power. But this actually decreases arm speed. The greatest power comes in your rotation and transfer, generated by the stronger muscles of your torso, back, chest, and shoulders. Your arm is like a whip, adding its own power only at the very end of the swing. So keep your arm loose, like spaghetti, so your swing can whip freely with the power of your whole body.

Now that you see how to apply corrective SMARTS to your serve, you may need to troubleshoot problems in your existing serve. The troubleshooting guide below can help you pinpoint what elements of the SMARTS skills can help you improve.

Troubleshooting Your Serve

I imagine myself double-faulting and then I do.

Seeing: Improve your imagery. Watch pro players deliver winning serves and then, in your mind's eye, put yourself in their shoes. On the court, see the path your successful serve will take.

My serve goes into the net.

Seeing: Keep your head up until impact is complete.

Adjusting: Is the toss too low or too far in front of your body? Add more height and spin. The rhythm of the toss and backswing may be too quick or you may not be extending your legs enough. Check your balance by adjusting your stance. Your feet may be too close together. For the second serve, toss above your head more and brush up on the ball as if you're hitting a ground stroke with topspin. Rely on your wrist more; keep it loose. Aim higher and deeper over the net.

Rotation: Too little rotation of your forearm (pronation) may be creating too much slice on the ball. Try using a different spin, such as a kick serve, or flattening out your slice.

Transfer: You may not be using your legs enough to push yourself upward to the ball. Or you're hitting down on the ball.

Swing: You may be pulling down with your elbow too soon. Try putting more spin on the ball, especially on a second serve. Also, your toss may be too low—your backswing may be ready before your toss is finished. Think of it as a race to the ball. The tossing arm needs a head start to get fully extended; the racquet arm will catch up.

I'm footfaulting.

Rotation: If you're stepping over the baseline with your back foot, your hips are opening too soon or not rotating enough at the start of the coiling motion.

Transfer: If you're faulting with your front foot, be sure you're transferring weight from the back foot to the front foot, angling your hip while keeping the front foot anchored to the ground. Practice serving with your weight just on the front foot angling your hip over the baseline to transfer your weight. Accentuate the extension of your tossing arm, and bend your hip over the baseline, but keep your feet on the safe side.

I have no power on the serve; I'm just arming the ball.

Adjusting: Your body may be straightening too soon. Get your legs into it, bending and extending them more. Then check other power sources: rotation, transfer, swing.

Rotation: You could be standing too open when making contact. Check your swing path.

There's a hitch in my serve.

Adjusting: Check your timing. You may be tossing the ball too high and taking the racquet back too quickly. Practice the whole sequence step by step. Toss first, then start the backswing.

Swing: Perhaps your racquet head is not staying up but dropping between your shoulder blades too soon.

I'm jumping at the serve.

Adjusting: Your feet should only leave the ground as a result of your upward extension. Don't jump to reach the toss. Your toss may be too high or your swing too soon.

I lose control of the toss.

Adjusting: Be sure you're not releasing the toss with a flick of your wrist. Also check that you're opening all your fingers at once and only when your arm is fully extended. Try tossing the ball as if you're holding an ice-cream cone.

My serve goes long.

Adjusting: You're moving under your toss, so move your toss more in front of you. Speed up your wrist to move the racquet through impact more quickly. Add spin and reduce pace: aim shorter in the box.

Swing: You may be hitting the ball too low. If you have a forehand grip, try a continental grip to put spin on the ball. Pronate your wrist and forearm. Accelerate your wrist more to get the racquet through impact faster. Speed up the follow-through.

My serve goes wide.

Adjusting: Pronate your arm more, meeting the ball with a flat racquet face. Aim with greater margin of error away from the lines.

Rotation: You have too much spin on the ball due to an open racquet face at contact and an over-rotation of the hips and shoulders. Focus on using the tossing arm as a decelerator across the body to stop rotation.

My elbow seems as if I'm not bending it properly during the serve.

Rotation: You may be serving from your elbow, commonly known as the "waiter serve." The problem may be that your right hip is opening prematurely. Try a closed stance for several weeks as your whole body learns to rotate in to the serve.

Swing: If your elbow is not bending at all, go back to the trophy position and serve with the racquet head up for a few days. Dennis Van Der Meer suggests taking a full backswing and tapping your back twice with your racquet before making contact, then after a few more serves tapping once, then not at all.

My legs aren't bending at all on the serve.

Transfer: Check the cadence of your serve. You may be rushing the backswing and decelerating the finish. Emphasize your stance and trophy pose.

My opponent repeatedly kills my serve.

Seeing: Look at your opponent's grips before you serve. Let that help you decide how and where to serve the ball.

Transfer: Your weight transfer actually may be going backward, giving it less power, making it easy to return. Transfer your weight upward and forward into the ball, and get a strong push off the ground. Then follow your serve into the court a step or two.

My rear end sticks out when I'm serving.

Transfer: Your upward transfer occurs too soon. Check your trophy pose. Load and explode. Fully extend before impact when the toss is on the way up.

I can't hit the serve with enough spin.

Swing: First be sure you're tossing in the right place for spin serves (1 o'clock for slice and 11 o'clock for topspin for right-handed players). Then from the trophy pose extend upward to your toss, keeping your wrist loose at contact, so the racquet quickly can brush the ball.

Returns

The unit turn is your most basic move when returning serves. So work on this move until it's second nature to you. As you practice returning ground strokes, develop your rhythm. Along with the guidelines below, I've provided you with cues to use as you are drilling each aspect of your returns.

Seeing

As with the serve, see if any environmental conditions could pose difficulties for you. Is there a brisk crosswind, tailwind, or wind in your face that will affect your return? You may be able to use this to your advantage. Perhaps there is a light pole or something directly behind the server, which makes it difficult to see his toss. Adjust as necessary.

During your warm-up, notice what types of serve your opponent is using (flat, slice, or kick), and look for cues that might tip you off about what kind of serve is coming—any differences in stance or routine that accompany a particular type of serve. Generally an open stance indicates a slice or flat serve and a closed stance means a kick.

Once you've stepped into your ready position, visualize the return you're going to hit. Have a good idea of where you want to put the return, based on your opponent's strengths and weaknesses. If you're playing a baseliner, try hitting the ball deep to a corner to put your opponent on the defensive. If the other player is a serve-and-volleyer, return the ball low at the feet. As you set up, see this in your mind's eye. But don't give away your intentions by staring at your target area. Survey the whole court, but let your mind discreetly pick your spot.

During the match, keep track of where your opponent likes to serve on important points such as deuce, ad out, or key points in a tiebreaker. You may see a pattern developing, which you can then exploit by being ready with the right grip for the return.

As you play, you'll quickly get a good idea of what kind of server you're facing. If your opponent hits well-placed first and second serves with varying paces and spins, you're going to have to stay on her closely. But at the beginner and lower-intermediate levels of play, you're likely to face players who blast a first serve, hoping it hits the box, but weakly push a second serve, just trying to get it in to avoid a double fault. Other players regularly put a good spin on the first serve, but they don't have confidence in it and so they just push a second serve. You can pick up this pattern pretty early, being ready for the blast, spin, or push serve. Try not to salivate too much at those weak second serves, but take advantage of them and rapidly gain the upper hand in those points.

Remember also that how you see the ball is enhanced by setting up in your ready position with your dominant eye closest to the ball. As your opponent begins to serve, focus on three areas:

1. See how your opponent is bouncing the ball. Watch the ball like a hawk, especially if you're playing someone who disguises the ball or quick-serves you. Some players have the sleight-of-hand of magicians, and you easily can lose track of the ball—especially if you're also dealing with glare from indoor lights or sun.

2. Watch the toss at its highest trajectory and try to distinguish how your opponent's racquet face is meeting the ball. This strategy will help you determine the ball's direction, height, spin, pace, and depth.

3. To cue your timing and rhythm on the return, watch the ball as it hits on your side of the court to give you last-minute information as to what the ball is doing.

Notice how Yevgeny Kafelnikov has lined up his head, eyes, hands, and torso to the ball.

Using Video for Improving Your Game

As a professional coach I cannot encourage you enough to beg, borrow, or rent a video camera to tape yourself playing. If you cannot get someone to take the video for you, use a camera with a tripod. Video will improve your imagery skills faster than anything. Seeing is truly believing. I particularly like using a camera that has immediate playback available.

Try different camera angles, depending on what skills you're checking. Side angles emphasize seeing skills such as head position point of contact, the swing point of contact, and amount of transfer. Rotary skills such as backswing, coiling and uncoiling, and adjusting skills such as moving around the ball are best seen by shooting from behind. It also emphasizes other seeing skills, specifically anticipation, movement skills such as first step and recovery, adjusting, rotation, and swinging skills specifically. Shooting from a forward angle emphasizes the position of the head and body for the see-ing skills and shows how they affect your stance. Adjusting skills such as movement around the ball and movements into the court can be viewed as well as weight transfer and swinging skills (specifically the follow-through and racquet-head acceleration).

If you are taping matches, try to get a wide angle so you can capture the balls being sent and received. Slow motion can help you to pick the finer nuances of your swing—such as racquet face at point of contact, uncoiling for rotary skills such as the relation of the hips and shoulders at contact, and pronation on serves and smashes. You also can analyze the timing of weight transfer on the serve to see if you transfer your weight from the back foot to the front foot. By watching yourself on video and analyzing the other players, you start to build your own personal library of images that you carry inside your mind. You'll then refer to these images to improve your game while you play.

Using Your Eyes

Darlene Kluka, PhD
Sports vision expert at Grambling State University in Louisiana

Athletes have to learn how to play from the eyes down. They should make sure that their visual systems have the best chance for receiving and processing information. That means training both eyes to observe as much relevant information as possible and not processing less important pieces of information.

In baseball, pitchers distract hitters with elaborate windups—lots of irrelevant movement. The same thing can happen in tennis. You don't need to watch everything the server does. Lock onto the ball—in the hand, at impact, and when it lands in your court.

Movement

You're going to need to move quickly to reach any good serve, so the best thing is to be moving even before the serve. Get used to bouncing on the balls of your feet as you set up in the ready position. When your opponent tosses the ball, hop forward, taking a split step at the moment he makes contact. This puts you in an athletic stance with your weight moving into the return. As time can be a factor, take your first step with

····· **Cues** ·····

Two-part breath (inhale on bounce, exhale on your contact); bounce . . . hit

Turn, shuffle, set

Pivot, hit, step

Pivot, step, hit

Turn and set

the foot closest to the ball to assume a foundation from which you can drive the return. Here are some tips for particular types of returns:

Returning high-speed serves. After your initial split step, make a unit turn and simply deflect (block) the ball back over the net. Or split, unit turn, hit the return, and then step to recover. If the serve surprises you, you may only have time to split step and lunge for the ball.

Returning medium and slow serves. You'll use a split step and unit turn and then shuffle forward, backward, laterally, or diagonally to get into the best position to rip or rally your return.

Returning especially easy second serves. Try to transfer weight into the return to hit a winner. After the split step, unit turn, and shuffle, take a moment to set your feet before ripping the return.

Returning serves that break away from you. You'll need to split, unit turn, hit, and step.

Returning serves you can challenge, going to the net. Use the footwork for transition movements covered in chapter 1—split and carioca on the backhand side or power step on the forehand. These will quickly get you to the net after the return.

Practice all of these moves from different places on the court. Start from behind the baseline, on the baseline, and inside the court, and practice returning all types of serves from each location.

Adjusting

Returning service, you constantly have to adjust to differing direction, depth, height, speed, and spin. Remember the crosshairs of the rifle scope described in chapter 1? You need to adjust your feet, hands, and torso to the expected path of the approaching ball so it arrives (a) at your preferred strike zone, (b) at your preferred contact point, and (c) at a proper distance from your body. And this serve may be coming toward you at more than 100 miles per hour!

Let's say your opponent has just hit a serve toward your backhand. The ball is approaching fairly high over the net and you can tell by the way that your opponent has arched his back and thrown the toss slightly behind him that the ball has been hit with a heavy topspin. When the ball bounces, it will really kick. Now it's time for you to start your adjustments.

Do you want to meet the ball on the rise, at the peak of its bounce, or coming down? Then move forward or backward accordingly. If you plan to meet a kick serve at the peak of its bounce, you may watch it veer over your shoulder or over your head. It's best to meet that kind of serve on the rise, cutting it off before it can kick so high—or back up and let it come down to you. Line up on the foot closest to the ball, but allow for the expected sidespin of the ball. Since you know the ball is going to bounce high, you need to prepare your hands and racquet in a higher strike zone by taking a higher backswing.

Of course, every serve is different, requiring all sorts of instantaneous, instinctive adjustments. There's no substitute for experience. Learn as you play, discover how to anticipate certain spins and certain shots, and teach your body to adjust quickly to what you see.

Rotation

If you're lunging for a well-placed serve to either side, you won't have much time for rotation. And if you're fighting off a fast serve right at you, it may be all you can do to get your racquet on the ball. But these desperate moves make for weak returns, which give your opponent the edge. Rotation gives power to your return, so get in the habit of hopping into that unit turn as soon as you see where the ball's going.

The unit turn rotates your entire body and your racquet in a single move, putting you in position to unfurl a powerful return. Of course, the more time you have, the more you can rotate. Returning a weak second serve, you can fully coil your hips, shoulders, and torso.

Besides providing power, rotation helps disguise your intentions. As you turn your body, your grip and racquet position are hidden, leaving your opponent less time to figure out where your return will go.

Transfer

First serves that are pushed or second serves that are weak give you an opportunity to attack on the return. This requires a careful blend of rotation, transfer, and swing. This is much like receiving a short ball in a baseline rally (review the information on transition shots in chapter 1).

Thomas Muster transferring his weight backward to allow the ball to drop into his strike zone.

Or you might want to return a weak serve by simply moving around the ball to hit a solid forehand. Be sure you adjust quickly enough to have your weight transferring forward into the shot.

But you're not worried about the weak serves, are you? It's the ballistic first serve that nearly shocks you out of your socks—how will you ever have time to get any weight transfer into these returns? You probably won't. Many players like to prepare for return of service just behind the area in the court where they hope to meet the serve. On all returns, then, they split step and move forward. This gets their body weight moving forward, putting some natural transfer into the return. Boris Becker made this move famous winning his first Wimbledon. Even if you have to block the return—no time for normal rotation and swing—your forward movement will give some pace to your shot.

Surprisingly, not all weight is transferred forward. It's not uncommon today to see many top professionals such as Carlos Moya, Alex Corretja, or Thomas Muster (see photo above) especially on clay, using a backward transfer of weight. This is not to put power into the shot, but to allow the ball to drop into a strike zone where the player can take a full swing. In other cases, a player may move diagonally to reach a ball that's going wide and just line up the racquet to deflect the ball back. Some of that diagonal motion may add forward power to the stroke, as a well-placed sail can benefit from a crosswind, but most of the force comes from the incoming ball itself.

Swing

There you are, awaiting a 100-mph serve from Killer Kravchek. You're giving him lots of room, preparing behind the baseline, bouncing in place, timing your split step just right. Suddenly he loads his cannon and fires, and there's the ball, speeding toward you. You can get it; it's in your strike zone! You split step making a unit turn, take a wild backswing and meet the ball squarely . . . sending it high over Killer's head, into another area code.

The toughest thing to remember in returning a serve is to take a measured backswing. People often get excited and swing wildly, rather than meeting each type of serve in an appropriate way. Generally, shorten your backswing for fast serves if you're near the baseline or inside the baseline. If you're being forced on defense with fast serves or well-placed serves you have to stretch for, or spins of various heights, depths, and directions, the shorter backswing keeps you in control. The shorter your backswing, the easier it is to time your contact with the ball. If you have an easy ball back by the baseline, take a big backswing and let it rip. But tough shots and precision shots may require the extra control of a measured backswing. The following troubleshooting guidelines can help you improve your returns.

Troubleshooting for Returns

I'm often caught with the wrong grip.

Seeing: Is your opponent studying your grip? If so, let him know you're aware of this by constantly switching it or waiting until he starts his serving motion to establish your grip.

Swing: Do not grip your racquet too tightly in the ready position. Let your nondominant hand turn the racquet in your hand. If you still are getting caught, try preselecting a grip that's suitable for the spot where your opponent will likely serve. This will likely be a backhand; but even if you have to change, you can move quickly to a continental or eastern forehand grip or the grip of your choice.

My returns are going all over the court.

Seeing: Keep your eye where you're aiming.

Adjusting: Adjust your starting position.

Swing: Measure your backswing and take a shorter backswing.

I get aced in the same place over and over.

Movement: Take your split step as the ball is struck to get yourself ready to move quickly.

Rotation: Vary your position (deep in the court, on or inside the baseline).

I often can't reach second serves.

Movement: Start closer to the service box and use shuffle steps to move forward.

I always swing late on a return.

Seeing: Make sure you are carefully watching your opponent's toss.

Adjusting: If you're too close to the ball, start farther back.

Rotation: Make your unit turn faster.

Swing: Shorten your backswing.

I'm often jammed on returns.

Adjusting: Work on moving around the ball, running around the anticipated contact point to get proper position.

My returns go short in the court.

Seeing: Pick the spot where you would like to return.

Adjusting: Get proper distance to swing. Clear the net with more height and spin. Add pace to your return.

Transfer: If hitting in a closed stance, rotate and *transfer weight into your shot.*

Swing: Accelerate the racquet head and hit the ball with a complete follow-through.

My returns go wide.

Movement: Make sure your first step is powerful.

Adjusting: Do not jam yourself. Give yourself proper distance from the ball.

Swing: Your swing may be late or not accelerating when meeting the ball. Aim away from the lines.

My returns go into the net.

Seeing: Pick your spot for the return.

Movement: Adjust your position by challenging the return with shuffle steps or transition movements.

Adjusting: Try to aim higher over the net. Try a different spin.

Rotation: Stay low and work on speeding up your unit turn so that you're waiting for the ball. Continue to adjust your location until the ball is being met at a height with which you feel comfortable.

Swing: Shorten your swing and open the racquet face slightly if you are blocking second serves. Add topspin or slice to give you more net clearance.

My returns go long.

Adjusting: Work on shuffle steps and adjust your position.

Transfer: You may not be transferring properly; your weight may be on your heels, especially if you're on the defensive.

Swing: You may have too big of a windup on second-service return. Work on your shuffle steps with a shortened backswing. Add topspin. Check to see if your grip is changing. Lower the height of your return. Aim shorter in the court. Close your racquet face more at impact.

My timing seems off.

Adjusting: Adjust your position further back so that you have more time.

Transfer: Use the two-part breathing (chapter 8) for timing the bounce and your stroke.

Developing Consistent Swinging Shots

Ground strokes such as forehands and backhands are the meat and potatoes of the game of tennis. If you manage to return your opponent's serve deep into the court, or if your opponent returns your serve deep, chances are you'll settle into some ground-stroke play for a while until one of you makes a mistake, hits a winner, or decides to come to the net.

Ground Strokes

Ground strokes, angles, passing shots, smashes, lobs, and swinging volleys, like serves and returns (chapter 2), are part of the swinging shots family. The primary source for power is rotation on swinging shots.

Seeing

Line up your dominant eye on your opponent's ground strokes. If you're same-side dominant (right eye and right hand or left eye and left hand), you can meet balls hit to your forehand side using an open stance. Keep your head straight as long as possible to keep your dominant eye on the ball. On the backhand side, the same holds true if you are left-eye dominant. You can take a more open stance if you have a two-handed backhand or keep your head more forward if you are a one-hander. Players usually have an easier time hitting down the line on their dominant side.

Let's say you've just run your opponent wide with a perfectly placed angle. The desperate return is bouncing in the center of your court, and it hangs there like a big plum. The other player is scrambling to get back into position. You have a wide-open court in which to hit. You move around the ball to line up an easy forehand. You just have to put the ball away. You take your measured backswing and . . . you shank the ball into the net.

What happened? It's quite possible you lined up on the ball with your nondominant eye. In your rush to rotate your body for the kill, you turned your head, letting the wrong eye zero in on the ball. As a result, you received inaccurate information about the ball's location. Not terribly inaccurate, just enough to convince your body to swing at an imaginary ball a few inches away from the real one. Just enough to hit the ball with the frame rather than the sweet spot.

Once you get accurate data from your dominant eye, you'll be able to read the motion of the ball—its direction, spin, height, depth, and pace—as well as you and your opponent's positions on the court. What you do with this information is a matter of tactical awareness, which I'll cover throughout this chapter with regard to ground strokes, angles, passing shots, smashes, and lobs.

Movement

On ground strokes you'd better be able to move in all directions, toward the ball, away from the ball, around the ball. It's a dance; you and the ball are like Fred and Ginger. The ball will hop, dip, and dive. You need to be right there with it.

With any dance, you need to learn the steps. There's a lot of by-the-numbers basic practice required before you go public. Here are the basic ground-stroke steps:

Split-unit turn—rotates your body and gets the racquet back quickly (see photo of Carlos Moya on page 47)

Split-step out—first step lines up the foot closest to the ball

Split-shuffle—steps in all directions

Split-unit turn-sprint—for a ball farther away

Split-unit turn-sprint-slide—on clay

Notice that I start every play with a split step; this gets your feet moving. The unit turn gets your body in position for a quick rotation. Shuffle steps adjust your position. For balls that take you wide, the crossover shuffle allows you to cover a lot of ground on your first step. If you have to cross the whole court, you could pivot and sprint as Monica Seles demonstrates on page 47.

After you hit the ball, the play continues as you recover, returning to a ready position. A lateral shuffle helps you here, to keep an eye on your opponent while getting into place and still allow you to change directions quickly if you need to.

Step-by-step practice is frustrating; it feels awkward, not like playing at all. But that's what you have to master at any level. Your body has to go through the paces. As you sweat through these practice moves, stop every so often to watch a pro tennis match on TV. Turn off the sound and ignore the score, just watch the movements. You can recognize the unit turn, the crossover shuffle, the split step, but now all those tactical moves are blending into one fluid sequence. One sequence flows into another as the player moves into place, adjusts, rotates her body, transfers the weight, executes the swing, and recovers to see the next ball approaching.

Split-unit turn with Carlos Moya.   Monica Seles demonstrating the pivot sprint.

Adjusting

As explained in chapter 2, lining up means planting the foot closest to the ball behind the perceived flight path of the ball, in the proper place so your whole body falls into alignment with the ball. If you line up well, your swing will meet the ball in your desired strike zone at the best point of contact. If you line up improperly, you'll be reaching for the ball (or too close to it), and your stroke will be a mess. You know how bad driving can feel if your car is poorly aligned. In the same way, the adjustments you make in lining up are crucial to the rest of your game. Here are some guidelines for adjusting your alignment for several types of swings:

Forehand. Plant your right foot (if you are right-handed). Then either step into your stroke with the left foot or stay open. The open stance forces your shoulder and arm to do more of the work, but it helps you see the ball longer.

One-handed backhand. You have a choice here, too. You can essentially reverse the pattern of the forehand stroke, planting with the left foot and stepping into the shot with the right (if you are right-handed). This is commonly done on backhands that you drive with topspin or flat stroke. However, if you're slicing, plant the right foot. In this case, you can see the "line" vividly all in perfect alignment from the right foot straight up to the hip, to the shoulder, and sometimes the chin resting on the shoulder.

Two-handed backhand. The two-handed backhand player may choose to line up first with the left foot and, with time to spare, step in with the right foot (if right-handed). When stretching wide for a ball, the two-hander may step across to line up with the right foot first.

Adjust Your Backswing

A big backswing can add power to your stroke, but there's a point of diminishing returns, literally. You can lose timing and control when you take the racquet back too far. In general, the more difficult a ball you're receiving, the shorter your backswing should be; the easier the ball, the more backswing you can add.

Of course, other elements also come into play, such as court position. The farther you are from the net, the more backswing you'll need. If you're near the net, you'll only need a short backswing to put the ball where you want it, so precision is more important than power. In addition, you'll make backswing choices based on the game situation. A big backswing puts you in a go-for-broke mode, like a baseball slugger swinging for the fences. If you need to play defensively, a short backswing makes timing your contact easier.

Rotation

Rotation is your primary power source on your ground strokes. The hips, shoulders, and torso, counter-rotated on a firm athletic stance, create a lot of stored energy.

Forehand. With the forehand the racquet arm pulls back and the other arm balances it, creating a full stretch across the upper body. Even in an open stance, the rotation of the upper body and hips is evident. The right shoulder lags back, causing a stretch through the chest. This is the coiling I've talked about, the preparation for the whiplike motion that provides power for your strokes. That racquet (right) shoulder eventually uncoils, rotating around until the body is squarely facing the net.

One-handed backhand. If you turn your shoulder early for the backhand, you'll be able to hide your moves from your opponent and also create a solid, powerful stretch of your back and trunk muscles. Notice how the body is rotated to the point that the chin actually rests upon the shoulder. From the front you can actually see the back of the player's shoulder. As you uncoil, the left hand goes back the other way, as a way of stabilizing the shoulders.

Tommy Haas moves back while rotating his hips and shoulders.

Two-handed backhand. As you will note in looking at the photo to the right, here the rotation is slightly different, especially on the uncoiling. As the racquet is drawn back with two hands, both shoulders uncoil toward the desired target, with the right arm being used to control the racquet and the left adding power (for a right-handed player). This can be executed from an open or closed stance. The two-handed backhand also provides disguise because your hands initially are hidden from your opponent's view by your body. Then, with two hands, you have the greater control you need to flick the racquet at the last possible second and change the direction of your shot.

Transfer

Transfer on the ground strokes can and does occur from open and closed stances. How much you choose to transfer your weight into your shots depends on your shot intent and the amount of time you have to move into the shot.

Chandra Rubin demonstrates the two-handed backhand.

Forehand. Rotation may be the primary source of power on ground strokes, but there is still weight being transferred. For a right-handed forehand, the transfer occurs from the right foot to the left as the player steps into the stroke. In a closed stance, the weight transfer is even stronger, occurring before contact with the ball.

Backhand. On the right-handed backhand, the right foot is pointing slightly forward at a 45-degree angle so that the hips are not blocked and can be rotated into the shot. The transfer of weight is earlier on the backhand than it is on the forehand, from the left foot to the right and typically heel to toe on the lead (right) foot. As the swing nears its completion, it's not uncommon on a two-handed backhand to see the left leg rotate through, squaring up with the right leg. This shows that rotation has contributed to the power of the stroke; it also helps the player recover, regaining balance.

Swing

Now that you are in position to swing you want to keep the following in mind: (a) keep your swing smooth, and (b) accelerate your swing on the ground strokes keeping your head still.

Forehand. From the athletic stance in the ready position, you've taken a split step and moved to the ball, adjusting to various factors on the way; you have obtained ideal striking distance to the ball, and you've rotated, taking the racquet back; and you're starting to transfer your weight into the swing and uncoil. Freeze the frame right there. What is going on with the swing?

As your shoulders uncoil, the racquet lags behind. This lag causes an additional stretching of your chest and shoulder muscles that are used to generate racquet-head speed. Note also the position of your wrist, cocked like the hammer on a pistol, at an angle from 45 to 90 degrees. This loading action with the wrist allows optimal control at the point of contact. Maintain this wrist angle as the rest of your body uncoils—remember your wrist and racquet are the tail of the whip. Once your shoulders are squared up, facing your target, and your arm has brought the wrist forward making contact with the ball—*then* release the angle of your wrist. You want to keep your wrist flexible at the end of your swing, but early release of that wrist angle keeps the whip from cracking with full power.

The follow-through depends on your shot intention. Obviously your follow-through varies if you're hitting an angle, improvising on a ball just to get it over, or meeting the perfect sitter in the middle of the court. For a flat stroke, the normal follow-through is outward and upward. The more spin and lift you put on the ball, the more upward your swing path will be. The follow through will depend on the height of the ball being met and the intended direction, in which case, if t may be over the shoulder or even across your body to the opposite hip.

Of course rhythm and timing are crucial in executing a good swing. This will be discussed more in chapter 4, but here's a simple approach to get you started, courtesy of Victor Tantalo in his book *USA Tennis Course* (page 56):

1. Visualize your hitting area as the ball travels toward you.

2. Say "wait" while your eyes and brain measure the approaching ball.

3. When the ball reaches your hitting area, say "Now!" Then aim and hit.

One-handed backhand. From your ready position, you have split stepped, completed a unit turn, and moved into position, lining up on the incoming ball. Your body is coiled to the point that your opponent can see about half of your back, and your chin rests on your shoulder. Your racquet also is coiled, with the racquet face open.

Either a straight or loop backswing will work, depending on your timing. You are ready to swing at the ball, making contact in front of your body. Your wrist is locked in and your legs are flexed. As you uncoil, you remain sideways to the net. Your follow-through is much longer, continuing toward your desired target.

Two-handed backhand. You use the same ready stance, split step, movement, and lining up. Rotating your shoulder, you take the racquet back with both arms. Then you step into the shot, with your right foot pointing to the ball. The uncoiling of your torso and the driving action of your left hand provide tremendous amounts of power. The follow-through continues out toward the target, until your arms are bent, allowing the racquet head to finish above your extended elbows.

To the left are a few cues to help you on your ground strokes. They may aid your timing or simply remind you of key aspects of the stroke.

Cues

- Set and hit
- Set and finish
- Hop, hop, hit
- Shuffle set
- Run and finish
- Brush and hit
- Short, extend, full extension, follow-through, short, and hit
- Move your feet
- Go to the ball
- Stay on your toes like an infielder
- Take short, quick steps
- Wait and hit

Troubleshooting Ground Strokes

I'm lunging for the ball, but not getting to it.

Seeing: More quickly identify the different ball controls (direction, height, spin, depth, and pace) of your opponent's shot intention. Note what shot you sent before you received the return forcing your lunge. Anticipate a similar return next time.

Movement: Your initiating movement may not be strong enough or you chose footwork unsuitable for the situation, or you didn't recover well from your last shot. Your last shot also may be the cause of the problem.

The ball doesn't go where I aim; I can't control the shot.

Seeing: Visualize the ball going to the target you have selected.

Adjusting: For directional control, line up your eyes, feet, hips, shoulders, hands, and racquet to the ball.

Swing: Control the racquet head. Work on follow-through. If you stop the follow-through abruptly, your stroke will be hacking, actually decelerating the racquet before you hit the ball. This lets the incoming ball (rather than your stroke) determine where it's going next. If you're using the one-handed backhand, you may not be physically strong enough, resulting in excessive body rotation, loss of racquet-head control, inability to impart spin, and meeting the ball too late. Check with a certified teaching professional to see if you should switch to a two-handed backhand.

I'm hitting into the net.

Adjusting: Get under the ball by flexing your knees and meeting the ball in your desired strike zone. Sometimes players meet a ball too high or too low. Line up your racquet hand on the ball so that the hand can drop under the ball to add proper lift. Aim higher over the net and try more topspin. Check ball controls: height, spin, direction, depth, and speed. Add height and spin, going for more depth. If the problem persists, try less speed and more spin.

Transfer: You may be straightening your legs too soon. This mistimes the release of power on your weight transfer. By the time you hit the ball, your leg strength has already been used. Perhaps you're transferring weight too early or uncoiling too soon, meeting the ball too far out in front. Some players, when uncoiling, dip the shoulder, causing the racquet to swing downward.

Swing: Check your swinging skills and swing path. Your racquet head is not getting under the ball. Work on swing skills. Your grip may be too tight. Your swing path could be too direct or from high to low. Try lifting the ball higher over the net with a low-to-high swing path. The racquet face also may be closed at impact, or you're rushing the timing of the stroke, making contact too far out in front. Check your adjusting skills and add more spin if necessary. Also check your point of contact—not too far ahead of your body or past it.

The ball goes short in the court. I'm not hitting it cleanly.

Seeing: Your head may be jerking or moving excessively, affecting your eyes.

Movement: Aim higher and deeper over the net. Or change the spin.

Rotation: Check your hitting stance. Do not block your hips by stepping with your lead foot across your body as this inhibits proper rotation. On your backhand, step out with your lead foot about 45 degrees for proper rotation. Keep your nonracquet hand on the throat of the racquet longer. This automatically turns your shoulders for you. If this is the problem, try an open stance (this can occur on either forehand or backhand).

Transfer: Back up a couple of steps. You may need more time to transfer weight into the shot.

I'm always too close to the ball to hit a solid ground stroke.

Adjusting: Practice getting around the ball to be properly positioned to take a full swing. Players who don't do this tend to drag the racquet across the ball, resulting in sidespin. They often hit the ball wide.

My ground stroke goes wide.

Adjusting: Don't aim too close to the lines; give yourself some margin for error.

Swing: Your swing path may be reversed, swinging from out to in, imparting sidespin on the ball. Try swinging in to out, so at the point of contact, you're sure that you're hitting on the outside of the ball and out in front of your body. The outside of the ball is always the side that's farthest from you (i.e., the right side if it's on your right). By meeting the ball on the outside, you naturally hit toward the center of the court. Aim away from the lines.

My ground stroke goes long.

Adjusting: Adjust your position to the ball. Work with different blends of rotation and transfer to get the proper amount of power in your stroke. Your racquet may be too loose. Reduce pace and add more spin. Aim lower over the net.

Swing: Shorten your backswing. Your racquet face may be too open on contact with the ball. Your swing may be too big. Your strings may be too loose. You may have hit in a strike zone that's too high. A different swing path could impart more spin. Make sure your wrist is firm at impact. Aim shorter in the court and use more topspin, reducing the pace put on the ball. Your swing path may be so direct that the ball is going out; try swinging more from low to high.

I take one giant step to the ball and become off-balance.

Movement: Move faster to the area where you'll hit the ball, using large steps at first, then shorten your steps as you near it, so you can make last-second adjustments if needed.

I always get sidespin on my backhand whether I want it or not.

Rotation: When you take the racquet back, be sure it's not too far from your body.

I can't seem to get any pace on the ball.

Swing: The point of contact may be outside your ideal strike zone. Check your other skills to be sure you have proper distance to the ball. Also check that you're not decelerating as you swing but accelerating and finishing the stroke. Maybe your swing is imparting too much spin on the ball, slowing it down. Keep going outward with your follow-through after meeting the ball in your preferred strike zone.

I can't change my grip in time.

Swing: Be sure you're not gripping the racquet too tightly. Your nonracquet hand needs to be ready to help with the change.

Angles and Passing Shots

For the most part, the strategic angles and passing shots follow the same form as normal ground strokes. But you need to be aware of a few special concerns.

Seeing

Since these are tactical shots that you can work into your strategy, you need to see the factors that make you choose such a strategy. That is, recognize your location and that of your opponent, as well as the direction in which he is moving (or where you expect him to move). Of course you'll recognize the characteristics of the incoming ball (height, speed, spin, etc.). If you're hitting a passing shot, pick the precise section of the net over which you want to hit the ball. This all will be happening in a matter of seconds.

Movement

When moving forward to either a passing shot or an angle, look to move diagonally into the court rather than running parallel with the baseline. This will put increased pressure on your opponent, giving him less time.

Adjusting

Stay low until the shot is completed. It's tempting to lift out of the shot, but that just drives the ball down into the net.

Rotation

The amount of rotation will vary depending on the ball you are receiving and how quickly you are getting to the ball and your court positioning. You may find yourself six feet behind the baseline and taking a full rotation to get the ball over, or moving forward into the court and measuring your backswing to gently place the ball past an opponent who is out of position.

Transfer

Full-weight transfer is nice when you have time for it, but angles and passing shots are usually quickly decided and quickly made. If you find yourself in a place where you can step into one of these tactical shots, go for it, but it's not necessary.

Swing

On these shots, the backswing usually is shortened to permit an acceleration of the racquet and to help the timing of contact. With topspin you impart on the ball; the follow-through is often across your body.

> **· · · · · ·Cues· · · · · ·**
> Down and through
> Load and explode
> Stay down

Smash

The smash is one of the best shots with which to attack and challenge. Occasionally it can be a defensive shot—when you get a very deep lob or you're caught sneaking in. Do it right and you can put away a winner. Do it wrong and you'll wonder how you let your great opportunity slip away.

Seeing

The smash is similar to the serve, especially when it comes to lining up with your dominant eye. Some players can keep their heads rather straight on to the ball while others have to turn.

Sighting and tracking the lob are extremely important. How high is it? What type of spin? Was your opponent hitting an offensive or a defensive lob? (If your opponent has time to reach the ball, that's an offensive lob, which probably has topspin. But if she is falling backward or lunging, it's defensive, which probably has backspin.)

Environmental conditions are especially important when tracking the smash. You may have to adjust your position to avoid looking up into a bright sun, or shade your eyes with your free hand unless you are wearing a hat or sunglasses. A blue sky or an indoor environment can make it tough to gauge how far away the ball is. Of course poor lighting will also cause problems. In windy conditions, the ball is moving constantly, so keep your backswing short and don't stand still. If you're not comfortable with the ball's movement, you can still play it on the bounce.

Movement

Your opponent is probably lobbing because you're at the net, so you'll have to go back to get the ball. For a strong push backward, use what is called a jab step. Just like a boxer transferring weight into a punch, step forward with one leg, and push off backward on it.

Pivot and *move* around a ball that's coming over your backhand side. For a ball you can reach anywhere from the net to midcourt, jab step, pivot, and shuffle *to get into* position. *For a deeper lob,* jab, pivot, and sprint *to it.*

There are some special moves you can add to your smash repertoire. For a lob you have to jump to, almost over your racquet, the scissors smash gives you some weight transfer in midair with a scissors kick of your legs helping you to maintain balance (see photo below). A backhand smash is an option if you don't have time to move around to your forehand. On a bounce smash, let the lob bounce first, just to get your rhythm right (a good idea on very high lobs or if it's quite windy). Pete Sampras has a hang-time smash, jumping off both legs like a basketball player on a dunk. If you're close to the net, you can try a knee smash, getting down on one knee and meeting the ball quickly on the bounce. These last two smashes may impress your friends, and they also may show up your opponent. You look great if you master them, but silly if you don't. Use them with discretion.

Goran Ivanisevic demonstrates a midair scissors smash.

Cues

Pivot-smash

Track-smash

Racquet back, ready, left arm up

Extend, reach, and pull

Turn and hit

Pivot, cross over, smash

Pivot, head up

Adjusting

If you're right-handed, keep your left arm up, tracking the flight of the ball, and the racquet head up, ready to pounce. Last-second adjustments are standard on the smash, so keep your feet moving. Coach Pat Etcheberry says, "Think of being barefoot on a hot tennis court." And of course you'll be making any adjustments necessary for the kind of smash you're using.

Rotation

Hips, shoulders, and torso rotate immediately, storing energy, while the flexed legs assume a solid base. There is an external rotation of the shoulder on the backswing followed by an internal rotation of the shoulder as the legs begin to extend. As the body uncoils, the arm is accelerated upward, toward the ball, and then the forearm pronates.

Transfer

Once you're lined up on the ball, try to transfer weight by moving forward and upward into the shot. Your weight transfers then from right foot to left foot. If you see the lob is going over your head, spring off your back leg and scissor your legs while your body leans up and back to reach the ball that is nearly out of reach. Scissoring your legs in this way acts as a counter movement to retain balance. With the backhand smash, you end up jumping off your left foot and landing on your left foot.

Swing

Various grips can be used but the continental grip is preferred for slice and flat smashes. You also may choose from a number of swing paths, stances, backswings, points of contact, and follow-throughs, whatever works for you.

On the backswing some players like to take the racquet straight up into the trophy pose while others take a longer swing path. From the trophy pose with the racquet head held up, the racquet pauses or passes continuously without a pause upward to the ball. As the legs extend from their flexed position and the hips, torso, and shoulders uncoil, the racquet lags back slightly. As the racquet accelerates with an internal rotation of the shoulder, the forearm pronates to the point of impact with the supple wrist allowing the hand and racquet to speed up. If you counted out the rhythm of the racquet being taken back and then sped up to the point of contact, it would be as follows:

1. Take the racquet back, with the racquet head held up, as on a serve, and the legs flexed.

2. Begin to straighten the legs and drop the racquet to its lowest point down the back, then propel the racquet upward to the ball with the body being fully extended at impact.

3. Hit the ball and the follow-through with the racquet continuing outward across the body.

Keep the grip loose until the point of impact to maximize acceleration. The body is straight and fully extended at impact. As with the serve, keep the elbow up as long as possible and pronate the forearm. The smash is struck in strike zone A, above the shoulder. Points of contact vary, depending on how well the lob was disguised, your court location, and the difficulty of the ball you're receiving.

Troubleshooting Your Smash

I'm missing the smash completely.

Seeing: Keep your head and chin up. Focus on the ball with your dominant eye until after contact. In practice, catch the ball with your free hand to get used to reaching up to hit the ball. If you're playing in extreme environmental conditions take a bounce smash.

Movement: Stay in motion with your feet until the last possible second.

Swing: Take an abbreviated backswing so you can focus on last-second adjustments.

My smash goes into the net.

Seeing: Keep your eyes on the ball.

Movement: Keep your feet moving on the court as you watch the approaching ball.

Adjusting: Adjust your body position to the ball as it approaches.

Rotation: You may be hitting the ball too low and in front of you. Work on the timing of your uncoiling.

Transfer: Be sure your weight is transferring forward and that your feet aren't stuck in cement.

Swing: Your point of contact may be too far out in front, so you're hitting down on the ball. Or the point of contact may be too low, which occurs when having trouble judging depth (indoors or at night against a dark sky). If you misjudge the ball position, it can drop too low before you reach up to hit it. Time it so you meet the ball high above you. You always can let it drop and smash it on the bounce.

I meet the ball too low and send it out.

Movement: You may not be getting in position early enough. Take a strong first step when backing up for the smash. Use the jab step, crossover shuffles, or other crossover steps to get into position quickly so that you can fully extend yourself and transfer weight into the shot.

Swing: Do some practice swings without the ball, reaching up to a fully extended point of contact. If you're using a forehand grip on the smash, you are probably hitting the ball too flat. Change to the continental.

My smash goes long.

Swing: Add spin and meet the ball more in front of you. Don't try to kill the smash; go for placement and varying depths.

My smash goes wide.

Swing: Do not slice the ball wide at the point of contact. Check your grip. (Are you using a continental grip?). Don't aim too close to the lines.

I'm putting too much spin on the ball.

Adjusting: Your racquet arm is not extending enough. Ask a certified teaching pro to show you how. Reach up fully. Also check your grip and use the continental not the forehand grip.

Swing: With the continental grip you can pronate your forearm.

My timing's off, so when I jump for the ball I shank it or miss it entirely.

Seeing: See where you are in the court. If you are ahead of the service line, you shouldn't need to jump.

Adjusting: You're not bending your legs enough. Flex your legs as you get into position.

When I go up for the smash, I'm always too far from the ball.

Movement: Practice initiating with a stronger jab step.

Adjusting: Track the flight of the ball with your nonracquet hand while doing the trophy pose.

I lose my balance as I go backward for the smash, and then I hit ineffectively.

Movement: Perfect your shuttle steps so they allow you to move forward and backward.

Rotation: The backward movement is dangerous and you're losing all rotation. Your shoulders aren't turning. Turn your whole body to run back, even if you keep your head forward to watch the ball. Keep that body rotation. Just before a smash, be in a trophy pose, as if you're serving, with hips and shoulders coiled back. In practice, try catching the ball with your extended left hand while your body coils in the trophy pose.

I'm always hitting the smash off my back foot.

Seeing: Watch and listen for cues that your opponent is planning on lobbing you. Look to see if their racquet face is open, if both of their feet are planted, and if they are dropping the racquet head and accelerating upward to hit a topspin lob.

Movement: The jab step is crucial to perfect.

Transfer: Get quickly into position to behind where the ball is dropping. Give yourself room to transfer weight into the smash. Sometimes you'll have to hit off the back foot, if the lob surprises you, but ideally you'll set up behind it and step in.

I always jump off the ground when hitting a smash. Is this OK?

Seeing: Look to see where you are in the court. If you are ahead of the service line, you shouldn't have to jump unless you are just being flashy.

Transfer: Hang time is cool, but it can make you mistime your smash. Keep your feet on the ground and transfer weight forward, using shuffle steps or small stutter steps to get into position, then set your feet and uncoil upward to the ball. You can jump on the more difficult smashes, when a lob pushes you deep in your court, past the service line. Then the bicycle or scissors smash may save you.

My smash lacks power.

Transfer: Adjust with your legs flexed, then push off the ground forcefully.

Swing: Your point of contact may be too far to the side or too low. Reach up for the ball above your head.

I'm always sidearming the ball on the smash.

Adjusting: Track the flight of the ball with your nonracquet hand.

Swing: Work on your swing path and pronation of the forearm to ensure that you're hitting the ball from left to right. On the smash, your swing path goes upward past your ear, not off to the side.

Backhand Smash

The backhand smash can be one of the most balletlike movements in tennis. And it's quite helpful if you're playing a crafty opponent who can repeatedly disguise his intent and then lob over your backhand side.

Seeing

The lob over your backhand normally catches you by surprise on your way to the net, so there's not a lot to see in advance. Just be sure you recognize it as soon as possible.

Movement

Not much here either. You have little time to move backward, as you would for a normal smash. You may just have time to step back with your right foot or take a crossover step.

Adjusting

You have a quick decision to make. Go for the backhand smash or run around it to hit a normal smash. The normal smash is usually your best option. But if you are pressed for time, then reach up for the backhand smash.

Rotation

Rotate immediately to your backhand side, turning most of your back on your opponent. On a forehand smash, your free hand tracks the incoming ball, but on the backhand smash the shoulder and elbow of your racquet arm must help you line up on the ball. That is, actually point your elbow at the ball and extend your arm to meet the ball. Note: when your arm goes up to meet the ball on the backhand smash, your body will counter-rotate *away* from the ball.

Transfer

Your weight has moved to your back foot. Depending on how high the lob is, you may need to spring up off that back leg and land on the same leg. You're not transferring weight forward, but upward, to reach the ball.

Swing

Keep your elbow high and extend your racquet up to the ball. Now your body is fully stretched out. Use your wrist and forearm to adjust the face of the racquet to angle your reply short crosscourt or deep down the line.

· · · · **Cues** · · · ·

Turn and extend

Elbow up

At first just practice getting the racquet up to the ball and directing it with your wrist. Don't worry about adding power until you feel more confident with the basics. But later you can accelerate more and more, snapping the racquet up to the ball and following the wrist down (on the follow through) in the direction of the target. This will improve your confidence in the shot.

Troubleshooting for Backhand Smash

I meet the ball too low.

Adjusting: Line up the elbow and shoulder on the ball, swinging upward to meet the ball.

Swing: Is the ball high enough to hit a backhand smash? If not, take a high backhand volley.

I can't get any pace on the ball.

Rotation: Rotate more at the beginning of your stroke. You may be sidearming the ball a bit if your elbow is too low.

Swing: Your swing may be too stiff or the grip on your racquet too loose. Stay loose when taking the racquet back; keep your forearm and elbow relaxed as you extend upward from the elbow.

I can't control my backhand smash.

Rotation: Practice rotating and extending your arm to the ball. Do not rotate your body in the direction of the shot but away from it as a counter movement.

Swing: Stop the racquet at the point of contact and use your wrist and lower forearm to direct the ball.

Lob

The lob is a strategic ploy that lofts the ball over a net-minding opponent. A well-placed lob can turn a point around, putting your opponent on the defensive. Too high or too low, and you could be facing an impossible smash. The lob is less about power and more about touch, but even here the SMARTS skills can help you.

The lob can be used offensively or defensively. The offensive lob can chase your opponent back from the net. It usually is hit with topspin, so it bounces away from the retreating player. The defensive lob buys you time when you're in trouble. It usually is hit with backspin.

Seeing

For this strategic stroke, take in all the data that affect your tactical decision. Is your opponent closing in on the net, trying to pick off your pass? Is the sun behind you, in the other player's eyes? Are you lobbing into the wind? Does your opponent have a poor smash? If you answer "yes" to any of these questions, and you're set up to hit the shot, then go for an offensive lob. If you're not in a good position, you still can throw up a defensive lob.

Movement

Move as you would for any forehand or backhand, in an open or closed stance. The lob is basically a ground stroke with a higher trajectory.

Adjusting

The ball is soaring toward you, and you see your opponent rushing the net. Decision time. You have tried to pass, but your opponent reads your passing shots easily. Maybe it's time for a lob. Depending on your time and position, you'll choose either an offensive or a defensive lob. Once you've made these decisions, you need to make only a few minor adjustments to your normal ground-stroke stance. Your legs need strong flexion to help with the lift. For a slice lob (defensive), open the racquet face more. On a backhand lob, straighten your arm slightly before contact.

Rotation

On a forehand lob, your follow-through needs to rotate your body toward the target. On the backhand lob, the ball is lifted up from your shoulder and the upward swing path of the racquet.

Transfer

The weight transfer occurs on the lob about the same as on a ground stroke, except with a slightly larger step. Set up with your front foot pointing toward the oncoming ball. On the backhand lob, your right leg should straighten. With the lift of your shoulder, your body should counter with a slight backward movement.

Swing

The swing is what really makes a lob different. The swing is low to high, with the open racquet face creating lift. On the forehand, the racquet arm remains slightly bent. On the backhand it's straighter.

Cues

Lob and rob (rob your opponent of an advantageous position at the net)

Under and lift

Under and accelerate for a topspin lob

Troubleshooting for Lobs

My opponent picks off the lob and easily smashes it.

Seeing: Before you lob, be sure your opponent is coming in all the way and not hanging back waiting for you to lob.

Rotation: Use rotation to disguise your intention for the lob for as long as possible.

My lob goes short in the court.

Movement: Execute all the same movements that you normally would use for a ground stroke, but give the ball added lift by opening the racquet face.

Adjusting: Straighten your arm on the backhand. Your backswing may be too large and you may not be getting under the ball. Extend your follow-through. Adjust the racquet face by opening it more for slice. Hit with more height on the lob. On the offensive lob, you may be putting too much spin on the ball.

Transfer: On the defensive lob, you may be transferring weight while falling backward, lunging to the side, or stretched out in an open stance. Give your ball extra lift when in trouble.

I can't control the lob.

Seeing: Check to see if the wind is a factor.

Adjusting: Add height and spin.

Rotation: There's not enough rotation. You're letting your arm do all the work. Get your body into it, too.

My lob is too low. My opponent reaches it.

Swing: Create more lift with a low-to-high swing path. Lengthen your follow-through, letting your arm extend high.

My lob goes long.

Swing: Swing more upward, putting a higher (and shorter) trajectory on the ball. Or add topspin.

Slice

The slice typically floats low over the net but longer into the court. It requires less energy because of the downward swing path, and it's possible to be late and still slice successfully. It's a good stroke for low balls that you can't get good lift on, and some opponents may have trouble returning strokes hit with the slice.

Seeing

Keep your eye on the ball. If it's coming in low, you'll need to speed up the racquet head as you lift the ball over the net trying to achieve depth.

Movement

Use the same movements you did on your other ground strokes to move toward the ball and away from it. Shuffle and carioca steps put you in a position to transfer weight into the shot while maintaining a closed stance. In an open stance, you can use a power step with your slice.

Adjusting

On the slice it's especially crucial to achieve proper distance from the ball by moving around it. Line up on the ball with the foot closest to the net.

Rotation

The forehand slice starts off with the right foot and right leg rotating to the side. The upper body rotates with the stroke as well. The backhand slice requires a rotation of the body with the upper body coiling a little bit more to get the extra power stretch of the torso, back, and shoulder muscles. There is also a counter movement backward with the nondominant hand. The last bit of that whip-cracking rotation is the rolling of the forearm (supination) to square the face of the racquet at contact.

Transfer

On the forehand slice, your weight transfers from the right foot to the left. On the backhand slice, it's from the left foot to the right, with the left dragging across the court for sensory awareness and balance.

Swing

Use a continental grip. The swing path is down and across the ball with the follow-through going outward and upward toward the target. Keep the backswing short. The racquet head starts up on the backswing (as compared to a ground stroke that's driven with topspin, which has a low-to-high swing path). Use the rally or defensive point of contact, in line with the body or slightly past it, to allow maximum extension of the arm into the shot. The elbow locks in for better control, then relaxes after contact.

> **Cues**
>
> Slice is nice (low balls)
>
> Bend and extend (the elbow)

Troubleshooting for Slices

I'm not making clean contact with the ball.

Seeing: Line up your dominant eye on the ball.

Movement: Line up the foot closest to the net with the incoming ball.

Swing: Check to be sure you are not meeting the ball too far out front.

The ball has no bite when I hit a slice. It sits up for my opponent to handle easily.

Movement: Your stance may be too open.

Adjusting: You may be too far away from the ball, and your arm is overextended. Adjust your movements around the ball. Aim lower over the net.

Rotation: Your preparation is too late. Take some pace off the ball. Shorten your backswing until you acquire the feel of acceleration.

Transfer: Sometimes players step forward for a slice onto a straight leg. This keeps them from stepping in to the swing properly. Keep your legs bent and accelerate your swing through the point of contact.

Swing: Shorten your backswing so the racquet can accelerate properly. The ball will float if the racquet face is too open on contact. Your wrist will naturally supinate, closing the racquet face at impact. Try a later contact point. Be sure you're using a correct grip.

My slice has sidespin.

Rotation: Make the swing path out, down, and across the ball. Sidespin also can be due to improper distance to the ball or inadequate adjusting. You may not be rotating enough and pulling your racquet across the inside of the ball.

Swing: You're uncoiling with the upper body in the direction of the shot, so you make contact with the near side of the ball. Swing down and across the outside of the ball.

The ball goes into the net.

Rotation: Your shoulder should not dip as you uncoil.

Swing: Make sure the point of contact is not too far out in front.

On my backhand slice, I can't control where the ball goes.

Rotation: You may be over rotating on the follow-through.

Swing: Your point of contact may be too early. You may not be extending your arm fully, or the finish may be too abrupt.

The ball lands short in the court.

Adjusting: Adjust your movements around the ball, so you're not getting jammed on your stroke.

Swing: Your swing may be coming from the wrist. Reestablish a proper swing path: down and across. Imagine hitting down and across the ball. Aim deeper in the court, adding pace and spin, causing the ball to float longer.

Drop Shot

The drop shot is considered a touch shot or specialty swinging shot because it requires an understanding of the correct timing and use of the shot. Use it

- when your opponent is deep in the court, after your previous shot has driven him behind the baseline,
- if you see that your opponent has difficulty moving forward, or
- to surprise your opponent.

Of course, the drop shot is most effective when it's disguised as if you're going to hit a ground stroke on the forehand or a backhand slice. A good drop shot typically clears the net with a safe margin (two to four racquet widths) and is hit with underspin, so the ball hits and stops on the court. In Europe the drop shot is often called a stop shot, because the ball will basically stop and bounce three or four times in the service box. Some professional players such as Fabrice Santoro and Goran Ivanisevic are so good at hitting drop shots that the ball will land on their opponent's side of the net and then bounce to their own side.

Seeing

Note your own location in the court and your opponent's. If you're inside the baseline, your chances are better for executing a successful drop shot. If your opponent is not, that's even better. Note also your opponent's condition: is she tired, winded, or injured? Of course you also need to see the ball you're receiving. If your opponent rips a ball at your feet, obviously you'll have difficulty coming up with a successful drop shot. But if you're receiving an easier ball, inside the baseline, from a player who will have difficulty reaching your shot—then drop shot away.

Movement

The beauty of the drop shot is that your opponent never knows when it's coming. Use the same movements as for the backhand slice: a closed stance commonly is used, with carioca and shuffle steps to maintain the stance.

Adjusting

Line up on the ball with your foot closest to the net. The racquet head starts high and follows a high-low-high swing path, similar to a slice. The racquet face is open on the backswing and stays open as contact is made. As with the slice, it's crucial to get proper distance by moving around the ball. You can drag your back foot across the ground for sensory awareness.

Rotation

On the backhand drop, your racquet arm bends and extends. But on the forehand, your elbow remains fixed and the rotation comes from your upper body turning in the direction of the shot.

Transfer

Step forward to the ball, bending your leg and then straightening.

Swing

The point of contact is to the side of the body. The continental grip is preferred, but other grips may be used, as long as the racquet face can open properly. On the backswing keep the racquet face open, with the racquet coiled back around your body. The swing path is under and through, lifting the ball over the net with height and backspin, meeting the ball with an open racquet face. Pronate (turn the palm of your hand downward) on the backhand and supinate (turn your palm upward) on the forehand—that is, rotate your forearm to open the racquet face. If you receive a ball with considerable pace, keep your swing path under and forward, which will impart backspin and lift, and it will help you direct the ball to go where you want it.

Cues
Under and lift
Cup it

Troubleshooting for Drop Shots

My opponent easily puts my drop shot away.

Seeing: Observe your opponent's strengths and weaknesses. Do not play into her strength by directing a drop shot to her better side. Selectively choose when to use it.

Swing: You may need to put more backspin on the ball, so swing low to high.

My drop goes into the net.

Seeing: Aim higher and extend your follow-through. Also, you may be too far back or trying to handle a difficult ball. Don't try the drop shot if you're behind the baseline or receiving a tough shot.

Movement: Take the time to set up the shot; move

inside the baseline to hit this shot.

Swing: Swing under and through the shot. Keep your arm locked on the backswing before making contact; don't generate the spin by chopping the ball with your wrist.

My drop shot goes wide.

Adjusting: You may not be getting around the ball enough. Aim toward the center of the service boxes.

Swing: Check your swing path to be sure you're not going down and across but under and through.

My drop shot sits up too high, allowing my opponent to reach it.

Rotation: Look at your rotation. You're probably too open. Rotate fully; this also disguises your

intentions. The swing should then come from your shoulder, your arm, and finally your wrist, giving the ball height and increased backspin.

My drop shot goes too deep in the court.

Rotation: You're supinating your forearm (on the forehand) or pronating it (backhand) too soon. Keep the swing under the ball and upward.

Swing: You may be attacking the ball with too much spin and follow-through, causing it to float long.

I can't control my drop shot.

Transfer: You may be relying too much on your wrist. Bend your front leg slightly, transferring your weight easily into the shot.

Swinging Volley

The swinging volley is an aggressive stroke hit inside the baseline. It requires confidence, balance, and timing. You can hit a swinging volley two ways, depending on the height and speed of the ball. If you can contact the ball above the net and it's approaching at moderate or slow pace, then use a basic swinging volley. It's similar to a ground stroke, with a measured backswing followed by an acceleration of the racquet to the ball. If the ball is below net level, or coming fast, then you need a block swinging volley. Again, measure your backswing, but then punch the ball, without the full rotation of a normal swing.

Mini-Tennis

If you need work on your short game, and the touch shots involved in net play, try the mini-tennis exercise with a partner. In mini-tennis you use two diagonal service boxes or two service boxes opposite on another and hit softly back and forth until one player makes a mistake. Play using normal tennis scoring, or just play games up to seven. In the early going, you may want to outlaw smashes, since the purpose of the game is to develop finesse, not power. Be sure to rotate between your right service box and your left, so your forehand and backhand are tested equally.

Seeing

As with other strokes, line up your dominant eye on the ball. This is especially important on the volley, since you have less time. You need every millisecond you can get to judge the position of the ball speeding toward you. The swinging volley is an attacking shot. You are going for the winner. Commonly you are standing between the service line and the baseline. Preferably you are looking for an easy to moderate pace that is high over the net.

Movement

Your movements depend on the type of ball you're receiving, but virtually all volleys require a well-timed split step. Take that step when your opponent hits the ball. Your next movements depend on how the ball approaches you:

- If it comes close to you, go into your unit turn.
- If it's two to four feet away, try a unit turn and shuffle or step out to meet it.
- If it's low or you're moving toward the net, try a balance step (step and hit).
- If it surprises you or you have to travel far for it, you'll need a lunging or diving volley.

There's not a lot of form involved in this; just get your racquet on the ball. Remember to control your body movements and to get back into a ready position after you hit the swinging volley.

Adjusting

When hitting the swinging volley, you have to adjust to balls of different heights and different directions. For the ball coming directly toward you, adjust your hands and feet to get out of the way! Preferably adjust into a position where you can hit a forehand. Other adjustments, of course, are the shortened backswing (sometimes as simple as laying the wrist back) to add topspin (for lift or to keep the ball in the court).

Rotation

On the forehand swinging volley and the two-handed backhand swinging volley, turn your shoulders, hips, and torso in the direction of the target to meet the ball in front of you. On the one-handed backhand, you want a slightly later point of contact, since the upper body will not rotate toward the target, but remains sideways. Also, your nonracquet arm will go the opposite way, to provide a counter movement, help stabilize the shoulders, and maintain balance.

Transfer

You can use a closed or open stance with the swinging volley. As always, the closed stance involves more weight transfer as you step into the stroke.

Swing

Your point of contact will vary depending on the type of ball you receive. On high volleys, swing on the same plane and let gravity carry your shot into the court. On low balls and to impart topspin on the ball, take a low-to-high swing path with upward acceleration of the racquet. To drive the ball, take a high-to-high swing, preparing high and finishing high, hitting it with less spin.

Troubleshooting for Swinging Volleys

My volley goes into the net.

Seeing: You may not be seeing the ball height properly. If it's beneath the level of the net, block instead of taking a full swing.

Adjusting: On low balls, open the racquet face and flex your ankles and knees to reach them. Aim higher and volley over the lowest part of the net when possible.

Rotation: Transfer your weight forward. On the backhand volley, rotate your hips and shoulders to swing the racquet from your shoulder to the desired target. On the forehand volley, rotate the hips and shoulders toward the target as the volley is struck.

Transfer: If the ball is low stay low and move through the volley, keeping your shoulders level.

Swing: Open the racquet face, check your grip, and adjust your body to the height of the ball. Shorten your backswing keeping your wrist firm, and punching the ball with a compact swing.

I'm shanking easy volleys wide, long, or in the net. I can't seem to control the shot.

Seeing: Line up on the ball with your dominant eye. Take aim for a larger part of the court, and try not to hit too closely to the lines.

Movement: Your split step is too late or not at all. Time the split step when your opponent meets the ball (one exception: when you're receiving an easy ball that you can move toward without a split step and volley in the air).

Adjusting: Line up your eyes, hips, shoulders, hands, and racquet on the ball so you can direct the ball where you want it to go. Wisely blend your ball controls of height, speed, and spin, so you're not overhitting the shot—the temptation on the swinging volley. Be sure your balance is steady. Add spin, take some pace off, and hit the ball lower over the net if necessary.

Rotation: During your measured backswing, keep your wrist at a firm 45- to 90-degree angle.

Swing: Measure your backswing and try to meet high balls in front of you at shoulder height. On low balls, flex your legs and try to meet the ball in a strike zone between your knees and shoulders. In the ready position your hands should not be together on the grip; your nondominant hand should hold the throat to stabilize the head of the racquet. Leave your left hand on the racquet longer if more control is necessary. Or try choking up on the racquet.

I hit volleys on balls that would go out, or I let them go and they drop in.

Seeing: Note your court location. Watch the ball and try to determine its flight plan as well as how your opponent has hit it. Pay attention to wind conditions.

I'm having trouble getting the timing of the swinging volley.

Movement: Move out into the court to meet the ball at its highest point. You may be letting the ball drop. Shorten your backswing to make the timing of the contact easier.

Transfer: You may be taking your split step too soon, throwing off your whole weight transfer.

I'm great on the first volley, but if it gets returned, I'm in trouble.

Movement: Stay low on your recovery. Work on your split step and initiating movements.

My volley goes long.

Movement: Aim lower over the net and shorter in the court.

Rotation: Supinate your forearm to add backspin on the forehand and pronate your arm to add backspin on the backhand.

Transfer: Do not transfer too much weight into the shot. Rely more on rotation.

Swing: Measure your backswing. Decrease pace if necessary. Don't swing at the ball; punch it. Close the racquet face a little more.

My volley goes wide.

Swing: Have your contact point in front of your body as you punch the ball to help you volley straight. Have a greater margin of error by not aiming for the line.

I get jammed by the approaching ball and my volley goes wide.

Movement: In the ready position, hold your racquet head up and away from your body.

Adjusting: Move around the ball, staying low.

My volley has no power.

Rotation: Rotate your hips and shoulders with a unit turn, then transfer weight forward and punch the volley.

I can't hit a strong backhand volley.

Adjusting: Adjust your position further from the net to practice stepping.

Transfer: Look to transfer weight into your volley.

Swing: You may be volleying with a forehand grip. Change to a backhand or continental grip. Be sure your point of contact is not too far in front of your body. If you lack physical strength, practice a two-handed volley for a while; then try releasing your left hand on the follow-through; when you're more proficient, go back to a one-handed volley.

My volley lacks depth.

Movement: Move closer.

Transfer: Transfer weight by stepping forward.

Swing: Focus on short punching action with the racquet face open for underspin and the follow-through going toward your target. Increase pace.

I can't get down to low volleys.

Transfer: When transferring weight on low volleys, turn your back foot on its side, or drag the top of your foot to get low enough. Many good players wear out the tops of their shoes from plays like this.

My volley lacks bite. It sits up for my opponent to easily hit it.

Swing: Accelerate your swing more and open the racquet face so the ball stays low.

I'm late getting to the ball for a volley.

Movement: Check your ready position. Is your racquet in front of you?

Swing: Be sure your swing is not too big. The preparation for it may be slowing you down.

Adding Accuracy to Punching and Transition Shots

Various game situations make it more advantageous for you not to use a full swing, but to punch the ball, using weight transfer more than rotation to provide power. If you master these punching shots—first volleys (including half volleys or lob volleys) and second volleys (including angle volleys, drop volleys, or lob volleys)—and transition shots, you'll be fearless in approaching the net or adapting to any number of less-than-ideal situations on the court.

The primary energy source for punching shots is the transfer of weight and simply returning the power of the incoming shot. Surprisingly, the actual weight transfer doesn't have to be completed before the ball is met but can occur after contact, with a recovering step. On lower volleys, the weight-transfer step usually occurs before or during contact. On higher volleys, it happens after contact.

The First Volley

Though they are both considered punching shots, I differentiate between the first volley and second volley. Your approach and intention in using each type of shot can be quite different. Follow your SMARTS for first volleys.

Seeing

As you approach the net look at your opponent and time your split step when you opponent makes contact. Using soft focus, track the direction, spin, pace, height, and depth of the incoming ball.

Movement

Take your split step when your opponent hits the ball. Step out with the foot closest to the ball if it is moving away from you. This step will create a foundation on which you can transfer your weight into the shot. Square up and move through the shot.

· · · · · · · Cues · · · · · · ·

Low and through (on low volleys)

Split and hit

Punch and hit

Punch the volley, short, freeze, open the face

Racquet head up, firm (wrist), low (with legs)

Around and through (moving around a ball hit right at you)

Accelerate punch

Punch and extend (counter movement)

Adjusting

Work on getting your hands and feet lined up on the approaching ball while moving your torso around the ball or diagonally toward the side of the ball.

Rotation

How much you are able to rotate will depend on the amount of time you have.

Transfer

Weight transfer is your primary source of power. Try to get as much of your body weight moving forward as possible.

Swing

Judge the height of the ball with an abbreviated swing. Open your racquet face to impart backspin as you punch the ball for low and midvolleys.

Half Volley

A specialty shot, the half volley, meets the ball on a short hop. If you've ever drop-kicked a football or soccer ball, it's the same idea. You're hitting the ball almost immediately after it bounces. The half volley is usually hit near the service line when a return or passing shot dips toward a player's feet. But it also can occur near the baseline if a player doesn't back up in time to catch the ball on a normal bounce. The half volley requires distinct rhythm and timing with a short backswing. Weight transfer is its primary source of power. Good balance and timing can make this a successful shot. Usually, you want to put this shot deep in the opposing court, but if you're approaching the net and your opponent is back at the baseline, you might want to softly dump this shot over the net.

Seeing

Like the other volleys, this shot needs quick judgment, based on good visual data. Where are you and where are you going to meet the ball? If you're caught between the net and the baseline, too close for a ground stroke but too far for a normal volley, try the half volley. The same situation can present itself if you're on the baseline and the ball comes right at your feet. In fact, all sorts of factors—wind, bad bounces, topspin—can put a ball at your feet and put you in need of a half volley. Keep your eyes open.

Movement

Pivot on the balls of your feet while doing a unit turn. Then line up and step into the shot.

Adjusting

Adjust your position by moving forward or stepping backward to volley or half volley the ball. Maybe you will make an error if you try to volley the ball before it bounces, so don't hesitate to do what Pete Sampras does so well. Stop and back up, hitting an aggressive half volley.

Rotation

The amount of rotation you can use depends on the ball speed, height, and depth. If the ball is coming short, low and fast, take a shortened swing as you assess the incoming pace of the ball to play it back over the net. If the ball is slower, take a full swing to generate your own pace.

Transfer

You need to bend deeply in your ankles and knees and keep your back straight. Make contact as far out in front as possible. The foot nearest the net steps forward (balance step) and the transfer occurs during the swing.

Swing

Swing your racquet parallel to the ground. Sometimes a player gets lazy and does not want to bend his body low to the ground; rather he will dip the racquet to get the ball. This may work sometimes, but its success is inconsistent. For better results, get in the habit of getting low. Keep the racquet face open. Use an eastern grip and a measured backswing. Meet the ball in front of you and follow through in a forward direction. All you need for recovery is to bring your trailing leg forward. Then you're squared up again for your next split step or to move on to the net.

Notice Pete Sampras' body
adjustment low to the ground
to strike the ball.

Troubleshooting for Half Volleys

The ball comes directly at my feet, making it nearly impossible to hit a half volley.

Seeing: See the height and spin your opponent is using.

Movement: Do not compromise your swing—back up and hit a ground stroke as Pete Sampras does.

Adjusting: Adjust your position so you can meet the ball as it comes off the ground.

My half volley goes into the net.

Movement: Move forward faster to volley, or be prepared to back up and hit a ground stroke if you're not comfortable with the half volley.

Adjusting: Stay low, bending from your ankles and knees instead of your lower back. Adjust your backswing to the height of the ball so you're not swinging high to low.

Transfer: Be sure the timing of your weight transfer into your shot is not throwing off your balance.

Swing: Check your grip to be sure the racquet face is open enough. Transfer with your back leg bent.

My half volley goes long.

Adjusting: Aim shorter in the court.

Rotation: You may be relying too much on rotation and not enough on transfer.

Swing: You may be taking too big of a backswing.

Second Volleys

You have hit your first volley and closed in for the put-away. Your choices now are to angle, attack the ball, or hit a drop volley.

To hit the angle your racquet face determines the direction of the ball. Hit angled volleys when you are close to the net or when the ball is low to use the lowest part of the net versus hitting down the line.

Drop Volley

The drop volley is another specialty shot. Use it when you have good position at the net and

- your opponent is deep in the court,
- your opponent has difficulty getting to short balls, or
- you're playing on a surface on which it's difficult to get traction (grass or clay).

When properly executed, the drop volley is a magnificent shot, since it's usually an outright winner, taking an opponent's power shot and responding with touch and finesse.

Seeing

Before using a drop volley, note your opponent's situation and estimate your tactical advantage. Is your opponent off balance, deep behind the baseline, or playing on a difficult surface on which to get traction such as clay or grass? Watch the incoming ball. Is it manageable? Evaluate your own position. Are you inside the baseline? If so, then go for it!

Movement

If you recovered well after your first volley, squaring up to the net with your trailing leg, you should be close enough to the net for a second volley. Keep your upper-body movements smooth.

Adjusting

With a shortened backswing, take the pace off the ball by decelerating the racquet at impact. You're using touch now, feeling the position of the racquet face and soften your grip on the racquet, directing the ball where you want it to go.

Rotation

Rotate your hips and shoulders as you normally would for your volley and using a short, compact swing, take the pace off the ball using soft hands and not gripping the racquet so tightly.

Transfer

Step in on a bent leg (the leg nearest the net) and keep your racquet arm loose. You're actually not trying to throw weight forward, as with other shots, but you're cushioning the approaching ball, taking power off of it.

Cues
Touch
Massage
the ball

Swing

The swing of the drop volley is almost as if you're trying to catch the ball on your strings. Think of an egg toss, in which you pull back to catch the fragile egg, or a bunt in baseball. I recommend using the continental grip, but you also can drop volley with an eastern forehand or eastern backhand grip. Keep your backswing short. The point of contact is out in front. Supinate your forearm on the forehand, and pronate on the backhand.

Sometimes a hard-hit ball causes the racquet to rebound, resulting in a wild volley. To counter this, keep your arm bent and your wrist firm, stabilizing the racquet face so the ball will bounce more predictably off the racquet.

Troubleshooting for Drop Volleys

My opponent always seems to know when I'm going to try a drop volley. She gets there and beats me.

Seeing: Your previous shot may not be deep enough. Or you may be showing your intent.

Swing: Prepare and execute as if you were volleying normally but disguise your intent with your hand. Use your hand to take off the pace.

I can't get this touch thing. I've got hands of stone.

Adjusting: Practice playing mini-tennis (see page 64) to help you develop the feel necessary to hit with touch.

Swing: Your wrist may be too loose.

My drop volley goes too deep.

Swing: Shorten your backswing and aim shorter in the court.

I can't hit the drop volley.

Swing: Check your point of contact and the strike zone. Is the ball coming too fast or too high to make good contact?

Goran Ivanisevic moves his torso toward the ball and transfers his weight forward for a drop volley.

Lob Volley

The lob volley is more often used in doubles games. You have to catch your opponent by surprise, or else you'll be eating felt. As with any volley, you meet the ball before it bounces. As with most lobs, you're lofting the ball over an opponent who's at the net. It's a way to counter his net approach with a quick shot over his head, sending him scurrying back to the baseline.

Seeing

If you see your opponent quickly moving to the net, you may decide to answer with a lob volley. Your movement, adjusting, rotation, and transfer are all the same as for the volley.

Swing

Open the racquet face at the last second. Keep your swing path upward, lifting the ball over your onrushing opponent.

Troubleshooting for Lob Volleys

My opponent smashes my lob volley.

Seeing: Lift your lob higher if you can. Try using the lob volley over his backhand.

My lob volley is too short.

Transfer: Transfer more weight into the shot, giving you more lift.

Swing: Open the racquet face more to give the ball height and punch it more.

Transition Shots

So, you're in a rally with your opponent, and you're blasting deep shots at each other from the baseline, running each other ragged, when finally your opponent hits short. Now you move into the court, lining up your dominant eye, and you have to decide how you will play the shot. Will you set your feet and go for an outright winner, attacking the ball? Or will you move to the ball, challenging it by taking it early and placing your shot, trying to get a good position on the net?

Seeing

Line up your dominant eye on the ball as always. Be on the lookout for the ball controls your opponent is using—depth, spin, speed, height, and placement. Identify the short ball.

Movement

Here are some of the different movements you will need to execute for the approach shot:

- **Attack approach**
  Shuffle set
  Around and set
  Sprint and slide
  Power step

- **Position approach**
  Power step
  Carioca step
  Spring step
  Sprint and slide

Adjusting

Line up your hands and feet. Get your body in position to attack or position yourself at the net.

Rotation and Transfer

The power of your transition shot comes from a blending of rotation and transfer. For the attack approach in which you go for the outright winner, rotation on a solid base is necessary. When you're on the move, however, your weight already is transferring forward, and that force will naturally go into the shot. So you don't need the full rotation of, say, a ground stroke. Measure your swing. Add some rotation if you are receiving an easier ball.

Swing

Your swing path will vary depending on the type of ball your are trying to come in on and your intent. The strike zone is the height of the ball wherever you can get to it. If the ball is coming in low, lift your shot with spin swinging low to high. If you are attacking, meet the ball in front of your body and drive it, swinging outward toward your target.

> **·····Cues·····**
> Attack approach
> Shuffle set, around, and set
> Placement approach
> Hit and go

Karsten Shultz, who has coached Sabine, Hack, Manuella Maleva, Slava Dosedel, Sergio Casal, and Tommy Haas recommends reaction drills to help a player develop his or her transition shots. Reaction drills involve having a player make the shot from any direction. The player should not know from where the ball is coming. Such drills put a player under pressure and force the player to improve his or her reaction time. The player has to go to his forehand or backhand and then recover back to middle as fast as possible between each shot.

Troubleshooting for Transition Shots

I'm not always sure whether to attack or play for position.

Seeing: Learn to note whether the approaching ball can be attacked. Look for balls lacking pace but with topspin which may land short in the court, allowing you to approach the net. Look for balls that have a lot of spin that just clear the net or that your opponent may not have hit cleanly.

My shots go to the center of the court.

Seeing: Keep your target in mind as you approach. Then adjust and rotate to impart the desired pace and direction to the ball.

Adjusting: Adjust your position to make enough room to swing, especially if you hit an inside-out forehand.

Rotation and Transfer: It varies, depending on shot intention.

The ball goes into the net.

Seeing: Look and listen for relevant cues that the ball will be short so you can move in more quickly. Perhaps your opponent shanks the ball off of his racquet or simply does not meet the ball cleanly.

Movement: Make your move to the net sooner (or faster), so you can hit the ball before it gets too low. (This may involve honing your seeing skills so you quickly can discern the balls that invite you to the net.)

The ball goes wide.

Adjusting: Move around the ball more to get enough striking distance.

The ball goes long.

Rotation: Use less rotation, keeping your backswing short, and more transfer.

Transfer: Use more transfer.

Swing: Your swing is too big, or you are meeting the ball too high or too far in front. You need to change your swing path to put more spin on the ball. If you still are having problems, check your point of contact.

When I get an easy sitter, I miss it and put it in the bottom of the net.

Swing: Again, you may be meeting the ball in too low or too high of a strike zone or hitting the ball too flat. Or keep the racquet on the same plane if you're driving your approach shot and low to high if you're adding topspin.

Improving
Shot Selection

How did you learn to play tennis? Likely, by going over the strokes. Your instructor or coach hit the ball to you in the same place over and over so you could develop consistently good form. But then what happened when you played a real match? Suddenly the ball was not always coming directly to you. It was bouncing above your shoulder or kicking out wide. The neatly controlled shots of your practice sessions weren't working anymore. When you did manage to use your good form to deliver a solid ground stroke to the center of the court, your opponent killed it. This chapter will help you develop your tactical awareness and select your shots within a game situation.

So far you've been using the SMARTS system to analyze and improve your tennis strokes. Now you need to use your own smarts to choose the best shots at the best times. There's nothing wrong with working on consistency of form. But don't stop there. Learn to read a game situation and select the tactics that will win you the point. Brett Hobden, coauthor of *Five Keys of Tennis,* has come up with what he terms "System 5" as a means to improve court awareness. Hobden graciously allowed me to highlight parts of his System 5 here and kindly let me interview him about his system.

System 5 Court Awareness

Brett Hobden
Coauthor of *Five Keys of Tennis*

Your court awareness and shot selection must be right before the stroke execution can be even close. You can hit the ball with great form, executing SMARTS to perfection, but if you're not hitting the ball to the right spot at the right time, it won't do you much good. Form follows funtion. Choose tactics with this in mind.

Tactical intention and stroking skills go together like heads and tails on the same coin. First decide what you're going to do, and then do it. Tactics and technique are both essential to tennis success. Form follows function. Choose tactics with this in mind.

We break down our tactical intention into two parts—awareness and response. First read your situation—court location, phase of play, and characteristics of the approaching ball—and then make a decision about your own strategy. You might take the ball on the rise, return it with speed, vary the pace or spin, or place it at varying depths. Keen awareness leads to realistic responses, which result in a natural execution of the SMARTS skills.

Awareness of Court Location

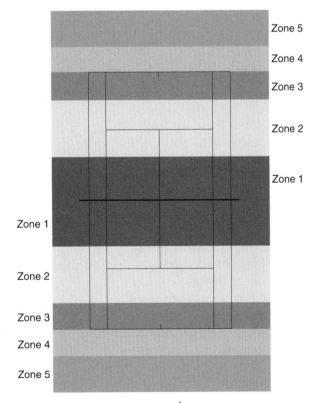

Figure 5.1a—Five zones on the court.

Tennis has one constant—the layout of the court. People play with different racquets, techniques and tactics change from coach to coach, even court surfaces vary. But the court always has the same dimensions. The first part of good awareness is proper understanding of the court. At any given time, you must know the following:

- Where are you on the court?
- What type of ball are you receiving?
- Where is your opponent?
- What type of ball will you send back?

Zones

Hobden divides the court horizontally into five zones, as shown in figure 5.1 *a* and *b*.

Zone 1 is the put-away zone. You're so close to the net, you can easily put the ball away. In this zone, you have more angles available to you, creating more opportunities to put a ball out of your opponent's reach.

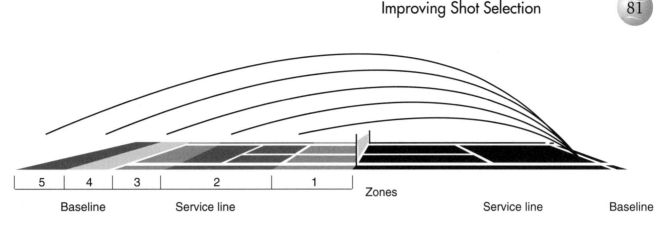

Figure 5.1*b*—Side view of the five zones.

Zone 2 is the attack zone, where you can pressure your opponent. On a ball hit short, you can challenge and approach the net.

Zone 3 is the zone of choice. Attack, challenge, or counterattack, depending on the type of ball you are receiving and where your opponent is. Attack going for an outright winner, challenge going to the net, or counterattack by hitting a deep shot and running back to the baseline to create a better opportunity.

Zone 4 is the rally zone, where you play most of your ground-stroke points.

Zone 5 is the defensive zone. If you're forced to play back here, it will be hard to stage any sort of attack.

Tactical Skill Progression 1: In the Zone

Identify the five zones.

The best players have a sense of where they are on the court. They pick up the cues of the approaching ball—its sound, the opponent's location, trajectory, spin, speed, etc.— and they figure out where the ball is going. Already they are planning their response, based on their court location.

Step 1: Based on figure 5.1 *a* and *b*, mark off the five zones using tape or chalk on a hard court or using your shoe on a clay court.

Step 2: Have a friend feed you balls of different heights. As you return them, call out the zone you're in as you make contact.

Step 3: Repeat step 2, but now have your friend hit at different speeds.

Step 4: Do the same thing, but vary the spin.

Step 5: Now receive balls of varying heights, speeds, and spins, but call out the zone before you get there. That is, as soon as you think you know where the ball is going, name that zone and get there.

After going through these exercises, make a note of which zones are easiest for you to anticipate and which are the hardest. Take your list and note which types of balls and which zones gave you the most problems. Work on those that you feel need improvement.

Runways

We also can divide the court lengthwise into five runways. For our purposes, the side and middle runways are the same on each side, so we'll deal with only three different types of runways, calling them (from left to right) C, B, A, B, C. See figure 5.2.

Runway A is about eight feet wide and runs down the middle of the court. Nowadays players are encouraged to run around a ball in runway A and hit a forehand. Because you don't have to move too much to get to runway A, you generally can rally balls from here, attack, or counterattack if someone hits the ball with pace. That is, you can take control of a point if you receive a ball in the middle of the court, because you have a little more time to deal with it. But don't be lazy. You still have to adjust to the ball to achieve proper striking distance. Sometimes that's difficult when the ball is hit right at you.

Runway B starts at the singles sideline and continues about halfway to center court. In the pro game, players constantly are using runway B by hitting angles and passing shots down the line. This is a more difficult area to play in, because you're usually on the run. If you're forced to play the ball in runway B or if your opponent is running you from C to B, you'll probably respond with a defensive shot, but if you can shorten your backswing when running to this shot, you may be able to counterattack this ball or rally it to your opponent's weak side.

Runway C is outside the singles sideline. (Remember, it's not where the ball bounces, but where you make contact.) Obviously, this is a difficult ball to retrieve. If you find yourself out in runway C, you want to play defensively, stroking the ball with the proper height over the net to allow you to get back into position for the next shot. In some game situations, however, runway C might give you an opportunity to go for broke, trying an aggressive, low-percentage shot. Hey, you're already on the run and at a disadvantage. What do you have to lose?

Pay attention to runways and zones the next time you watch a professional match. Where do those players spend most of their time? Hardly ever in runway A. They're routinely in B and often running back and forth between the C runways.

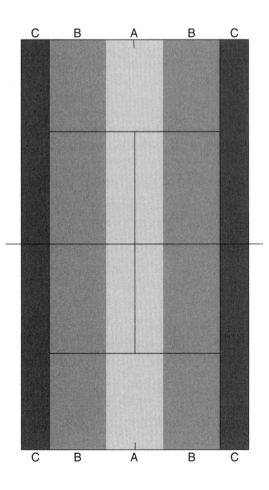

Figure 5.2—The three runways.

Tactical Skill Progression 2: On the Runway

Identify the three runways.

Step 1: Along the base of the net, mark off the five runways using tape, chalk, or your shoe.

Step 2: With a friend hitting to you, practice returning balls in runway A. Note the amount of time you have to get around the ball and achieve proper striking distance. Then take several balls alternately in the two B runways. Keep the pace slow at first; just get the feel of running between runways. Then have your friend hit angles that put you in the C runways.

Step 3: Now have your friend hit ground strokes deep, in any of the runways. As soon as you know which runway you'll be hitting in, call it out.

Step 4: Ready for this? Put runways and zones together. Have your friend hit anywhere, and as you're running to the spot, call out the zone and runway from which you'll be hitting.

Videotape one of your practice sessions and analyze it later. Where do you make most of your errors? Which zone? Which runway? Do you have problems anticipating balls hit to certain spots? If so, what cues could help you?

Do you struggle when you have to run wide for the ball, say, from runway A to C? If so then you need to work on your pivot sprint, keeping the racquet in front of you and staying low while you run for the wide ball. If runway A is where you make most of your mistakes, then you have trouble adjusting to balls that come right at you. Practice the adjusting skill of moving around the ball to hit your forehand.

Do you try to do too much or too little in certain zones like rallying from zone 5, trying to put away a shot from zone 4, or getting stuck in zone 3? If your mistakes are in zones 1 through 3, then you need to work on your transition and net game like punching shots, seeing and adjusting skills, and footwork. If your mistakes are back in zones 4 and 5, work on your ground stroke, developing your basic movement, rotation, and swing.

Awareness of Game Tactics

Game tactics are the parts of the game that make up your overall set strategy. Game tactics require a keen sense of tactical awareness. You have to be able to identify quickly and spontaneously which phase of play you are in and select an appropriate tactic that fits into your particular strategy and style of play based on your strengths and weaknesses.

Phases of Play

A player may come off the court saying, "My backhand was terrible today," when that's not really the whole story. That player may have played a great rally backhand throughout the game but merely had trouble counterattacking a fast serve. It's not just a particular stroke this player needs to work on, nor is it only a particular court location, it is a phase of play.

Phase of play = court location + type of shot received

There are five phases of play:

Defensive—when you're forced to run a great distance to the ball; when the ball is hit with placement behind you or directly at you; when the ball is coming quickly, deeply, or very low; or when the ball bounces higher than expected, or lower, or kicks out with a surprise spin. In stoplight terms, we'll call this situation red.

Rally—when the ball's height, speed, depth, spin, and direction are comfortable and you can hit a strong return. We'll call this situation yellow.

Challenge—when you can do something with a ball, putting pressure on an opponent. This situation is green (and sometimes yellow).

Attack and counterattack—when you can take a risk, grabbing the offensive from the other player. You can attack on "green" balls that are slow or sitting up in your strike zone, when you have a good court position. You counterattack on "red" or "green" balls when you turn the tables, ripping a passing shot off your opponent's approach or blocking a fast serve back over the net. In chapter 9, you will learn differing responses to the different phases of play.

In any zone or runway, you may receive an easy ball or a difficult one. In zone 1, for instance, someone may blast a ball straight at you and you'd just stick your racquet up for a reflex volley, or you might get a floater that you can step up to and put away. Same zone, but different responses, all because of what kind of ball you're getting. And yet a floater in zone 4 or 5 calls for a different response. Same ball, but a different location, and so you try a different tactic.

Frankly, this is what makes tennis fun. Up until now, we've been focusing on technique. The SMARTS skills are physical patterns you need to teach your body to adopt. Theoretically, a robot could learn to do that. But now we're talking about the creativity of the game; problem-solving; and choosing the best tactic, in given circumstances.

Brett Hobden calls choosing the best tactic an open skill, since it involves responding to a continuously changing environment. In a tennis match, you never know what you're going to get, so you have to be ready to apply your skills to any challenge and to expand your skills to have one for every challenge. Closed skills, on the other hand, are those robotic movements you can drill with a ball machine. Don't get me wrong, closed skills also are important to master: they are the fundamental skills that make up your game. There are plenty of hacks who play very creatively but keep losing because they've never disciplined themselves to develop a consistent serve or a powerful ground stroke. Honing your fundamental skills now allows you to have more fun later.

Ball Controls

Any ball coming at you has five characteristics. I call these ball controls. As you learn to recognize and interpret these controls, you'll be better able to anticipate where the ball is going. The characteristics are as follows:

Direction. This is the most obvious; the direction of the ball launches your lateral movement. Is the ball going to your right or left? To which runway is the ball headed? How far will you have to run for it? Of course, the farther you have to run, the more defensive your options will be. Let's say your opponent has approached the net taking you off the court with his approach. As you play the ball back from runway C, your opponent is standing at the net and he volleys crosscourt, for which you take off. You just won't have time to do much with the ball, unless you try a daring counterattack.

Steffi Graf assesses the direction, speed, and depth of the ball coming at her and moves into position for her next shot.

Speed. How fast is the ball approaching? This challenges your timing, anticipation, early positioning, and early racquet preparation. Balls traveling at the same height, but with different speeds, will go to different zones. In general, extremely fast balls will put you in a more defensive phase of play while slower balls invite you to challenge or attack. Rally speed is the pace at which you feel comfortable and have the best control. That's your midpoint, your yellow light. More or less speed than that will turn the light red or green.

Height. You have to learn to judge ball trajectory. What is the course it will follow? Note its speed on the way up to determine how soon it will peak. Once it peaks, you get a pretty good idea of where it will land. In general, higher balls are easier to handle, inviting you to challenge or attack, especially if they're shorter in the court. Low balls that zip by the net with a few inches to spare are tough for challenging. Here again, your experience in determining your rally speed will help you find your yellow-light level. What height balls do you like to hit and what height gives you difficulty?

Depth. The depth of the incoming ball will, of course, determine your up-and-back movement (zone location). The height and speed that you already are observing will help you guess the ball's depth. In general, the deeper the ball lands in the court, the more difficult it is to challenge or attack.

Spin. This is the most difficult ball control to recognize, and it can be devastating if you don't read a spin correctly. You need to see how your opponent strikes the ball to know what bounce to expect. With topspin, a low-to-high swing makes the ball spring up and come toward you with forward rotation. If you're not ready for it, it will get to you sooner than expected, throwing you on the defensive. With underspin, an under-and-through swing puts backward rotation on the ball. This will surprise you as the ball lands and then appears to stop and sit up not quite getting to you. Underspin and a slice put a backward or sideways rotation on the ball, causing it to skid, stay low, or move sideways.

Generally, the less spin on the ball, the easier it is to judge its bounce. More spin means more dramatic surprises and more adjustments that are necessary. However, some players find certain spins easy to read and return and have difficulty with others. If you're used to playing a heavy topspin player and you suddenly face a player with great backspin, you could be forced on the defensive for most of the match until you adjust to the lower ball. But if you're facing a foe who uses only underspin, you can start pouncing on those short bounces which may be floating over the net and take the advantage.

Tactical Skill Progression 3: In Your "Phase"!

Determine how ball controls affect your phase of play.

Step 1: Have a friend hit the ball to different runways. Note how this affects the phase of play you're in. When you're running for the ball, can you attack or challenge? Pay special attention to which directional changes are the most difficult for you and which ones are the easiest.

Step 2: Now change the pace of the balls you receive, but keep them coming to different court locations. As you return soft, medium, and hard feeds, determine which balls you can attack, challenge, counterattack, rally, and defend. Evaluate how your location (zone and runway) and the different paces combine to create various phases of play.

Step 3: Rally a ball back and forth and have your friend hit at different heights. Note which heights and locations make it easiest or most difficult for you to attack, challenge, counterattack, rally, and defend. For example, maybe you notice that you (like most players) have difficulty in zone 5 with high balls or that in all zones and runway locations it is very difficult to attack low balls.

Step 4: Have your friend hit to you at different depths, intentionally hitting short into the court, then deep, then midcourt. Which ball depths are the most difficult for you to play? Which zones are the easiest?

Step 5: Have your friend feed you balls with differing spins (topspin, slice, flat, underspin, oblique). Which spins do you like and which ones do you have to work harder to return?

Step 6: Take some time to review what you've learned. Put the different ball controls and locations together and figure out which are easiest for you and which are most difficult. Which combinations create an attack phase of play and which put you on the defensive? For instance, you might have trouble with a hard flat ball hit deep into zone 4, or a soft drop shot hit with underspin into zone 2.

Step 7: Play ground-stroking points with your friend and ask yourself after each point which phase of play you were in when you hit your last shot.

By now you should have developed your tactical awareness of knowing where you are receiving the ball (zone and runway) and which phase of play you are in based on the ball controls your opponent is using. You are now ready to execute your tactical response.

Reading Your Opponent's Intention

On the tennis court, every split second counts. The faster you can distinguish your phase of play based on where you are in the court and the ball you are receiving, the faster you can choose the response you will send back.

That makes it crucial to recognize the incoming ball as soon as possible. And if you have keen powers of observation, you can gain a lot of information about the incoming ball even before your opponent hits it. "A good player can tell largely what they are going to receive before their opponent hits the ball," says Brett Hobden, "based on their backswing, how they line up to the ball, how their racquet head is approaching

Michael Chang concentrates on anticipating his opponent's next shot so he can plan his response. His opponents, however, often have difficulty reading his intention until the last possible second.

the ball, and by the sound of the racquet hitting the ball."

The better you are at applying the SMARTS to your own game, the better you'll be at analyzing your opponent's shot-making capabilities and intentions. We're talking about anticipation. This becomes a game within the game. If you know where and how your opponent is going to strike, you can prepare for it, blunting his offensive ability and taking control of the game for yourself. Players often disguise their intentions until the last possible second.

Michael Chang, for instance, is fantastic at running toward the ball looking like he is going to rip the passing shot and then at the last second stepping back and flicking a topspin lob (see photo above). Boris Becker would look like he was completely out of position on the dead run trying to hit a forehand—and then he'd hook the ball back into the court.

At the core stage, you don't need to worry too much about faking out your opponent; that can end up distracting you. But you should do all you can to read your opponent's intention and to prepare for the incoming ball. Later, you can work more on your ability to disguise your shot intention.

Tactical Responses

Hobden notes six basic tactics to use when returning a tennis ball:

1. Be consistent.
2. Put the ball in a particular zone and runway.
3. Change the pace and spin.
4. Increase ball speed.
5. Hit on the rise.
6. Combine any of the above.

The better you become, the more you'll integrate and execute these responses in your game. But don't rush. Work on these tactics one at a time, and eventually they'll become valuable weapons for you.

Consistency

Consistency may seem like cowardice. The "pusher" who just keeps getting the ball over the net is boring to watch, frustrating to play. Is that what consistency is? Playing it safe?

In the defensive and rally phases of play, that's correct. But as we've seen, those phases do not call for heroic attacks or challenges. Consistently getting the ball over the net in those situations is not boring or cowardly—it's just smart tennis.

Moreover, consistency in the counterattack, challenge, and attack phases of play is far from playing it safe. You need to learn to take chances wisely when the situation calls for it. Jump to smash a lob, catch a short ball with a half volley, and follow your shot to the net, or catch an easy floater and drop it way short in your opponent's court. Consistency does not always mean placing the ball in the center of the court. It means taking the best shot at the best time and executing it as well as you can.

Of course, you don't want to make unforced errors. But in the challenge, attack, and counterattack phases of play, aggressive errors demonstrate your ability to recognize easier balls and to try and do something with them. There is a big difference between missing a tough shot in a challenge situation and passing up a challenge for a safer rally but then losing concentration and putting the ball in the net anyway. Take smart chances and work on consistency of execution.

When Navratilova played Mandlikova in the finals of the 1985 U.S. Open, how many balls do you think Navratilova hit into the net during the first set? Twenty? A dozen? Seven or eight?

Two. In that 6-7 set, Martina was remarkably consistent, with only two net balls out of the hundreds she played. You may not be a Navratilova, yet. But you can set a goal for that kind of consistency.

Tactical Skill Progression 4: Being There

Develop consistency in all phases of play.

Core and Mileage

Step 1: Have a friend feed you balls that put you into the differing phases in each zone and runway. For example, you are in zone 1, runway A, and the first feed is low on your feet (defensive phase of play); the second feed is right at your body (counterattack); the third feed is about waist height (rally); and the fourth feed is a floater that you can then move in on (challenge) or put away (attack). Move on to the other zones and runways.

Step 2: After isolating various court locations, mix them up; have your friend hit anywhere. Test your consistency in the rally, defensive, and challenge phases of play.

Fine-Tuning

Step 3: Try to keep one ball in play while you hit down the line and your opponent hits crosscourt. This keeps you running and tests your ability to adjust to difficult balls and practice ball control.

Step 4: Do the same as fine-tuning step 1, but alternate. Hit crosscourt while your opponent goes down the line. This continues to develop your consistency at moving your opponent.

Step 5: Cover the full court, but hit to just one corner of your opponent's court. This develops your ability to consistently attack an opponent's weakness in all phases of play. Play a game to seven points.

Step 6: Repeat fine-tuning, step 3, but now add different spins and paces.

Step 7: Play the approach game. Start playing a normal point, but when the ball goes short, the receiving player must approach the net, hitting the ball down the line (that is, straight ahead, not crosscourt). The other player must attempt a passing shot, getting the ball past the player at the net. This develops consistency in using the passing shot as a counterattack.

Step 8: Take two broomsticks and attach them to the net posts. String a rope across the top and hit balls over the rope. Play a game, keeping the ball over the rope. This develops consistency in your rally and defensive phases of play, as you hit with height, depth, and spin.

Placement and Depth

Placement is your ability to control the direction and depth of the ball. In the core level, good depth is anywhere past the service line. In the mileage and fine-tuning levels, hitting within a yard or two of the baseline is considered good depth and placement. Varying depth with angles can make your opponent run more. So can hitting the ball side to side. Or you may want to pinpoint your opponent's weak spot. Some players have trouble adjusting to balls hit up the center of the court, so even this might be an effective placement for you.

Tactical Skill Progression 5: Put It There

Vary the placement and depth of shot.

Core and Mileage

Step 1: For depth and placement, play a game with your friend to 11 points. Each time you hit a ball past your partner's service line it counts as one. Each time you hit short, deduct one shot from your total. Both of you are trying to do the same thing. To work on your volley, stand at the net, with your friend still at the baseline, and see how many consecutive times you can volley the ball past the service line.

Step 2: For direction, divide the court in half using the center line of the service box. Can you successfully hit into each half? Alternate sides of the court while maintaining consistency in all phases of play. The same can be done with the volley. Twenty repetitions is a good goal.

Fine-Tuning

Step 3: Monica Seles drills using a slightly different version of step 1 above, according to Renee Gomez, her former traveling coach. Between the service line and baseline, they set up a chair, which Monica would have to hit over. Try it. Play to 11 points.

Step 4: Try the Andre Agassi box game. Mark off a box in the corner of the opposite court. You get a point each time the ball lands in the box and lose one each time it doesn't. Play to 11. Practice crosscourt, then down the line, using both your forehand and backhand ground strokes. Vary height, spins, and paces. You also can practice volleys while on the net.

Step 5: Try the Andre Agassi dual-box game. Set up two boxes in the corners of the opposite court. Now your partner should move you around the court while you aim for the boxes. Work on volleys, too.

Step 6: For varying depth, divide the court into four boxes. The service boxes make two, and imagine the center line continuing to form two more. Play a game of four-square, in which you're not allowed to hit into the same box twice in a row. Play a game to four points, using ground strokes, volleys, smashes, and returns. When you consistently can place balls into the four boxes, varying your depth, move on to step 5.

Step 7: For target practice, using cones, racquet bags, or whatever you choose, make eight separate targets. With a ball machine or friend feeding you balls, see if you can hit all eight targets within 30 tries.

Step 8: For the no-center game, mark off a square in the center of the opposite court and try to keep the ball out of it. Play a game to seven points, losing one each time you hit that box.

Step 9: For double or nothing, see how precise your down-the-line shot is by playing a game to seven points, keeping the ball in the doubles alley.

Change of Pace and Spin

If you vary the pace of your shots and the spins you put on the ball, you will directly affect your opponent's rhythm and timing. Some players struggle with certain spins and paces and enjoy receiving others. If you can create uncertainty, then you'll start to break your opponent's confidence.

Tactical Skill Progression 6: A Change Will Do You Good

Change pace and spin.

Step 1: Rally with a partner and, whatever type of spin she puts on the ball, try to counter with the same spin when possible.

Step 2: Go back through steps 1 and 2 in tactical skill progression 5 (page 90)— getting it past the service line, or alternating sides of the court—but vary the pace and spin of balls that you hit.

Step 3: With a partner, play a ground-stroke game to seven points, but start varying the spins, depth, height, direction, and pace you use in challenge situations. For instance, try a drop shot if the occasion calls for it.

Step 4: Go back to the placement-and-depth section, playing the games in steps 1 through 7 in tactical skill progression 5 for the fine-tuning player (page 90), but vary pace and spins.

Increased Pace

When you increase ball speed, you challenge your opponent's timing, giving her less time to respond effectively.

Tactical Skill Progression 7: Speed Thrills

Increasing ball speed in the course of play.

Step 1: Practice attacking easy balls with your best shots using pace.

Step 2: For offense-defense, play to four points. You attack and challenge while your partner works on rallying the ball and playing defensively. Then switch.

Step 3: Pick a box on the opposing court. Decide that, in an attack situation, you will put the ball in that box with pace.

Step 4: The Tommy Haas direction drill: Rally with a friend crosscourt. When you see a ball you can rip down the line, do so; that starts the point. Play a game this way to seven points. For the next game, begin rallying down the line and wait for an opportunity to go crosscourt. Play to seven.

Step 5: With a ball machine or having someone feed you balls, practice taking swinging volleys in zone 3. Hitting swinging volleys from this zone helps you solidify your strokes. This stroke in this zone is a naturally powerful shot. It puts pressure on your opponent using pace.

Taking the Ball on the Rise

Taking balls on the rise gives you an advantage because you give your opponent less time to respond. As you play, you quickly can settle into an easy rhythm with your opponent, hitting deep ground strokes, perhaps crosscourt. In that exchange, you're positioning yourself so the incoming ball bounces up, crests, and drops into your strike zone. But if you step forward, striking the ball as it crests, you're changing the rhythm. You're taking initiative and being aggressive. If you make a strong shot, you put your opponent on the defensive.

As you step forward to take the ball on the rise, you need to measure your swing to accelerate it properly and to correctly time your contact with the ball. It does you no good to take a ball on the rise if you decelerate your racquet. It's best to step into the shot, catching the ball as it comes off the court at the peak of its bounce.

Andre Agassi taking the ball on the rise.

Tactical Skill Progression 8: Rise to the Occasion

Take balls on the rise.

Step 1: Practice taking short balls on the rise as a friend hits to you.

Step 2: Play ground-stroking points and practice taking balls on the rise in all phases of play.

Step 3: Inside the baseline, you are only allowed to step out of the court with one foot. This forces you to take deep balls on the rise. Play to seven, alternating *who starts the point, as in a tiebreaker.*

Step 4: The goalie game develops your ability to read the intention of a server and react quickly to the incoming serve. It teaches you how to stay low but light on your feet, rotating your hips and shoulders quickly to line up the racquet behind the incoming ball. Set up the game with your partner serving from the service line. Start behind the baseline. Each time you make a return it counts as a goal. Each ace or service winner your partner hits counts as a score. For every goal you have to take one step forward. Players who have practiced this game eventually can reach the service line. Play a game to seven points.

Step 5: With the volley-volley-smash, hit forehand and backhand ground strokes up runway A (center). When you get a short ball, take it on the rise and go to the net, where you will receive two volleys that you rally up the middle of the court. Your partner should lob the next ball, which you smash back at three-quarter speed up runway A. (The idea is that you want your partner to be able to return your smash to keep the drill going, so don't kill it.) Your partner then approaches the net off your smash and does what you just did—volleys twice, then smashes, etc.

Step 6: With the Michael Chang drill, stand at the net and hit volleys to a friend. You're not allowed to hit a winner, but your friend can lob you, hit through you, or wait for an error. Next game, switch roles—put your partner at the net. Play to 7 or 11 points. This game will teach you how to counterattack balls and take them on the rise so you avoid being run all over the court.

Tactics and Technique

If you are consistently having trouble with certain parts of your game, it's either a technical problem or a tactical one. Keep going back to review the elements of SMARTS to brush up on your technique. We all can get lazy on certain aspects of movement, rotation, or swing. But if your SMARTS are good and you're still having trouble, it may mean you're not so smart in your tactical decisions. You may be choosing the wrong shot.

There are many different shots in the game of tennis, as the six basic tactical responses previously detailed show. At any given moment of a game, your court location and your quick analysis of the ball you're receiving determine your best phase of play. Will you defend, rally, challenge, attack, or counterattack? The game itself tells you what to do, if you pay attention.

Another element that affects your choice of shots is your skill level. If you know your net play is weak, you can be forgiven for choosing defensive or rallying tactics a bit more than necessary. Of course, as you become a complete player, you'll want to work on those weak spots so you'll have a complete arsenal of tactics to employ.

I've discussed your general tactics, but how do you take these tactics and build them into specific strategies? How can you know the best shot to take? Say you receive an easy short ball after some baseline play. The ball and your court location make it a challenge situation, but how will you make your challenge? Where will you hit the ball?

That puts us in another strategic area—percentages. I'm not going to crunch numbers, but I am going to discuss high-percentage and low-percentage shots in different situations. Obviously, players who choose appropriate high-percentage shots wind up winning consistently.

Percentage Tennis and Baseline Play

I list the following strategies in the order I recommend you practice them. Spend a month or more hitting to these spots. Being able in all phases of your game to effectively neutralize whatever your opponent sends with a ball deep up the middle of the court will really help you to get out of some difficult situations.

With crosscourt rallies you will be in a dual against your opponent matching your strengths and weaknesses against his. The down-the-line play will be the quickest way to get your opponent in trouble and to test his recovery. Challenge or attack behind him trying to wrong-foot him. Position yourself aggressively when possible inside the baseline by taking the ball on the rise to control the center of the court. You will be pulling all the strings while your opponent dances like a puppet.

Neutralizing

Hitting deep up the middle of the court allows you to play over the lowest part of the net and makes it difficult for your opponent to hit winning angles. By placing the ball deep up the middle, you position yourself in the middle of the court to bisect her possible return.

Here's another advantage of hitting up the middle. Sometimes you can catch your opponent moving forward and unable to back up quickly. For instance, your opponent serves and follows up by moving into the court, but you neutralize this movement with a deep return up the middle of the court. Your opponent has to go on the defensive, backing up for the ball. Many players do better running to wide balls rather than making the more intricate adjustments to move around a ball hit right at them.

Crosscourt

If you find yourself in the deep corner of your court, rallying, counterattacking, or playing defensively, your best percentage play is to hit the ball crosscourt. This way, you're hitting the ball over the lowest part of the net and into the most court (you have 82.5 feet from corner to corner versus 78 feet down the line). Then wait for a "green" or "yellow" ball to challenge or attack down the line.

Since it's the best percentage play, your opponent also is more likely to hit crosscourt, so you can settle into a lengthy baseline rally between opposite corners. Because of this, it makes sense for you to position yourself to bisect the probable crosscourt return (see figure 5.3). That is, instead of running back to the center hash mark after every stroke, stay in runway B. You still want to be able to reach something down the line, but you can set up for the expected crosscourt ball.

Have you ever watched a pro match and wondered, "Why do they keep hitting crosscourt, again and again and again? Why doesn't anybody hit a down-the-line winner?" Well, they're simply playing the percentages. When someone gets a "green" or "yellow" ball to challenge or attack, he goes for it—but not until he gets that advantage. In fact, a professional player's perception of a yellow or green ball is much different from yours. Crosscourt rallying is foundational to the game of tennis. If you can out-rally your opponent in this way, you'll win consistently. So work on putting the ball deep in the opposite corner. Then develop your skill with angles, slice, and topspin to gain even more advantage in crosscourt play. These shots open the court by forcing your opponent to play in runway C or zone 5. You still are hitting to your high-percentage area, but the ball is bouncing into a wider area and your opponent has to cover more ground.

You will play longer points hitting crosscourt and you will hit more balls, but this is a great way to help you get your feel if you have lost it. Let yourself get into the game's rhythm, and be patient. Don't be gulled into trying for a low-percentage winner (which easily could become a loser). Let your opponents make those mistakes. Once in a while, they'll get lucky and score, but that's the percentages. Even a lowly .100 hitter in baseball gets a hit once every 10 times up. You may lose a few points on your opponents' risky shots, but you'll win many more by sticking to high-percentage play.

Down the Line

If you decide to change the ball's direction from crosscourt to down the line, it probably will be because you receive a ball that is easier or you are going for broke because you are so far off the court becoming fatigued, or your opponent is at the net covering your crosscourt pass. Make sure you are balanced and accelerating your swing. This is a lower-percentage shot because you have to be precise when hitting over the highest part of the net and using the shortest part of the court. In the challenge and attack phases of the game, take short, easy balls down the line and follow your approach to one of the three spots. When trying to get a good net position, take first volleys down the line. By hitting a volley down the line, you force your opponent to pass you by hitting crosscourt, which takes longer and gives you a split second longer to react and move to the ball. If you're at the net, be sure to cover a down-the-line return, and be ready to move for a crosscourt passing shot or lob.

Wrong Footing

What do you do when your opponents start to anticipate your shots into the open court? Hit behind them. It's a great way to keep them honest. By hitting behind players who already are beginning the pivot-sprint to the open court, you force them to stop, recover, and move in a different direction. Sometimes this gets them to hit off the wrong foot, resulting in weak returns.

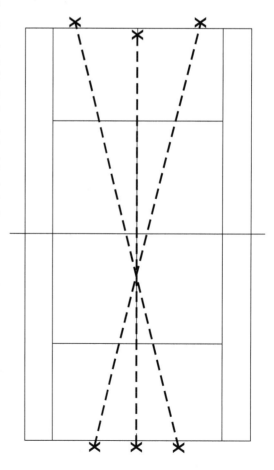

Figure 5.3—When you determine crosscourt play is your best bet for keeping the ball in play, position yourself to bisect the likely crosscourt return.

Controlling the Center

Tennis is a territorial game. It's not just about hitting a ball over a net, but about controlling the court. Taking control of the center of the court is just like boxing out in basketball, or fighting for position in front of the net in hockey or soccer. It's much easier to score and control the action when you have that control. In tennis this is typically inside the baseline or at the net.

This doesn't mean that you have to be in the center of the court. You just have to control your opponent's access to it. That may mean keeping your opponent deep in a crosscourt exchange or positioning yourself at the net to cut off her angles.

In a baseline exchange, if you draw an easy yellow or green ball from your opponent, then you are in position to attack, challenge, or counterattack. That puts you in control of the other player, to a degree. You have the opportunity to run him, forcing him to rally, counterattack, or play the ball back defensively. The more defensive he is, the more likely he is to:

- try a low-percentage desperation shot, which will probably fail; or
- launch an easy high-percentage shot to the center of your court, which you easily can return, putting him on the defensive even more.

Even if your opponent manages a defensive return or two, you will gain more and more control. In many cases you'll be moving more and more to the center of the court as you do.

Percentages at the Net

Net strategy is just the opposite of baseline strategy. Now the play is to volley down the line, keeping the ball in front of you so you can bisect your opponent's passing shot.

When coming to the net behind a ball that you have challenged or attacked, try to bisect the angles of your opponent's possible returns. That is, put yourself smack in the middle of the range of where the ball might go. Depending on which side you have approached, you want to position yourself at one of the points shown in figure 5.4. From this position you will cover the down-the-line passing shot and have a fraction more time to move for the crosscourt pass, which you could then volley into the open court.

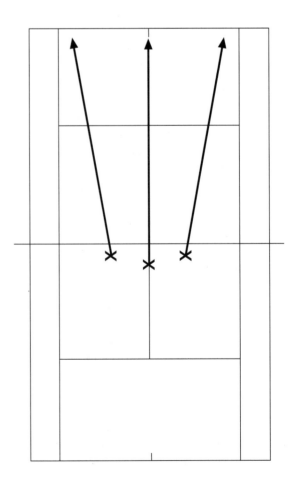

Figure 5.4—Net strategy positions.

Tactical Skill Progression 9: What's Your Position on That?

Make the connection between shot placement and positioning.

Neutralizing Balls

Step 1: Play ground-stroking games in which your friend has the entire court in which to hit and you only neutralize balls up the center of the court. Then switch, so you're hitting to the whole court and your friend hits to you in runway A.

Step 2: Do the same as above, but have your friend serve and you return deep up the middle of the court playing out the point.

Crosscourt

Step 3: Play a crosscourt game with both players using only half of their court. Play games to seven points, alternating right side and left game by game. Work on all phases of play, especially recovering back to position after each crosscourt shot.

Down the Line

Step 4: Play ground-stroking points again, and when you get a short ball try to challenge or attack the ball down the line, hoping to force your opponent into hitting a weak crosscourt or up-the-middle shot.

Step 5: Play the approach game, in which you challenge the first short, easy ball you receive, sending it down the line and getting into position at the net.

Wrong Footing

Step 6: Play a ground-stroke game to four points. On any ball that you can challenge or attack, hit behind your opponent.

Segmenting Your Swing

Where you are and what you get: that's what makes you decide what to send back over the net and how much of a swing to take. Measuring your swing, (i.e., taking the racquet back to differing points depending on where you are and the type of ball you are receiving) helps give you better control in certain situations and helps you to time your contact better, not hitting the ball out.

Say you're standing inside the baseline, waiting to return the serve of Greg, the league pusher. His serve usually resembles a dying quail, so there's no problem with where you're standing. The slow speed of the incoming serve will allow you to take a full swing and launch a solid return.

Now let's say it's a different Greg serving to you, Greg Rusedski, only the possessor of one of the most powerful serves on the pro tour. Now there's a problem between where you're standing and the speed of the incoming serve. I know, you're tempted to stand in the next town, but let's say you stay there, inside the baseline, awaiting that rocket serve. You simply don't have time for a full backswing. You take the racquet behind you, and the ball already is whizzing past your ear. In cases like this, you need to shorten your backswing and meet the ball as best you can. All the other SMARTS skills still apply, but you won't have as much rotation. Still, if you merely step in to meet a powerful serve, you can send the ball back with power.

Different situations call for different measures of your backswing. Imagine yourself lined up on a ball, ready to strike it. Now take your racquet back about one racquet-head width from your desired point of contact. This would be a measure 1 backswing, which you generally would use in zone 1. You're close, the ball comes at you quickly, and you don't need to send it far, so measure 1 is all you need. Of course if the ball is coming slow, then you can take a larger backswing and put away a killer shot. But a measure 1 backswing is standard for zone 1.

Now draw your racquet back two racquet widths from the point of contact. That's a measure 2 backswing, generally used in zone 2 for volleys and half volleys. Go through the motions of hitting some volleys with a measure 2 backswing. See what I mean? That's all you need. Now go back three racquet widths. Then four, and five. Backswings with measures 3, 4, and 5 generally are used for ground strokes in, you guessed it, zones 3, 4, and 5, respectively.

You need to make these measures your own. Racquet-head width is an approximate distance. Your full backswing may be more or less than five racquet-head widths (and your racquet may be wide or standard). The point is this: a measure 5 backswing is your complete or maximum backswing on a ground stroke. However far back that is, that's measure 5 for you. Segment your backswing into five measures, based on that maximum.

We all have different interpretations of the segmented swing, and your style of play has a lot to do with it. Take John McEnroe's backswing compared to Andre Agassi's. McEnroe takes his backswing straight back while Agassi has a big windup. Being able to measure your backswings, learning the difference between a measure 5 and a measure 3, and getting the feel of a 4 or a 1 all take practice.

Please note that the speed and difficulty of the incoming ball is always a factor. This may lengthen or shorten your backswing. If you catch a rocket in zone 5, forget about your measure 5 backswing, you may only be able to manage a 3. But if you see a floater in zone 2, don't limit yourself to a measure 2 backswing. Wind up and nail it!

I've been discussing backswing. Now a look at follow-through. A follow-through starts from your point of contact and proceeds forward in five measures. Note that the point of contact will differ, based on your swing preferences and your phase of play. For example, an eastern forehand grip has a different point of contact than a full western grip. A ball you're attacking can be met farther in front of your body than a ball that backs you up, putting you on defense.

Now count one racquet-head width forward, then two, three, four, and five. As with the backswing, adjust this to your own style. Measure 5 is your farthest point on a complete follow-through. A player with a western grip will have a very different finish than a player with an eastern grip. Your style, grips, stances, and tactics all affect your follow-through. And you can take your measurement across your body or straight out, depending on your intent. A full follow-through will look different on a forehand angle and on a forehand drive down the line, but both are measure 5.

Now the measure of your follow-through has more to do with the type of shot you're attempting than your court location (although your shot selection will be affected by your location). On punching shots including the first volley, second volley, angle volley, and drop volley, your range on the follow-through is typically anywhere from measure 1 to measure 3. On all the swinging strokes and transition strokes, I encourage players to use a measure 5 follow-through and to vary the swingpath depending on the intent.

You can think of your shots now with a pair of measurements, backswing and follow-through. A 2-5 swing, for instance, is a rather short (measure 2) backswing with a full (measure 5) follow-through. This combination becomes important when you're running for wide balls or reaching for low ones. Ideally, on an easy ball in zone 5, you'd take a measure 5 backswing and a follow-through at 5. That way you do not lose control of the shot. With a shortened backswing on a tough shot, you still can accelerate the follow-through. The swing also is easier to time, since the racquet starts off closer to the point of contact plus, contact is made much easier with a shortened backswing.

Pete Sampras's measure 5 backhand backswing.

Tactical Skill Progression 10: Measure for Measure

Learn proper measures of the backswing.

Step 1: Measure your backswing according to your zone location. Start in zone 1 and, with a machine or friend feeding you the balls, measure your swing according to the zone in which you're standing. Hit with a measure 1 backswing from zone 1 for a while, then move to zone 2 and use a measure 2 backswing, and so on, back to zone 5. Then mix up the zones. Feel how the backswing increases in length as you move further back from the net.

Step 2: Now put together backswing and follow-through. Try a 1-1 volley and a 2-2 volley. But then practice a good number of 2-3 punching shots, as well as 3-5, 4-5, and 5-5 swings, from the appropriate zones.

Step 3: Now measure your backswing according to the speed of the approaching ball. Start by standing in a particular zone and have balls hit to you at different speeds. You will quickly notice that your rhythm, timing, and consistency are affected. On fast balls, you can't take your normal swing. To successfully counterattack or rally the faster balls, you must take a shortened backswing. Try this in all five zones.

Step 4: Now have your partner feed balls to you that require you to move up and back and side to side. When the ball is too low, you're stretched wide, or you're just having difficulty, then shorten your backswing. Note that the faster or more difficult the ball is, the shorter the backswing needs to be.

Height Over the Net

Stand next to the net and put the edge of your racquet on it. Memorize this distance—one racquet width above the net. If you're in zone 1, that's where you want to hit the ball, clearing the net by approximately one racquet width. Now raise your racquet so it's two widths high. That's where you want to hit the ball from zone 2.

So, from zone 5, how many racquet widths should you clear the net by? Yep, five. And that's a minimum! This gives your ball height and depth from the backcourt so your opponent cannot attack you. Brett Hobden notes some exceptions, such as underspin shots that should clear the net by half the recommended height (a slice backhand from zone 4 should clear the net by exactly two racquet widths). Other spins have other requirements, and specialty shots such as angles, passing shots, drop shots, and lobs require more or less height. But consider this "one racquet width per zone" a general rule for most shots.

Another exception: "red" balls. If you're receiving a difficult ball—due to height, spin, speed, direction, or depth, combined with your court location—increase your margin of error by hitting with more height over the net.

Tactical Skill Progression 11: Scale the Heights

Learn the approximate heights for clearing the net based on court location.

Step 1: Carve five equally-spaced notches into two old broom handles. Attach the broom handles to extend each net post and tie a rope between the extended posts. Set the string height so that it's one racquet width over the net (at the middle), then two, then three, four, and five. Now rally with your partner, hitting over the stretched rope. Start by taking turns at the net, hitting volleys at the one-racquet height. Then set it at height 2 and play mini-tennis (see page 64), always making sure the ball clears the rope. Then move back to zones 3, 4, and 5, resetting the rope accordingly. Be sure to play in the different runways, too.

Step 2: Practice hitting one ball over the rope and the next shot beneath the rope.

Step 3: Set the rope at three racquet widths and play a ground-stroking game in all zones. You're still trying to hit at a height appropriate to your zone location. If you hit the rope, you win the point only if you hit it from zone 3.

Step 4: Play the same ground-stroking game as in step 3, but add some other elements. On difficult balls, double the height to increase your margin of error. As you do this, yell, "Double!" Try some slice or underspin shots and cut the height in half. As you do this, yell, "Half!"

Core Match Tactics

Tennis strategy can be intricate or simple. I've tried to keep it simple so far. On any given point, the basic elements that determine your strategy are the characteristics of the incoming ball and your position in the court. These combine to create a phase of play—a general intention for that particular shot. Will you try to defend, rally, challenge, attack, or counterattack?

Once you've decided what you're trying to do, you choose the best way to do it (tactics). This involves high-percentage shots, good positioning, appropriate backswing and follow-through, and the proper distance over the net. I've given you general rules to follow, based on the ball, your position, and the resulting phase of play. Beyond these, the game itself will tell you what to do. Be alert to each game situation as it develops, follow the principles I've given you, go into each match with the following intentions, and you'll do the right thing.

1. **Be steady.** At the core stage, consistency is key. Fight the temptation to try the trick shot or to smash everything that bounces higher than your eyebrows. Keep the ball in play. Of course challenge and attack when you get green balls (short and easy), but wait for those opportunities. If you work hard on your consistency, chances are your opponent will goof before you do.

To be truly consistent, become completely aware of your own strengths and weaknesses. If your backhand is weak, for instance, run around the ball and hit your forehand. Should you have to play a backhand, don't try to hit it as a weapon like your forehand, but lift the ball with height and depth over the net so you don't put yourself on defense. Keep the ball in play by hitting up the middle and crosscourt if need be to out-rally your opponent. Neutralize your weaknesses by playing to your strengths.

2. **Move the ball around.** Some players have a difficult time running side to side, while others have a hard time running up and back. Sometimes you can grind down your opponent by keeping her on the run. Keep the ball deep side to side, or intentionally hit short, varying the heights and types of shots (e.g., hit angles and drops, then hit deep, forcing your opponent to move up and then quickly backward). If you've been hitting consistent crosscourt shots, and your opponent has been consistently returning them, you might want to switch to this tactic.

3. **Attack your opponent's weakness.** Think through the SMARTS as you watch your opponent warm up. Look for weaknesses in her game. For instance, a player might have movement problems, lunging for balls or using sloppy footwork when moving side to side. Or she might swing poorly on certain balls, perhaps chopping weakly at high bouncers. Once you have found a weakness, then play to that weakness. You don't have to hit a winner each time you do this. By consistently using placement and depth of shot to exploit your opponent's weakness, you will gradually gain an advantage, both mentally and strategically.

4. **Make the playing conditions work for you.** Remember to check for COWS (Court, Opponent, Wind, Sun). Obviously, these environmental factors can hurt your game, but if you're smart, you can take advantage of them. Observe what varying conditions, such as wind from behind you, to your face, or across the court, do to the flight of the ball. Note what it's like to serve into the sun and attempt to hit smashes while the sun is in your face. Play when it's cold and experience balls that don't bounce very high. Play when it's very hot and feel the sweat running down your back and arms. Practice and play on hard courts, grass, and clay, noting the differences among these surfaces. Use different types of balls—feel them, smell them, and see which ones you like the best. But also note their playing characteristics. How do they bounce and spin?

Now, with all these conditions in mind, how can you make them work for you? The wind will blow your ball farther, shorter, or to one side. So hit deep into a headwind and short with a tailwind. If you're playing into the wind, you might want to approach the net more often, knowing that your opponent's lob or passing shot might be carried out of play. With a sidewind, the effects of a slice or a kick might be more pronounced. Use your observations to select your tactics and technique carefully.

If the sun is tough, prepare to run around high balls to get a better angle. Know which direction to face on a smash. (And you might want to loft some lobs for your opponent to deal with.) If it's hot and you're in better shape than your opponent, keep him running. But if you're likely to wear out first, take a few more chances, to get it over with faster.

On a clay court, direct the ball side to side and hit behind your opponent. (Clay is a bit slippery and quick turns can be tough.)

Tactical Skill Progression 12: Putting It in Play

Apply core match tactics to an actual match.

Play three to five sets with a friend, trying out the core match strategies. Take a notebook or logbook with you and jot down your thoughts during changeovers. Then as soon as possible after you play, do a more thorough analysis of how your strategies worked. Here are the things to consider and questions you should answer:

Step 1: Rate yourself overall from 1 (needs improvement) to 10 (outstanding) in the following areas:

Being steady		1 2 3 4 5 6 7 8 9 10
Moving my opponent		1 2 3 4 5 6 7 8 9 10
Attacking opponent's weakness		1 2 3 4 5 6 7 8 9 10
Making playing conditions work for me		1 2 3 4 5 6 7 8 9 10

Step 2: *Being steady*

In what location on the court did you play the most?

About what percentage of shots did you make successfully in the defensive and rally phases?

About what percentage did you make successfully in the challenge, attack, and counterattack phases?

About how many times did you challenge or attack when you shouldn't have?

About how many times did you rally or stay on the defensive when you should have challenged or attacked?

Based on this, next time out should you be more offensive or defensive in your play?

Step 3: *Moving your opponent*

Do you think your opponent had to run more than you did, less than you did, or about the same?

About what percentage of your shots had your opponent running five or more steps?

Step 4: *Attacking your opponent's weaknesses*

What weaknesses did you notice in your opponent's game?

How did you attack these?

On the points when you directly attacked these weaknesses, about what percentage of those points did you win?

Step 5: *Playing conditions*

What significant playing conditions did you notice (sun, wind, heat, surface, balls)?

How did you take advantage of these?

Did that work?

Upgrading Your Equipment

In chapters 1 through 4 I've provided workouts to drill your SMARTS (stroking skills) and in chapter 5 I've applied your SMARTS skills by developing your tactical awareness (playing skills). Now I'll prepare you for choosing the right racquet, string, and string tension for you as well as provide guidelines for ensuring your footwear is appropriate for your game. Your playing potential and longevity are at stake, so taking care of these equipment needs is important for becoming a complete player.

Selecting the Right Racquet

If you walk into a tennis shop looking to buy a new racquet, you quickly can be overwhelmed by the many options available. Today racquets come in different shapes, lengths, widths, weight, flexibility, string bed patterns, and materials. How can you determine which racquet is best for you? Try the following step-by-step approach.

Evaluate Your Current Racquet

Before you go ditching your old racquet, get to know the features of a tennis racquet (figure 6.1) and answer a few questions about the one you're currently using.

For this checklist I'm indebted to Tom Parry, a renowned racquet stringer who has worked with numerous players on the pro circuit.

☐ **Why do you feel you need a new racquet?** If you're just tired of your old racquet, and you're craving one of the hotter, newer models, that may not be a good enough reason to switch. Many of the top professionals use racquets that were built in the mid-1980s—even though racquet manufacturers are offering them a lot of money to adopt their latest, greatest models. But these players realize that their livelihood depends on their consistency of play, and they've grown accustomed to their old racquets. A change might throw off their whole game.

☐ **When was the last time your racquet was strung?** Later in this chapter I'll talk more about stringing racquets with the proper string and tension. For now, just realize that the racquet itself is just one-third of your performance triangle. If you're unhappy with its performance, you may have the right racquet but the wrong string or tension. Don't throw it out until you know what the problem is.

☐ **Is your racquet's grip the right size for you?** Typically, players use grips that are too small. Sometimes teenage players still are using racquets from their younger days, and sometimes the grips wear out and essentially shrink. When you grip the racquet, there should be at least an index finger's width between your thumb and your longest finger.

☐ **What do you like about your racquet?** Certain aspects of the racquet's size and shape may be perfect for you. Even if you decide to get a new one because, say, the grip is too small, take other measurements of your old racquet (i.e., length and swimg weight) and look for a new racquet with those same specifications.

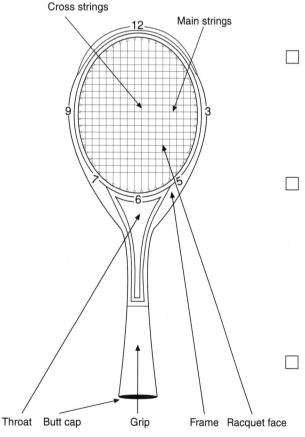

Figure 6.1—Features of a racquet.

Cross strings

Main strings

12

9

3

7

5

6

Throat   Butt cap   Grip   Frame Racquet face

☐ **What do you dislike about your racquet?** If you had specific problems with your racquet, make sure your new racquet doesn't give you the same problems. Make a thorough analysis of your old racquet and how you play with it, and make sure your new racquet purchase improves on all the trouble spots. Be sure to take your old racquet with you for comparison's sake.

☐ **Do you have any wrist, arm, elbow, or shoulder problems?** If so, they could be caused by a bad interaction with your racquet. If your racquet is not whipping through to meet the ball smoothly, you're probably compensating with extra effort from the wrist, elbow, or shoulder; this puts strain on those body parts and causes injury. Choosing a better racquet may ease those problems. If you are suffering from arm problems, you may need to consult a tennis professional to see what kind of racquet you need.

☐ **Are you happy with the head size of your racquet?** Swayed by fads, some players have bought big-head racquets and now they're paying the consequences. I'll admit that I did that, purchasing a wide-body racquet a few years ago. It was great for my serve, but the rest of my game suffered.

☐ **Do you break strings a lot in your racquet?** If so, it might reflect on your choice of string gauge or tension, but it also may mean the racquet's string bed pattern is so open that the strings wear out more quickly.

☐ **What's your preferred style of play?** Do you stay on the baseline, hitting ground strokes? Or do you tend to serve-and-volley? Or do you play mostly doubles? Different racquets are better for a power game and a finesse game.

☐ **Do you hit a lot of topspin, or do you hit flat shots?** Racquets with open string patterns (fewer strings) hit better topspin.

☐ **Do you need more power or control in your game?** For a power game, you'll be looking for a racquet with a larger head and more flexibility. For a control game you'd want a standard or midsize racquet with more stiffness.

☐ **Do you use a one-handed or a two-handed backhand?** A larger head size will help you on a two-handed backhand.

☐ **How much money are you looking to spend?** Good racquets cost anywhere from $75 to $250 (U.S.). Don't assume that the most expensive racquets are the best.

☐ **Are you right-handed or left-handed?** New frames come gripped for right-handers. If you're left-handed, you'll need to ask the shop to regrip the racquet you choose.

What Do You Want in a Racquet?

"Most players do not know what they want," says Ulrich "Uli" Kuehnel, the racquet consultant behind one of the greatest players of all time, Boris Becker. Working with players at every level of the game, Kuehnel has noticed that almost all players have the same problems. Either they don't have enough power in their racquets or they're struggling to control the ball. Many also are experiencing shoulder and arm problems, and many have racquets that actually turn in their hand while stroking the ball.

What Kuehnel has done for Boris Becker since the early 1990s cannot be underestimated. Becker has seen many coaches come and go, but he always has made it a point to take the best care of Kuehnel. Why? Because when it comes to racquets, Kuehnel is one of the best. He knows that when his work is exact, his clients' confidence is secure because their ball placement, depth, spin, power, and control improve. Improved confidence means more matches won.

Your confidence also will improve when you are able to play the ball the same way repeatedly.

Uli Kuehnel takes Boris Becker's racquet back for restringing.

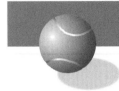

The Performance Triangle

Ulrich "Uli" Kuehnel
Racquet consultant

Translated from Uli Kuehnel's German original and used here with his cooperation.

Ivan Lendl was considered by many to be a worker on the court, working to achieve the most out of his game and not as naturally gifted as, say, John McEnroe. Still, Lendl spent a lot of years at number one in the world. What was his secret? He stuck to his racquets—Adidas GTX at that time—and he made his shots repeatedly. When he ran for a ball hit wide, he knew that his return was going to hit the back part of his opponent's line. Boris Becker has the same confidence. If he is running for a forehand wide, he can hook the ball from outside the court back into the court. This is possible due to a performance triangle made up of the racquet, strings, and the playability of the racquet (strings and racquet working together; see figure 6.2).

Just like the professional player, you need to be able to trust the racquets you use. A golfer can count on a particular iron hitting the ball a certain distance. You need to have this same dependable feeling from each racquet you pull out of your thermal bag.

It could be that the tension you are now using is not the best for the string and the string is not the best for your racquet. Racquets of differing lengths and not weighted and balanced correctly, as well as a dirty grip, can result in a three- to six-foot shot variance. With this variance you have no chance to hit a ball repeatedly deep in the court with the control you need. More than likely, you're also on your way to problems with your elbow, shoulder, or lower back. All because of a bad performance triangle—wrong racquet, wrong strings, wrong tension.

I've worked the inconsistencies out of Becker's performance triangle. Pete Sampras may be playing with a racquet that is too tight or strings that are too thin. His string breaks in the first 10 to 15 minutes or with the first mis-hit. Andre Agassi's earlier wrist problems also may have stemmed from a bad racquet situation—something was wrong with that performance triangle, so he was overcompensating with the wrist. My judgment of these matters may be right or wrong, but the point is that even pros need to tinker with the details of their performance triangle, adjusting racquet, strings, and tension to fit the unique aspects of their style of play, their location, and the playing surface.

Preparing this performance triangle for your racquet, string, and tension takes some time. On the pro tour the performance triangle is done at least two to three months before a big tournament. This is because the reaction of a racquet differs for each shot you hit among the backhand, forehand, volley, serve, and smash. You need time to get to know the feeling of the racquet and what it is doing.

There is a lot to know about your own racquet. Be serious about it and take time to find out exactly what you like. After a week or two of playing with a racquet that is suited to your game, you will start to improve dramatically because of the greater amount of control and power you can direct at your will.

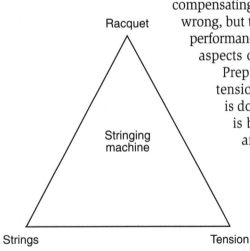

Figure 6.2—Performance triangle.

Weight

The weight of a racquet is measured in grams in Europe and ounces in the United States. A light racquet weighs 320 grams (11.28 ounces) or less; a heavy racquet weighs about 350 grams (12.35 ounces). A heavier frame tends to generate more power, vibrate less, and have a larger hitting area. With the newer materials used in racquets (e.g., titanium and hyper-carbon), manufacturers are making lighter, stiffer racquets that are more maneuverable and are very powerful.

The lighter racquets, however, are not for those who have experienced arm problems. Lighter racquets have a greater tendency to twist in your hand on off-center shots. You can reduce this tendency by increasing the racquet head size, but you need to be aware of this tendency. Beware of the "pick-up feel" of a racquet that the manufacturers realize impresses potential buyers. Just because it feels different doesn't mean it is necessarily the best racquet for you.

Balance

More important than the racquet's overall weight is the swing weight of the racquet. It is important that your racquets are weighted and balanced equally. A weight difference of just five grams or a fraction of an ounce difference in the swing weight of your racquet can mean your ball is landing three feet too long or too short. Many younger players who play with heavy topspin have their balls bouncing before the service line, allowing their opponents easy returns. Make sure your racquet is properly weighted so you can consistently hit to the baseline. Any reputable tennis shop should be able to help you with weighting and balancing your racquet.

So the weight and length plus the balance point of your racquet gives you an idea of its swing weight. The balance point is just that—where the racquet's center of gravity is. You can find it simply by laying your racquet handle on the edge of a table and letting the head of the racquet hang over. How much of the racquet can extend off the table before it falls off? When it's just teetering on the edge, you've found the balance point. The average balance point for most racquets is 32.5 centimeters (12.79 inches) from the butt cap. This may seem trivial, but a difference of just half a millimeter in the placement of the balance point can make a difference of up to three feet on the court.

If you have a high balance point, the racquet head will feel heavier, because a greater portion of the racquet's weight is in its head. This adds to the whip effect, giving you more power but less control. A lighter racquet with a high balance can give you greater depth than a heavier racquet with a low balance point. Generally, baseline players like a racquet that's head-heavier, while serve-and-volley or doubles players prefer a racquet with a lower balance point, making it feel head-light. Which one is best for your game really comes down to personal preference. Knowing your style and what the balance weight is for your racquet will at least give you an idea of whether moving the balance point up or down might improve your game.

Head Size

In racquet heads, you have your choice of standard, midsize, mid-oversize, or oversize. A larger frame tends to generate more power, since the strings are longer, creating a larger "sweet spot" hitting area on the racquet face. It's also more resistant to twisting, which is good if you tend to have arm troubles. I recommend a larger frame for those players who only play once in a while. You can gain confidence knowing that, with the larger racquet head, it's harder to miss the ball.

The oversize racquet popularized in the mid-1970s by Howard Head has done wonderful things for novice and intermediate players. But it also led to the midsize and mid-oversize racquets, which have about 25 percent and 35 percent more racquet face than the standard size (the oversize has about 50 percent more racquet face). I recommend a midsize racquet for the advanced competitive player and the serious weekend player who has good technique. The midsize and mid-oversize are the racquets of choice for an estimated 80 to 90 percent of players on the pro circuit.

The International Tennis Federation (ITF) has established the maximum width of a competition racquet at 31.75 centimeters (12.5 inches). Racquet manufacturers have realized that racquets are best with 16 to 18 main strings and 18 to 20 cross-strings. So count the strings of the racquets you want to buy. Racquets most frequently come with 16 main strings and 20 cross strings (16/20), 16/19, 14/18, or 20/21.

Stiffness

You might assume that the material of a racquet determines its stiffness, but that's not the whole story. Actually, the shape has more to do with it. If a racquet has a smooth transition from the widest part of the head to the handle, it will be stiffer than a racquet that rounds off suddenly to a long handle.

Materials do play a role, however. Graphite has proven stiffer than aluminum, and now boron, titanium, and hyper-carbon have emerged as stronger materials yet. Sometimes racquets have composite materials, and this affects their stiffness; a fiberglass composite will be more flexible, while titanium or graphite reinforcement should stiffen it.

What kind of racquet stiffness do you need? If you're a serve-and-volley or doubles player, a stiffer (and lighter) racquet will be more maneuverable at the net. But baseline players benefit from more flexible racquets, which add their own bending to the whip-like motion, taking the strain off the arms. Yes, a stiffer frame generates more power, has a larger sweet spot, and provides a more uniform ball response across the strings—but the bad news is that a stiffer frame transmits more shock to the arm. So if you have arm problems, you want a more flexible racquet. Unfortunately, the flexibility of a racquet can be tested only in a laboratory. You can call the manufacturer of your racquet or ask a knowledgeable sales representative the RA value of your racquet. An RA value of over 70 is stiff, 60 to 70 is medium, and under 60 is soft. Theoretically, if you had a racquet with an RA value of 100, then it would not bend at all when hitting the ball. The stiffest racquets available now have RA values of 80 to 90.

Proportional stiffness is the racquet's ability to resist torque, when the ball is not struck cleanly in the center of the strings. Placing lead tape on the racquet frame at three and nine o'clock (section B on figure 6.3) also can help with stability. I recommend that you take your racquet to a professional stringer who is certified. Wilson, with its Perimeter Weighting System, has built weight into these two areas of the frame and patented the idea, allowing players to benefit when mis-hits occur. Almost all players in the top 20 have lead tape on their racquets to create a more stable effect and to produce a continuity of weight among all their racquets. My research shows that most balls are struck with the top third of the racquet, so another

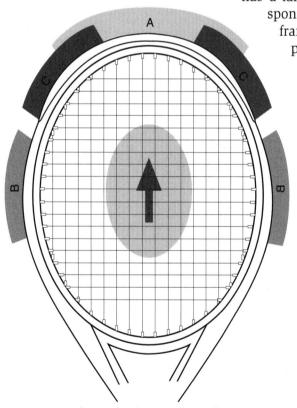

Figure 6.3—Placing lead tape on specific edges of your racquet can effect the sweet spot.

good reason to place lead tape at the top of a racquet (sections A or C in figure 6.3) is to give it more mass in this area.

Length

In the past few years, long-body racquets have hit the tennis scene, the latest innovation in a competitive industry. The ITF sets the maximum length at 81.23 centimeters (31.98 inches), but the average racquet these days is about 69 centimeters (27 inches). Long-body racquets are coming in at about 70.5 to 71 centimeters (27.75 to 28 inches).

Uli Kuehnel notes that players under 5 feet 8 inches could benefit from longer racquets as Michael Chang did, especially on serves, but it may take up to three years to get used to the different playing characteristics of a longer racquet. If you are switching lengths, warns Kuehnel, consider your age, strength, and stroking preference. Children basically should use a graduated-length method starting with their particular coordination level, height, and strength. Some kids can swing a standard-length racquet at an early age and others have to mature. I do not encourage children under the age of 8 or adults with a one-handed backhand to use the long-body racquet.

Grip

Most of today's grips consist of foam angled differently at the cap and at the top. That's why it's necessary to measure the grip in the same place on each racquet—I recommend a spot 6 centimeters (2.36 inches) from the butt cap.

Grips come in varying sizes—4-1/4, 4-3/8, 4-1/2, 4-5/8. How can you determine what's best for you? Test them out! When you hold the racquet there should be at least one finger's width between the tip of your finger and your thumb. For many racquets, grips are interchangeable. If you like a racquet but find the grip too small, you probably can have the shop put on the grip you need.

Grips also can be customized for right- or left-handers. If you're right-handed, you want the grip of your racquet so the angle of the grip (where the grip overlaps itself) goes upward to the right. If you're a lefty, it's just the opposite. (Thus your grip should be wrapped counter-clockwise if you're right-handed and clockwise if you are left handed). Be sure the butt cap and grip wrapping have no sharp edges that could injure your hand.

Some players use overgrips, wrapping extra material around the grip to absorb sweat or to increase the grip size. The most common is Tournagrip. This is fine in moderation, but some overdo it, using two or three wrappings. This can take away the feeling of the panels of the grip, the information you need in order to change grips effectively during play. That is, if your grip was completely rounded, your hands would have no way of feeling an eastern, continental, semi- or full western, or backhand grip. You'd have to look each time, to see how your racquet face was positioned.

If your hands sweat a lot during play, you have other options besides overgrips, which can get expensive, since they have to be replaced frequently. Ivan Lendl was famous for reaching into his pocket for a handful of sawdust before serving. Another product, called Fusion, is a sawdust-like material that absorbs sweat and adds friction. Prince has a spray-on grip enhancer that dries your hands effectively.

Making Your Choice

A good racquet won't make you play well, but it can help you play to the best of your ability. A bad racquet will sabotage your efforts, forcing you to play under your ability level.

The perfect racquet for you is one that fits your unique playing style. Don't get wowed by bragging manufacturers or salespeople. The latest, greatest model is not necessarily your salvation. Check out the materials, head shape, grip, length, width, and stiffness. Know what you need for your game, and test out several options. This is a crucial purchase for any complete player. You need to be completely satisfied with the choice you make.

Test-Driving Some Racquets

According to Phil Irish, a Tampa, Florida, tennis pro, the best way to find the right racquet is to test several out. Most reputable shops allow you to put down a refundable deposit and test-drive a new racquet. If a particular store won't let you leave a deposit and "test-drive" a racquet, find one that will. Don't be afraid to ask questions, and if a salesperson doesn't know the answers, find one who does. Take five to eight racquets from the shop on a demo tour. It's best to find a court with a ball machine and try out all your different strokes with each of the racquets. You can have a friend hit to you, but the machine offers you a consistent feed, helping you to make more accurate decisions about the racquets you're testing. Plan to spend a good couple of hours with all the racquets, sorting out which you like best.

As you hit your strokes, consider which racquets feel most comfortable, then hit a few with your old racquet and compare the sensation. Which ones give you control or power for your game? Pay special attention to your wrist and elbow. Are they working together well with the racquet or are you putting too much strain on those joints? (This also could be a matter of stringing, which I'll cover later.) And don't be swayed by price tags. Just because a racquet costs $250 doesn't mean it's the best one for you.

Line up the racquets at the side of the court in order of your preference (it may be tough to remember each racquet's performance if you're not organized about this). Narrow down your choice to two or three racquets. Then forget the ball machine and play a few sets with a partner, using the different racquets. There are always improvised shots that occur in game situations that are hard to test out against a ball machine.

How many racquets should you buy? Well, it really depends on how serious you are about your game. If you are an occasional player, then one is all you need. The weekend warrior can benefit from having two racquets of the same make and model and strung the same. Should a string break, he can walk over to the sideline and pick up another one confidently knowing how it is going to feel and perform. Competitive players and professional players tend to have six or more racquets so they can string them at different tensions. They use specific frames for practice and others for match play, etc.

Once you have selected a racquet that you like and you know its weight, balance point, grip size, head size, stiffness, and length, it is important to then order another racquet or racquets with the same specifications from the supplier or manufacturer. For example, it will do you no good if the racquet you like weighs 12.2 ounces and all the rest in the store weigh 12.8. It is easy to add weight onto a racquet, but taking weight off is more difficult and expensive. Purchase racquets with similar specifications and have a professional stringer weight and balance the racquets for you.

Stringing Your Racquet

Don't underestimate the value of having a professional racquet stringer. Earlier I introduced tennis racquet expert Uli Kuehnel, who introduced me to the concept of the "performance triangle"—the racquet, the strings, and the playability of the racquet. That "playability" is basically the string tension. All three elements need to blend together, matching a player's style, to attain optimum performance.

Stringing the Perfect Performance Triangle

Uli Kuehnel

The whole tennis industry is very young. Racquet manufacturers and string manufacturers forget to look for synergy. They forget that a racquet is only as good as the string job will be. If you string a racquet in the wrong way, then the advantage of the racquet is gone. On the other hand, the string manufacturers have worked only on finding better materials, better elasticity, or less elasticity.

Bringing the string type, racquet, and stringing together was important to me when I started stringing racquets 16 years ago. I knew there had to be a connection between a perfect racquet and a good string job. The basic point to understand is that the main strings and cross-strings are working together to take the ball and let it go. Because the main strings are longer, they require more tension than the cross-strings.

What is the best tension? One way to find out is by measuring the string bed with the Swiss-made Master Tension Meter. With this machine we can say that an average player would play with a dynamic string tension of about 40. That means that you need 40 kilopoints to move the string bed one centimeter down. With fewer than 40 kilopoints, you have power and control, which I refer to as a soft string job. With a dynamic tension of more than 42 kilopoints, you have control—a hard string job. Between 40 and 42, you have an optimum string job.

When a player comes to me for stringing, I ask him to show me a racquet that feels good to him. Then I check it myself by sound and by dynamic tension. Then we make sure we have all the information we need about what tension the player wants and needs. We then figure out the tension of the main strings and the cross-strings and the thickness of the string, as well as the best type of string to use.

You want your racquet to be strung on a machine that has a good prestretching system, or you should ask the person stringing your racquet to prestretch your string: based on the elasticity of that particular string. Strings lose up to 10 percent of their tension in the first 12 hours, no matter how they're strung, and they lose even more if the string was not prestretched. Prestretching increases the relaxation of the string, which simply means that the string bed does not fall down too much after being strung, and that can lead to longer play.

Step 1: Select String Type and Gauge

- Which player type are you? (Circle one)

  Straight stroker (you hit the ball flat)
  Topspin slicer

- How often do you play tennis? (Circle one)

   Occasional (Less than once a week)

   Weekend (Once or twice during the weekend)

   Tournament (Three to five times a week)

   Professional (Year-round)

Step 2: Select Your String

- What type of string is recommended for you? (Circle one)

   Synthetic

   Gut

   Middle synthetic

- What gauge of string does table 6.1 recommend for you based on your frequency of play, your types of swings, and the size of your racquet? Note: Eighty percent of the string sold in the United States is 16-gauge string, according to Ian Arthur of Head racquet manufacturers. In Europe it is 15-gauge because it lasts longer—and stringing is more expensive there. (Circle one)

   15   16   17

Now for the final part of the racquet performance triangle—bringing racquet and selected string together with the correct tension.

Step 3: Assess String Tension

Keep the following environmental conditions in mind if you are a tournament or pro player when assessing your string tension. Remember that if the meter registers under 40 kilopoints the tension is soft, between 40 and 42 is optimal, and above 42 is hard.

- Outside temperature: < 40°F = string softer; 40 to 90°F = optimal; > 90°F = hard
- Altitude: Sea level to < 2,500 feet, string softer; > 2,500 feet, optimal or hard
- Humidity: > 80 percent = optimal
- Strong wind: optimal

If you are playing on grass or clay where the ball picks up dirt or if you are playing with a ball that feels heavy, then you want your tension to be a few pounds looser (softer). Also, ask the professional stringer to whom you are taking your racquet when was the last time his machine was calibrated. Stringing machines become inaccurate if they are not calibrated. Every machine on the market does the job a little differently, so try to find out how the machine your stringer is using pulls the strings. Is there a tendency for the machine to pull true to the tension shown or does it pull looser or tighter?

- What type of stringing machine is used? (Circle one)

   Prince   TruE

   Babolat   Tension

   Ektelon

Player type	Straight stroke			Loop or semiloop backswing (topspin/slice)		
Head size LL in mm	Normal 300 mm	Mid 320 mm	Over > 320 mm	Normal 300 mm	Mid 320 mm	Over > 320 mm
Occasional beginner	Good elastic synthetic 15/16	Good elastic synthetic 15/16	Good elastic synthetic 15/16	Good elastic synthetic 15/16	Good elastic synthetic 15/16	Good elastic synthetic 15/16
Occasional nonbeginner	Gut or good elastic synthetic 15/16	Gut or good elastic synthetic 15/16	Good or middle elastic synthetic 15/16	Gut or good elastic synthetic 15/16	Gut or good elastic synthetic 15/16	Good or middle elastic synthetic > 16
Weekend	Gut good elastic synthetic 16 or 17	Good elastic synthetic 16 or 17	Good or middle elastic synthetic 16	Gut or good elastic synthetic 16	Good elastic synthetic 16	Good or middle elastic synthetic 16
Tournament	Gut or good elastic synthetic 17	Gut or good elastic synthetic 16	Gut or good elastic synthetic 16	Gut or good elastic synthetic 16	Gut or middle elastic synthetic 16	Gut or middle elastic synthetic 16
Professional on clay or hard court	Gut or good elastic synthetic 17 or 16	Gut or good elastic synthetic 17 or 16	Gut or good elastic synthetic 17 or 16	Gut or good elastic synthetic 17 or 16	Gut or good elastic synthetic 17 or 16	Gut or good elastic synthetic 17 or 16

Table 6.1—String Gauge Recommendations

- Did you ask if the string was prestretched? If it was not, then be sure to prestretch your string either on the machine or by tying one end to a door handle and pulling on the entire length of the string.

Step 4: Try Out Your Strings

Now string one racquet and go play with it. Give yourself a week or two to get used to it. When the racquet feels good, have a professional stringer test the dynamic tension (the flex of the entire string bed).

- Based on the stringer's reading the finished dynamic tension = _____
  < 40 is soft; 40 to 42 is optimal; > 42 is hard

Step 5: Complete Your Customization

- String all your racquets on the same machine and by the same stringer.
- Repeat the weighting and balancing of each ready-to-play racquet (strings now included).
- Add your stencil on the strings.
- Place racquets if possible into plastic bags to protect from dirt and humidity.
- Always keep racquets in your thermal bag when not in use.

Record periodically in your training notebook just how you feel your racquet performs. Include the date used, the power and control rating on a scale of 1 (low) to 5 (high), as well as what the dynamic tension is, who strung your racquet last, and when.

Taking Care of Your Racquet

Heat and moisture are your racquet's worst enemies. A comfortable temperature for your racquet is 17 to 25 degrees Celsius (60 to 80 degrees Fahrenheit), with a humidity of 75 to 80 percent. Leaving your racquet in the car is one of the worst mistakes you can make. The temperature inside a car can be well over 30 degrees Celsius (85 degrees Fahrenheit), leaving the strings in your racquet exhausted. The heat robs the strings of their life and leaves them in a condition where they easily could break. Try to keep your racquet out of direct sunlight, protected from moisture, and always in the thermal bag when you're not using it.

When the professional stringer has finished weighting and balancing all your racquets the same and you have selected the type and tension of the string that you will be using in your racquets, then your performance triangle is complete. You now are armed with a quiver of racquets that you can go to with confidence, as you know how each of the racquets will respond.

Now it is time to make another important and educated decision—how best to take care of your feet and improve your game.

Choosing the Right Footwear

Though we tend to treat our feet with disdain, they're probably the tennis player's most important body part. They bear your weight, and they get you where you need to be. If your feet are happy, you'll be happy. If not, you'll be miserable.

What Is Your Foot Type?

Unfortunately, feet are not one-size-fits-all commodities. You know, of course, that some folks have huge feet and others tiny feet, but did you know there are different types of feet? Your feet have a precise shape and certain ways of moving that affect your game. Your whole physical alignment is built on your feet, with your legs and upper body compensating for the kind of support your feet provide. Foot type also is linked with specific injuries. By identifying the structure of your feet, you may learn to avoid some common foot problems.

You'll also be able to choose the best possible shoe for your foot type, with proper support and cushioning. For years running shoes have been designed to provide for the special stability and motion-control needs of the runner. But only recently have tennis players recognized that they, too, can benefit from shoes matched to their specific foot types and the demands of the game. Feet fall into three broad categories: pronated, neutral, and supinated (see figure 6.4).

- **Neutral.** One quick way to determine your basic foot type is to examine the soles of your old shoes for the pattern of wear. Which part of the shoe is most worn?

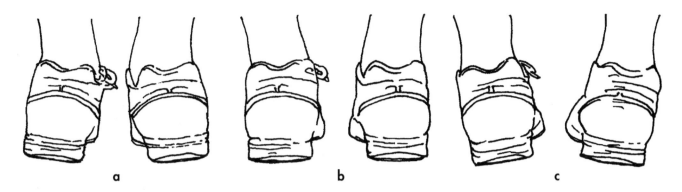

a   b   c

Figure 6.4—Categories of feet: (a) pronated, (b) neutral, (c) supinated.

A player with neutral feet wears shoes relatively evenly, stepping squarely on the center of the foot. The stride also is even, with the front of the foot and heel aligned with the ground and positioned directly beneath the lower leg (not twisting to the side). The arch is neither too flat nor too high.

• **Supinated.** A person with a high-arched foot puts pressure on the outside of the foot. The technical term is "supination." You might notice an outward tilt in the walk of a player with supinated feet. The weight-bearing starts at the heel, transfers along the outer foot border, and ends with weight distribution in the forefoot. Supinators usually have calluses on the balls of their feet and may suffer from ankle problems. The ankle joint is stiffer and less able to flex upward, contributing to conditions of excessive shock and stress to the bones and supporting structures. Potential injuries include tears or inflammation of the plantar fascia (plantar fascitis), bursitis, Achilles tendinitis or rupture, and ankle sprains.

• **Pronated.** Other players have flatter arches and more flexible feet. As they walk, the inner side of the foot hits the ground first and the foot appears to roll outward. This is called "pronation." Such players may get calluses along the inner side of the foot. Their arches may tire and they also may have problems with ankle instability. Since the arch is not doing its part in weight-bearing, the front muscles of the foot try to make up for it, resulting in fatigue. Common pronation problems are injuries of overuse, loss of shock absorption in soft tissue structures, and muscle pulls.

So are you doomed if you don't have a neutral foot? No. While it's true that too much supination or pronation can hurt your game in the long run, these conditions also have a few advantages. A high-arch (supinated) foot can work well for quick cutting, pivoting, and speed. And you actually need some amount of pronation for "setting the inside edge" in sports such as skiing and some golf or tennis stances. But you also need to be aware of the instability and potential injury involved. Be extra careful if your feet are supinated or pronated. Women's feet tend to be narrower in the heel and wider in the forefoot with a higher arch then men's. Be sure to find shoes that accommodate your needs. The exercise for ankle stability in chapter 7 also will help stabilization depending on how disciplined you are at practicing it.

Determine your foot type by getting an imprint of your step. You'll need baby powder and black construction paper. Get barefoot and place the paper on a level, noncarpeted floor. Rub powder all over one foot and then step onto the paper with all your weight. As you're making an imprint with one foot, be sure to keep equal weight on both feet. Repeat with the other foot. Then compare your imprint to those in figure 6.4.

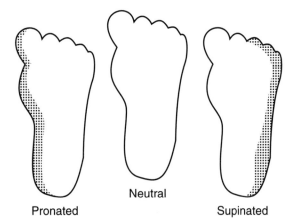

Pronated   Neutral   Supinated

Figure 6.5—Perform the powder test to help determine your foot type.

Healthy Feet, Happy Feet

Maybe it starts halfway through your second set: some nagging pain in your feet or ankles. It could be a blister or some kind of cramp, or maybe your feet are just exhausted from pushing you around so much.

Any pain is your body's way of trying to get your attention. Pain in your feet, ankles, or lower legs probably means your feet have something to tell you. Many tennis players just resign themselves to chronic foot discomfort. It goes with the game, they say. But that's not necessarily the case. You can do things to correct many of the problems that cause you pain. If the problem seems severe, or if other measures don't correct it, see a sports podiatrist. But before you go to that expense, check the following factors:

- **Do your tennis shoes fit properly?** Shoes that are too small or too big can cause corns, calluses, blisters, black toe, or other painful conditions. Tennis is especially demanding on your feet and lower legs, with quick turns and constant pounding. Your shoes must provide ankle support and cushioning for the balls of your feet.

- **Are your feet out of shape?** Like any other part of your body, your feet respond to conditioning. By performing the foot stabilization exercises in chapter 7 at least four times a week, you can strengthen your feet and reduce your level of discomfort during strenuous activity.

- **Do you abuse your feet?** Off the court, you may be overusing your feet, misusing them, wearing ineffective shoes, or walking barefoot in treacherous places. The serious player needs to make a 24-7 commitment to keep the feet in good playing condition.

Buy Shoes That Fit

Many people fall prey to advertising. An expensive shoe must be a good shoe, right? Well, no. If you just shelled out $150 for a hot brand name, I hate to break it to you—a good shoe is a shoe that fits well, no matter what the name is, or the price tag.

Still, it's true that most of those big-name shoe companies work hard to design shoes that keep pace with the changes in the game. Remember when any kind of sneaker was called a "tennis shoe?" Those days are gone. Today's players are more athletic and better conditioned than ever, pounding shots from all over the court—and giving their shoes a real beating. Now shoes are wearing out not just at the toe but around the inner side of the shoe, a result of hitting big forehands from an open stance. And players are tougher on the midsoles, jumping into shots and changing directions. It's not hit and giggle at the country club anymore. Tennis is a tougher game, and its shoes have had to step up to the challenge with beefier outsoles for hard-court abuse, bigger toe guards that employ advanced materials, and midsoles made from polymers that combine the best cushioning qualities of ethyl vinyl acetate (EVA) with the die-hard durability of polyurethane (PU).

Expensive brand-name companies may have the best shoes for you, but not necessarily. More importantly, the shoe still has to fit you and your game. So don't just grab a cool-looking shoe from a shelf. Try it on! Try on lots of shoes to see what gives you the best fit. Every shoe fits differently, even shoes made by the same manufacturer. Take your time in shoe shopping, and it will pay off on the court.

☐ **Get a complete fit.** When trying on shoes, most people push down on the toe to check the length, and they may check the width, but the most important area is the heel. You want a firm fit there; any slippage affects your balance and alignment on the court.

☐ **Measure both feet properly.** Tennis players often wear shoes that are too small, causing pain and reducing the necessary support and cushioning. That's why it's extremely important to measure your feet—both of them—every time you shop for new shoes. Examine the length and width of each foot. If one foot is slightly longer or wider, get a pair of shoes in the size that accommodates the larger foot.

☐ **Find your longest toe.** Once you have a shoe on, make sure you have a thumbnail's width between your longest toe and the end of the toe area in the shoe.

☐ **Shop late in the day.** Feet tend to swell during the day, so it's best to shop for shoes in the afternoon. If your feet are measured early in the day, you may end up buying smaller shoes that won't fit during your evening match.

☐ **Keep your foot type in mind.** If you're a supinator, you may want a shoe with extra ankle support and strength along the outside of the sole. Also pay attention to the arch area, making sure you have plenty of room there. A pronator's foot may need extra cushioning in the front of the sole and strength along the inside.

☐ **Buy a flexible shoe.** Shoes with mesh uppers or a combination of leather and mesh tend to be lighter and breathe better than shoes with canvas or all-leather uppers.

☐ **Make sure your shoes are completely flat across the bottom**. Some manufacturers have been cutting the midsole out to make the shoe lighter and more stylish. But in tennis you want as much contact with the court as possible. Anything less threatens your stability, balance, and alignment.

☐ **Get the right construction for your game.** Find shoes that best meet your playing surface. Today's outsoles are designed for grass, clay, or hard courts. A suitable tread prevents slippage or the possibility of tearing up the court. Also, check whether the shoes have EVA or PU midsoles. EVA provides a more cushioned, softer feel, while PU midsoles are firmer and more durable.

And after you've made the purchase . . .

☐ **Break them in slowly.** Wear your new shoes around the house for about an hour a day over a three- or four-day period. Too much too soon will punish your feet.

☐ **Lace your shoes all the way up.** You need a very snug fit around your ankle, and firm lacing is the best way to achieve this. And, please, no Velcro.

☐ **Don't wear two pairs of socks.** Somehow the myth has grown among tennis players that double socks can help your game. They really just create more slippage within the shoe.

"Choosing the right shoe is the most important decision a tennis player can make when wanting to improve," says shoe specialist Connie Bernard, who is a consultant for Diadora, Adidas, and Nike. "When you have the right fit, it allows your lower body to stabilize, freeing your upper body to move with confidence and letting the racquet swing uninhibited."

What Is an Orthotic Device and Do I Need One?

Dr. Simon Small
Leading sports podiatrist

Many of us have feet that are shaped somewhat distinctively. For many, one foot's a bit different from the other. All of this means that we can't just grab a shoe off the shelf. We need some expert help, including an orthotic device, something that corrects an irregularity in our foot structure or movement.

An orthotic is a unique, handcrafted correctional device that provides symptomatic relief for the most frustrating foot problems. It is a customized, cast-molded appliance made with layers for comfort. An orthotic is designed and manufactured to meet the individual needs of each athlete by correcting game-related injuries and preventing other injuries.

There are various levels of orthotics. If you are interested in trying them for the first time and don't want to invest a great deal up front, you can purchase an over-the-counter, inexpensive one. Once you have determined that you want to try orthotics, consult with a podiatrist, orthopedist, physical therapist, or chiropractor who can evaluate you, determine your needs and style, and prescribe an appropriate device. The podiatrist should collect the following information about you:

- Time of day of the assessment
- Type of shoe you wear presently
- Type of foot
- Length of right foot and left foot
- Recommended shoe for foot type
- Unique body build or special needs

- Preferable playing style
- Need for foot support
- Need for an orthotic
- Width of stance for evaluation
- History of leg or lower back problems
- Plan of action

Since my practice generally works with highly talented professional athletes who require perfect biomechanical performance for their sports pursuits, we develop a high-end, custom orthotic. This type is costlier than an over-the-counter device, but the highly technical combination of thermoplastic, cast-molded materials provides the ultimate in comfort, balance, and support for achieving active, efficient, and pain-free foot control, leading to athletic success.

Our client list includes Pete Sampras, Chris Evert, Gabriella Sabatini, Derek Rostagno, Michael Chang, John McEnroe, Larry Bird, and members of the U.S., German, Bahamian, and Australian Davis Cup teams, along with other sports figures in the NBA, NFL, and major league baseball.

The life span on your orthotics depends on the type you own. A graphite and plastic device could last for several years due to the inherent properties of those materials. But if you have an orthotic with accommodative, softer layers, they should be recast after a year or two to determine whether the foot has changed.

If you have just gotten orthotics, you need to break them in slowly over the course of two weeks. Start wearing them for 30 minutes at a time and work your way up to two hours until you begin wearing them full-time.

Condition Your Feet for the Game

A few exercises before and during a workout will go a long way to ensure that your feet are ready to work with you. By regularly including ankle limbering and strengthening in your warm-up, you'll prepare your feet and ankles for any match (see chapters 7 and 13).

Here are some additional helpful hints to keep your feet healthy and happy:

- If blisters develop, drain the fluid with a sterilized needle but don't remove the skin until it's ready to fall off; the skin serves as a natural, biological dressing. Be sure to keep the area clean and cover it with a bandage.

- Keep your feet covered, inside and outside unless, of course, you happen to be at the beach. Resist the urge to go barefoot after a long match on a hot, humid day. Walking around shoeless predisposes your feet to contagious athlete's foot fungus as well as splinters, glass, and needles, which always seem to find a way to lodge inside the soles of the feet (another good reason to keep your shoes on).

- How can your feet get relief from the heat? Bring along extra socks. Since feet perspire more heavily in the summer, you should probably change your socks twice a day even if you're not playing tennis, and more often if you are.

- Sitting for an extended period of time puts pressure on the muscles surrounding the nerve tissue, which can cause those nerves to compress. Feet retain fluid or become numb—especially for the driver of a car—and upon the resumption of normal movement, pain and stiffness can occur. Certain exercises can help stimulate circulation and prevent compression of the nerves, even in the car. Consider the following suggestions: (a) Draw your knees to your chest, resting your heels on the front edge of the seat, then gently flex the ankle joints by pulling your feet upward while allowing your heels to press into the edge of the seat; (b) perform figure eights with your feet to help reduce the stiffness in your ankle joints; and (c) try not to sit in the same position for too long, and if you decide to take a snooze, avoid crossing your legs to prevent that "pins and needles" feeling when you awaken.

- Once out of the car, start moving. Take a short walk or jog, do some stretches, and gradually begin working the muscles until they loosen up.

Maximizing Your Fitness Level

In chapters 1 through 5, I've covered some drills that focus on improving tennis skills; chapter 6 has provided guidelines for ensuring you're equipped for your best game. Now it's time to maximize your fitness specifically for the game. You'll find how to fit a workout into your busy schedule as well as how to improve your on-court performance with the right nutrition and sleep habits.

First let's cover the fundamental conditioning aspects for tennis. Tennis strength and fitness coach, Pat Etcheberry, has pinpointed the basic conditioning aspects on which a serious tennis player needs to focus to improve his or her game.

Note that much of your tennis-specific conditioning focuses on your speed, speed endurance, and strength. You can assess your strengths and weaknesses in these core areas by performing a series of specialized tests (see the bibliography for selected resources). For the purpose of this text, however, I've noted several key conditioning exercises that can focus your conditioning on increasing your strength, speed, and speed endurance.

Conditioning Focus for Tennis

Pat Etcheberry
Tennis strength and conditioning coach

Movement on the court is critical. You may have the greatest strokes in the world, but if you cannot get to the ball you will never be able to execute them. Better players find that when they can get to the ball, they can hit it wherever (and however) they want. Take Andre Agassi and his forehand, for example—he is so quick that he can adjust and hit the forehand wherever he wants. Your ability to move on the court can be evaluated by your speed endurance and speed.

Endurance matters, but not raw cardiovascular endurance as such. For example, I could put a marathon runner on the court, but he would not move well because he's used to traveling at one speed. Tennis is not a one-speed sport, rather it involves repeated bursts of speed with short recoveries between—**speed endurance**.

A few years ago we were in New York doing some agility drills with Pete Sampras. A massage therapist on the tour who also happened to be a very good marathon runner decided to join us for a light agility workout, and he was just about dead by the end. How is this possible? Well, in tennis your heart rate goes up very high and then has to recover. So your heart rate goes up then down repeatedly. In tennis you don't train like a marathon runner and you don't train like a sprinter either. Maurice Greene runs his race and then maybe three hours later or the following day runs the finals. As a tennis player you have a final every 20 seconds and you may play 150 to 170 points in a match. Every 20 seconds you have to be ready to sprint all out. So *speed endurance* is what is important for tennis players. You have to be able to repeat it and repeat it, duplicating your performance each time.

So who's the better tennis player? The one who runs 100 meters (110 yards) in 9.8 seconds, but only twice a day? Or the one who does a 10.2-second 100 meters over and over again? The latter. Michael Chang cannot beat many players on the tour in a 100-meter dash. But he can beat most of the guys with his first two or three steps over a distance of 5 or 10 or 20 meters.

Strength is perhaps one of the easiest physical qualities to improve. With proper strength development you can be at least twice as strong as you are now, but your strength training must be tennis specific, or functional. You're not trying to become a body builder or linebacker. Everything you do for tennis has to be specifically for tennis. You can improve your tennis-specific strength in the weight room with specific strength training exercises (see page 127).

Balance is required if you want consistency in your strokes. You can have great speed but poor balance. Maybe you run 10 to 20 yards very fast, but then when you adjust your step to run wide for a forehand, you have to take smaller steps and lower your center of gravity. That requires balance.

We work on this by controlling the eyes, which control the head. Do shoes have an influence on balance? Yes, but mostly it's a matter of strength in the legs. Tennis is a lower body sport. If you look at Becker, Sampras, Courier, and Chang each have a great set of legs compared to the upper body. This gives them a lower

Yevgeny Kafelnikov's explosive power and footwork allow him to change direction quickly.

center of gravity, which allows them to change directions quickly. When tennis players go to the gym, they often do the wrong exercises. They need to emphasize working with the legs.

Explosive power is important because you need to generate explosive speed for the first few steps, and you also need to change directions. Tennis requires explosive speed to take off, but you also have to plant and recover and that takes power. You see it often with players who don't have the leg strength to plant and recover. They end up getting stuck. The ability to plant the foot and push off is critical. This enables you to accelerate quickly and change directions. My theory is that footwork is like dancing: you have to be light on your feet.

Some people—especially older people—say they don't have good footwork. They *have* the ability, but on the court they get tight. If I took you to a hard court out in Las Vegas somewhere, with the temperature over 100 degrees Fahrenheit, and I made you take off your shoes, you'd have great footwork. Your feet would be moving all the time!

Look at Jimmy Connors—he was always moving from the time he hit the ball until he received the next ball. He kept moving so he didn't have to break inertia. But to do that you have to be in very good shape, which brings us back to speed endurance.

Flexibility is important to help prevent injury. Also, some shots require you to be flexible in order to make them over the net. Players that do not get down well for low volleys tend to be stiff through the hips. Edberg always had his back straight and played on the balls of his feet. If you are bending from the waist because you are tight in the hips, you will never have a good volley. Improve your flexibility with yoga exercises on pages 242 and 243.

Agility is developed as a separate skill, after you have developed the strength, balance, flexibility, and power. Then you start learning how to position your feet, hips, and shoulders to react before and after hitting the shot, how to hit the ball with control and balance, and how to make sure you're ready to hit the next shot. The best way to learn agility is to get into position to hit a ball without hitting a ball. Once you learn how to move into position, then you're ready to try it with a ball.

Eye-hand coordination is also necessary. Most good tennis players have quick hands (explosive power). But, good returners have good eyes and reflexes. To improve your eye-hand coordination you'll need to incorporate a variety of exercises that require hand/eye coordination such as playing other racquet sports (i.e., ping pong and badminton).

Relaxation is important, too. Notice how relaxed players like Marcelo Riosand Pete Sampras are on the court. Players who are obviously nervous and tense, on the other hand, get beat. You can train yourself to relax to a certain degree (see chapters 8 and 9).

I also want a player to go into a match with the right **attitude**. Something like: "No matter how tough the match is, I am better prepared than my opponent." As they say, if you fail to prepare then you prepare to fail. There is a physical-mental connection for tennis players. If you know you are fit and can work hard, then you will be lot tougher mentally. If you've worked hard physically to prepare for a match, you're not going to tank or give up. Chapters 8 and 9 provide guidelines and strategies for toughening your mental game.

Basic Conditioning

The first few weeks of conditioning form the foundation of your training as you head into your competitive season. Your objectives in this phase are to develop a base of strength, to correct muscle imbalances, and to improve cardiovascular fitness and speed endurance (the speed of movements lasting 15 seconds or more). Keep your on-court training focused on developing and honing your SMARTS skills. Spend at least 2 weeks in the phase before moving on to the next phase.

In this particular phase, regardless of the activity, maintain a work rest ratio of 2:1— if you are sprinting for 30 seconds, your rest should be 15 seconds. This interval works well if you are beginning your training program with good speed endurance, but if you don't, you may need to give yourself more rest at first and work yourself down slowly to shorter breaks.

Functional Strengthening

Functional strength development does not just focus on improving strength, but also on learning to apply your strength properly to your tennis movements.

Begin each strength training session with an easy 5- to 10-minute warm up on the bike or treadmill followed by 5 minutes of stretching. This warm up will help protect your body from injury while lifting. In addition, seek guidance from a professional athletic trainer or consult one or more of the references I recommend in the bibliography to ensure that you are performing each exercise correctly (see bibliography, page 256).

Determine Your One Repetition Max

The one-repetition maximum (1RM) is the basis used for how much weight to lift for a given exercise. To determine your 1RM for a particular lift, find the maximum weight you can lift for each exercise just one time. As you will see in the workouts below, you will then lift a certain percentage of your 1RM weight for that lift. For example, if you determine that the maximum amount of weight your can lift for one repetition for the bench press is 100 pounds, then a workout calling for bench press 70 percent of your 1RM means that you are to lift 70 pounds for that set (.7 × 100 pounds).

If it has been a while since you lifted weights, start at about 50 percent of your 1RM for the first two weeks of training. After these two weeks, increase 10 percent per week or until you reach the desired intensity as noted in the exercises below.

It is important to perform core strengthening exercises for the lower back and abdominal regions each day. Keeping these areas strong will help you prevent injuries. Get in the habit of performing three sets of 25 repetitions (reps) of each of following abdominal and back exercises.

- Sit-ups
- Crunches
- Free hang (hang from a bar with your hands; lift your legs up to the sides and forward)
- Back hyperextension (use a hyperextension machine)
- Lie face down and lift your upper body off the floor for the first set, your legs off the floor for the second set, and lift both your arms and legs off the floor for the third set

In addition to core strengthening, focus on the following four workouts each week of the basic conditioning phase.

1. Chest, triceps, and lower arms

Chest (choose three): Bench press, incline press, reverse incline press; dumbbell incline press, dumbbell lateral, dumbbell fly (supine), and normal or knuckle push-up.

Triceps (choose three): Military press; triceps pullover, triceps extension; push-up (thumbs and index fingers together), and dip.

Lower arm (choose two): Dumbbell wrist curl, dumbbell wrist extension, rolling a newspaper with your hands straight in front of body, and lateral pull.

2. Back, biceps, and shoulders

Back: Upright row, lateral pull, and rowing machine.

Biceps: Dumbbell biceps curl, curl bar standing curl, reverse row (rowing machine), and Superman (stand with holding two pulleys shoulder height or higher and curl each arm toward your head).

Shoulders: Military press (seated or standing), pull-up, push-up, handstand push-up, and lateral row.

3. Legs: Dead lift, leg press, leg curl, leg extension, toe raise, front squat, and inverted squat.

4. Total body: These exercises use dumbbells or barbells and develop strength and power due to the explosive nature of the lifts. Choose two of the three: Clean, jerk, and snatch.

For all exercises except the total body lifts, perform four sets:

- 10 reps at 50 to 60 % 1RM
- 10 reps at 70% 1RM
- 8 reps at 75% 1RM, and
- 6 reps at 80% 1RM

For the total body lifts, perform two to six sets of three to five reps at 60 percent to 90 percent of your 1RM. Take two to five minutes rest between sets.

Why Total Body Conditioning?

Hans Jurgen Montag

Past physiotherapist for the DFB (Deustche Fussball Bund) national football team and late founder of the Rehabilitation Center Montag in Oberhaching, Germany.

Montag and his team helped Boris Becker and the German Davis Cup Team rehabilitate through many of their injuries.

The game of tennis can push your body to its full potential; but if you're not conditioned to take the pounding, twisting, and other stresses of the game you may be asking for injury. The good news is that you can prepare your body for the unique stresses and strains of this activity. If you prepare well and play wisely, you can avoid serious injury.

Tennis requires certain movements that are specific to the game. For this reason specific training is necessary to balance the muscles and increase flexibility. The most common tennis injuries occur in the ankles, knees, various muscles, and the back. Due to the twisting nature of the game, the back is the basis for many of the problems that are felt in the legs. While injuries to the arms and shoulders don't occur often among top players, recreational players tend to develop arm trouble due to overexertion and improper technique. Most specifically, a lack of economy of movement cause some players to be late making contact with the ball. This happens more often as players get tired and, with their late contact, they try to "wrist" or "arm" the ball over the net. Poor conditioning also results in lower arm injuries for many nonprofessional players. The result—tennis elbow, the swelling of the flexor *carpi radialis* or the extensor *carpi radialis longus*.

Players also can develop shoulder injuries due to the massive pressure of serving. Again, bad form is the culprit. When shoulder pain starts, players often adjust their serve, which momentarily eases the pain but creates stress on another area. Or if a player has a lack of back flexibility, he or she can compromise the movement of the serve, trying to generate more power from the shoulder.

Tennis does a number on hamstrings, too, with its sudden spurts of movement. Players who don't stretch properly are inviting serious leg injury, but even pros are vulnerable. Common injuries also include a range of small but pesky problems of the hands and feet: blisters, black toe, calluses, etc.

General conditioning will help you avoid some basic sports injuries, but if you want to fend off *tennis* injuries, you'll need to engage in some tennis-specific conditioning. For example, lifting weights to develop chest muscles may make you look better, but it does not help you reduce the chance of injuring your shoulder while serving. Instead, throw a medicine ball in the same motion you would use to serve or play. Cross training with other sports such as basketball and soccer has benefits, too. These sports are fun and give you a mental rest from tennis. They can also improve your balance and coordination. Even gymnastics can improve your movement on court and help you prevent injury.

Note also that tennis is a very one-sided sport. You use one arm to stroke the ball, and all your twisting and turning results in setting up that one arm for the play. That can result in muscle imbalances in your arms and throughout your body, and that can set you up for injury on or off the court. So smart conditioning includes strength-building on both sides of your body.

Speed Endurance

In addition to building functional strength, the basic conditioning phase also concentrates on long speed endurance. For tennis players, a long point lasts approximately 10 to 15 seconds. So a sprint of 100 yards or 100 meters is the equivalent to a long point on the court. The objective in speed endurance exercises, therefore, is to develop your cardiovascular system and help you perform with a consistent energy output over the course of a match.

Do your speed endurance work on the same days as your lifting. Spend at least 10 minutes warming up and stretching before doing the following speed endurance workout. Try part of Step 1 one day and Step 2 on another day fllowed by Step 3.

Step 1: Choose one of the following

5 × 100 yards at 80% intensity 30 seconds recovery between each

4 × 200 yards at 80% intensity; 60 seconds recovery between each

1 × 400 yards at 80% intensity; stretch

4 × 100 yards at 90% intensity; 30 seconds recovery between each

3 × 200 yards at 90% intensity; 60 seconds recovery between each

2 × 400 yards at 90% intensity; 90 seconds recovery between each

1 × 800 yards at 90% intensity; stretch

Step 2: Next you will need three jump ropes of different weights:

5-pound jump rope—4 × 50 jumps.

3-pound jump rope—4 × 50 jumps.

Regular jump rope—6 × 50 reps.

Rest 15 seconds between sets. You can vary the number of jumps based on your ability and stamina.

Step 3: Finally, run 10 × 100 yards with 30 seconds recovery between each. Increase the difficulty by wearing a weighted vest or pulling a sled (see page 131). Start with a lighter weight and build according to your own strength.

Tommy Haas getting ready to explode into his serve.

Precompetitive Phase

In the precompetitive phase you take the strength and speed endurance gains you achieved in basic conditioning and work toward more tennis-specific power. Your objective in the next three to five weeks (prior to your peak competition phase) is to develop tennis-specific speed (on the court and off) via sprint loading, sport loading, plyometrics, power lifting, and shorter distance speed endurance. On the court you can start to play points, games, and sets, but be patient with yourself because your training and complete fitness are still under construction.

Be sure to begin each workout session with an easy warm up on the bike or treadmill followed stretching. The work to rest ratio in this phase is 1:1. After you finish your workouts in this phase, you should feel light and quick on your feet.

Overspeed Training

Overspeed training uses methods to increase your stride rate and length by giving you assistance to perform at a much higher level than you are capable of without assistance. Perform overspeed training at the beginning of practice right after you have warmed up. Build up to overspeed training slowly, performing maybe three repetitions of an exercise your first time, five the next, and then building from there. Gradually working into overspeed training will help prevent injury.

Here are some court-specific forms of overspeed training players can perform with a partner, a harness, and strong surgical tubing (6 to 10 yards long). Surgical tubing can be purchased at a medical supply store and can be attached to a harness or belt. Attach the harness with the surgical tubing around your waist; this will keep your hands free to hold your racquet. Your partner will hold the other end of the tubing. Be sure not to overextended the tubing during this exercise since it can break and can cause injury. Always inspect the tubing before using and replace any overstretched or damaged tubing.

- **Crossover shuffle.** Stand on the baseline with your partner to your right side and shuffle to your left until the cord is almost fully extended, taking a practice swing with your racquet. Then crossover shuffle to recover back to the center. Repeat six times. Then perform three practice repetitions in both directions without the elastic cord.

- **Pivot sprint for the wide ball.** Again, start on the baseline at the center of the court and have a partner stand in the doubles alley. The elastic band should be taut, so that all your partner needs to do is pivot and sprint toward the doubles alley. After taking a practice swing, shuffle back to the center and repeat. Perform three sets of six repetitions with surgical tubing and three times without resistance.

- **Full court.** This time your partner stands in front of you on the service line and will follow you in whatever direction you run, allowing you to stretch the cord, and then they assist you in pulling you back to the center. Perform three times in all directions.

- **Smash recovery.** Your partner now stands at the net while you crossover shuffle or shuffle back as if you're hitting a smash. The cord provides resistance and accelerates you back toward the net, preparing you to volley.

These additional overspeed training activities do not require surgical tubing:

- **Treadmill intervals.** A high-speed treadmill provides a great way to increase your stride rate. You will need to be assisted by someone as you practice getting on and off the treadmill while it is moving fast, holding onto the rails. Do 10 reps of 15-second intervals, gradually increasing the speed.
- **High-speed cycling.** Compete against yourself by sitting on a stationary bike and with moderate resistance spin the pedals as fast as your legs will allow for 30, 20, or 10 seconds. Do three trials to see what your top speed is.

Sprint Loading

Sprint loading involves adding resistance while performing runs or sprints. Some of my favorite sprint loading drills for tennis players are *hollow runs* (alternating repetitions of a short jog with a sprint) followed by walking or doing sprints of varying distances on the beach. Running several repetitions up hills or stairs is also effective. Sometimes right before a match I will have players run a few flights of stairs to get their legs warmed up. However, in general these intense sprint-loading workouts should be incorporated into the precompetitive phase of training, rather than before competitions.

- **Stadium run.** Go to your nearest football or basketball stadium and sprint up 10 to 20 flights of stairs and jog down. Vary each flight by running on every stair for one set, then every other stair for the next set, then every third stair. When descending the stairs, be sure to jog easily and hit every stair. This is also a great workout to do when if you are staying in a hotel.
- **Weighted hill run.** Find a 30- to 40-yard long hill of not greater than a 15-degree grade. Wear a weighted vest and start the first week by adding 2 to 3 pounds weight the first week, then increasing by 2 to 3 pounds each week. If you don't have a vest, then carry a partner piggyback. With the weighted vest, run 8 to 10 repetitions of 10 yards up the hill the first week and increase the distance 5 yards each week. With the partner, carry, walk, or jog up the hill three to four times. Follow by 10 sprints at 80 percent intensity over the same distance with no resistance.
- **Harness pull.** With a partner holding onto your harness, pull them along for 3 to 5 yards as they add resistance. After 3 to 5 yards your partner lets go and you sprint the remaining 6 to 12 yards. Doing this on sand makes it even more difficult. Complete 10 to15 sets followed by 6 sprints of about 12 yards.

Sport Loading

Sport loading involves adding resistance (weight) to your body or racquet for practice swings or tennis-specific exercises. You can load your body with a lead vest or a harness. Some players like to take practice swings with their racquet jackets still on their racquets.

Try this two-person sport loading drill. Wear a harness with surgical tubing while your partner holds the other end of the tubing. Start on the baseline and have your partner resist your movements by holding you back to balls that are being fed to you in all directions. Take 2 × 12 reps with resistance followed by 2 × 6 reps hitting balls without the resistance.

You can perform the same drill with volleys and smashes. For smashes, connect the partner end of the surgical tubing to the bottom of the net and have a friend feed you lobs that land around the service line.

Complex Training

Complex training is something I learned from Carlos Drenhardt, the former world record holder in the high jump, while he was working with Boris Becker. What is especially appealing to me about complex training is that it combines power weight lifting with plyometric exercises. Plyometric exercises enable a muscle to reach maximal strength in as short of time as possible, then releasing the energy. In the precompetitive phase of your program, a variety of exercises can provide this important part of explosiveness training such as hops, jumps, bounds, and using medicine balls.

As with the functional strengthening you performed in your basic training phase, you'll want to continue strengthening your abdominal and lower back muscles. Choose six exercises from the following. Use a medicine ball of 5 to 15 pounds for each and perform one set of 25 reps or two sets of 12 reps.

- **Sit-up throw.** Secure your feet and toss the medicine ball to a partner while performing a sit-up. Your partner should return the ball as you descend back to the floor

- **Medicine ball sit-up.** Secure your feet and hold the medicine ball with two hands and keep the arms raised throughout the movement.

- **Crunches.** Lie on the floor and lift your feet in the air with your knees bent at 90 degrees. Hold a medicine ball on your abdomen, and contract your abdominal muscles to lift your shoulders and head off the floor.

- **Free hang.** Hold a medicine ball between your feet and hang with your arms from a bar. Lift your legs to the left, right, and forward by flexing at the hips and keeping your knees straight.

- **Russian twist.** Sit with your back straight and feet straight in front of you. Holding a medicine ball with arms extended twist as far to the left and to the right as you can.

- **Sit-up bench throw.** Perform sit-ups on an inclined sit-up bench, while throwing a medicine ball over your head to your partner

- **Sit-up bench twist.** Perform the sit-up bench throw, but twist to alternate sides while holding the ball and before throwing it to your partner.

- **Manual back extension.** Lie face down on a bench and have a friend hold your legs. Hold a medicine ball behind your head and extend upward.

- **Back extension twist.** Lie face down and hold a medicine ball behind your head. Lift only your upper body off the floor and twist to the side.

Anke Huber unloads on a backhand with an exhalation from strong stomach muscles.

According to Donald Chu in *Jumping Into Plyometrics*, "Combining strength movement exercises like squats with speed movements like the depth jump, double leg hop, or standing triple jump can be an effective way to stimulate the neuromuscular system and provide variety for the athlete." For your three weekly strength training workouts in the precompetitive phase, you'll want to choose from the combination exercises listed below. For the lifting segment of the combination, work four sets—10 reps at 50 percent to 60 percent of the 1 RM, 10 reps at 60 percent, 12 reps at 65 percent, and 15 reps at 70 percent. For second part of the combination—the plyometric exercise perform the repetitions noted. The bibliography provides resources that can show you how to do the plyometric exercises named below.

Chest, Triceps and Lower Arm

Chest (choose three)

>   Bench press; medicine ball chest pass (2 × 12)

>   Incline press; drop and catch (2 × 12)

>   Reverse incline press; drop and catch (2 × 12)

>   Dumbbell incline press; incline pullover (2 × 12)

>   Supine dumbbell fly; single arm swing (2 × 10 each direction)

>   Push-up (normal or knuckle); medicine ball push-up (2 × 12)

Triceps (choose two)

>   Tricep pullover; overhead medicine ball throw (2 × 10)

>   Triceps extension; two-handed soccer throw (2 × 12 reps)

>   Push-up; overhead step and throw, alternating legs (2 × 12)

>   Military press; overhead bounce throw (2 × 10 to 12, only with rubber medicine balls) or single arm overhead throw (2 × 10 to 12)

Lower arm

>   Dumbbell wrist extension; tip up with a medicine ball (3 × 6 to 8)

Back, Shoulders, and Biceps

Back

>   Lat pull down; backward overhead throw (2 × 12)

>   Upright row; lat pull with Russian twist (2 × 12)

Shoulders (choose two)

>   Military press (seated or standing); two- or one-arm put (2 × 8 to 10)

>   Pull-up; one- or two-ball medicine ball push-up or crossover push-up (2 × 12)

>   Lateral rows; handstand push-up

Biceps

>   Dumbbell bicep curl; forward underhanded medicine ball throw (2 × 10)

>   Standing curl-bar curl; underarm medicine ball toss (2 × 10)

Leg (choose 3)

Dead lift; lateral cone jump (3 × 8 to 10)

Leg press; double leg tuck jump (2 × 8 to 10)

Leg curl; double leg speed hop (2 × 8 to 10)

Leg extension; medicine ball squat throw, catch after the bounce (2 × 10)

Toe raise; in-place squat jump (3 × 6 to 10)

Front squat; split squat jump (2 × 10)

Inverted squat; double leg ankle bounce (3 × 6 to 10)

Short Sport Endurance

Short speed endurance is trained with sprints of 40 yards. The purpose of speed endurance training is to prevent you from slowing down late in the second or third set and to develop your ability to recover after a long point. The distances are now shorter than they were for the long speed endurance, but the effort and intensity should remain the same. Stay as close to the 1:1 work to rest interval as possible and stretch after completing your short speed endurance session.

Competitive Phase

The goal of the competitive phase—the two to three weeks during which you are peaking for important competitions—is to maintain what you have developed to this point. Typically I have players do a maintenance lifting schedule during this phases in which they lift 60 percent to 70 percent of their 1 RM 2 × 10 or 1 × 12 on the day they play or the evening before. Some players like to lift on the day they perform because it "awakens" the muscles and gets them warmed up increasing blood flow to the muscles. Doing light lifting on game day is something you may want to try adding to your routine to see if it works for you.

After warming up and stretching, start with overspeed training first then proceed to power training. Usually players like to do a few of the plyometric exercises first, followed by sprints and then sports speed. The work rest ratio is 1:2 in this phase so there's a high intensity output followed by an adequate recovery period.

Overspeed Training

- **Ladder drill.** Place a 10-yard rope ladder in the grass or on the court and make 20 timed passes running forward, sideways, in, and out of the ladder. Emphasize quick foot and hand movement and compare your times on each pass. Rest 10 seconds between each.

- **360- and 180-degree hop**. Face a partner. When your partner calls out "ready," start pumping your feet as fast as you can. When she claps her hands and yells "right" or "left," hop 180 degrees in that direction and then pivot back to the starting position. If she claps her hands twice, hop 360 degrees exploding off the ground quickly.

- **Harness sprint.** With one end of a 10-yard piece of surgical tubing attached to your harness, anchor the free end at one end of the court and walk 20 yards from it. Once the cord is stretched as far as it will comfortably go, sprint back toward the anchor point. Perform 6 sprints with the harness followed by 6 sprints of the same distance without the harness.

Power Training

The following power enhancing exercises will help you maintain your power through your competitive phase of training. Choose from the following:

- **Lateral cone hop.** Jump sideways back and forth over a cone or bench—2 × 12 reps with a 15-second recovery between each set)

- **Forward cone hop with a change of direction.** Have your partner stand in front of your line of cones and when you have hopped over the cones using two legs or one, they will direct you right or left. You then sprint in the desired direction.

- **High knee.** Set up cones in a straight line and practice running over each cone with high knees. Make a total of six passes varying the number of cones that you jump over.

- **Step-up.** Step and down off a box or stair that is about knee height. Go as quickly as possible for 12 contacts. Repeat three times.

- **Single leg push-off.** With your left foot on the stair or box, explode off the ground with your right foot so that you gain as much height as possible, using your arms to gain height and balance. Land with the left foot on the box. Do two sets of 12, alternating legs.

- **Lateral box jump.** Start with one leg on top of a box and hop so that you alternate legs side to side, making 12 contacts as quickly as possible.

- **Depth jump.** Drop down off a stair or box and sprint 10 to 15 yards. Repeat 9 times. Then drop down and have your partner direct you left or right and sprint in that direction for five yards or more.

- **Jump rope.** Jump for 10 × 10 seconds as quick as possible

Sports Speed

Sport speed involves developing explosive speed for tennis. You want explosive acceleration in the first 2 to 4 feet on the court, so we'll work on agility and balance. As you are playing sets during the competitive phase, on-court drilling is of short duration and with an emphasis of 1 to 4 shots. Emphasize high-energy output with the challenge and attack phases of your stroke.

Timed sprints

Perform 15 × 20-yard sprints. Recover fully between each and record your time for each.

Sprint Intervals

Perform 6 reps each of 40-yard, 20-yard, and 10-yard sprints. Recover fully after each repetition. Start from different stances, such as sideways, starting off with a crossover step, backward, etc.

Partner Chase

Mark off 20 yards and sit down on the 10-yard line while your partner sits at 0. When your partner says go, stand up and sprint for the finish line before he can touch you. Vary the chase by lying down on the grass or sitting facing your partner. Do this 6 times being chased and 6 times chasing.

Active Recovery Phase

It's a good idea after your competitive season to take a break from tennis training—both mentally and physically. Performing the following activities for 20 to 30 minutes, four times a week will allow you to recover from your tennis training, but will also keep you active. Choose bicycling, rowing, water skiing, snow skiing, windsurfing, boxing, karate, or your favorite activity.

Maximal Fitness in Minimal Time

If you're a professional tennis player, you can put major blocks of time into developing your game and staying in peak condition. If you're not, well, you have to shoehorn your tennis practices between business meetings and driving your kids to soccer practice. You're probably serious enough about this game to want to put time into it. But it's still hard to make it happen.

I can't solve that problem for you. You simply have to look at your priorities, make a schedule, and stick to it. But I can offer you a training program that won't waste your valuable time, will accomplish your goals, will help you get the most out of your tennis game while reducing your chances of injury, and will have you practicing skills that enhance your performance. All this, and you still can live the rest of your busy life.

These exercises can be accomplished with as little as 5 to 20 minutes a day and by emphasizing proper nutrition and rest will help you improve and maintain your fitness. You may laugh at the thought that you could actually benefit from only ten minutes of working out one day, but let's look at the metabolic demands of tennis. Tennis is an anaerobic sport with almost 80 percent of the points lasting 20 seconds or less. Most points on a grass court last less than 2 seconds, on hard court 8 to 10 seconds, and 10 to 20 seconds is a long point on clay. This is followed by 20 to 25 seconds of recovery for pro players and about 30 seconds for recreational players.

For a point lasting about 10 seconds, metabolically we rely for power on two chemicals stored in our muscles: adenosine triphosphate (ATP) and phosphocreatine (PCr). Glycogen (stored carbohydrate) is the source of power for the muscles in a point that lasts longer than 10 seconds. The waste product produced when the muscles use glycogen is called lactic acid. A buildup of lactic acid in the muscles after a long point results in the burning feeling you start to get in your muscles.

The beauty of the following workouts is that they will stress your body's energy system in ways that are similar to actually playing tennis. The following workouts condition your body to use different energy systems by offering intervals that are longer than 20 seconds *and* shorter than 10 seconds.

Each workout starts with an important warm-up period. Jog, skip rope, or run in place to get your muscles warm and limbered up. Following the warm-up each different workout emphasizes different things, such as developing the energy systems you use on the court to play tennis or building strength (to balance the body and counter the one-sided nature of the sport). The sessions work on

- **power**, specifically explosive movements starting from the foot making contact with the ground and progressing upward;
- **speed**, using your strength and power to move quickly;
- **flexibility and balance**, incorporating tennis yoga exercises that challenge your

coordination and ability to stabilize;

- **agility**, putting it all together in appropriate court movement; and
- **speed endurance**, the ability to consistently produce bursts of speed.

Because time is at a premium, it's best to lay out everything you'll need to perform the workouts, creating different stations so you can proceed quickly from one exercise to another.

20-Minute Workouts

Due to the demands of tennis and its tendency to work one side of the body differently from the other, tennis players commonly have problems in their lower back, shoulder, elbow, and wrist areas. If you are playing three or more times a week, do this maintenance program at least three times a week to strengthen your body and prevent injury.

Workout 20-1

Step 1: Warm up and stretch for two minutes. Even if you've just finished playing tennis, you still should stretch.

Step 2: Focus on strengthening and injury prevention for seven minutes. In 1998 at Wimbledon and the U.S. Open, I saw Mark Woodforde and Todd Woodbridge doing these same exercises with surgical tubing after each match. You may use two light hand dumbbell weights (start at 2 pounds and progress to 10 pounds each) or a 6-foot-long piece of surgical tubing. For each of the following exercises, perform 3 × 10 reps slowly (unless otherwise noted). Your work-rest ratio should be 1:1. For instance, 10 seconds of exercising followed by 10 seconds of recovery.

- **Empty-can exercise.** Raise your arms out in front of your body and then down, approximately 15 degrees from your sides. Point your thumbs down (this internally rotates the shoulder). Don't raise your arms above shoulder level or back past your pants seam.
- **Shoulder flexion.** Standing, raise an arm out in front of your body as high as possible (thumb up) and hold for two seconds, then lower it.
- **Skydive.** Lie facedown on the floor. Lift your legs and arms up off the floor by pinching your shoulder blades together. Then work your legs and arms together and apart, just as if you were doing jumping jacks, only facedown. Do 2 × 20 reps.
- **Crunches.** Roll over and perform crunches with your legs lifted. Do 15 to 25 reps.
- **Bicycles.** Lying on the floor with your hands behind your head, keep your back on the floor but lift your knees and elbows, and pedal your legs as if you're riding a bicycle backward. Alternate touching your elbow to the opposite knee. Do 15 to 25 reps.
- **Shoulder internal rotation.** Lie on the floor, with a dumbbell in each hand and your arms out, elbows bent at 90-degree angles with your hands up in the air (field-goal pose). Now move your hands toward your toes, keeping your elbows in place. Return to the starting position.
- **Shoulder external rotation.** Use the same starting pose as the internal rotation, but lower your hands toward your head, and then back to the starting position.

- **Wrist flexion.** With dumbbells in the palms of your hands, do wrist curls, lifting your wrists toward you.
- **Wrist extension.** With dumbbells in the palms of your hands, drop your palms downward, letting the weight hang.

Step 3: Emphasize power for two minutes by focusing on explosively reacting off the ground. Try to flex (load) your foot as you land and then extend as a dancer would, pushing (exploding) off the floor. Perform as many of each of the following jumps as you can for 20 seconds. Recover 10 seconds between each type of jump.

- **Hopping split step.** Split step on the balls of your feet.
- **Lower-body jumping jack.** Work your legs, doing jumping jacks as quickly as possible.
- **Split-step crossover.** Split step on the balls of your feet and then jump, bridging your legs back together and crossing them as you land.
- **Jumping lunge.** Alternate right and left leg jumping lunges. As you move forward, bending your knee, keep a right angle—be sure your knee does not go past your toes.

Step 4: For speed (2.5 minutes): Mark off 20 yards and complete 8 sprints, starting in different positions (facing forward, backward, and sideways).

Step 5: For agility (4.5 minutes): Here is where you can start to add some cross training. Play one-on-one basketball or Colombian soccer in which you try to kick a tennis ball through your partner's legs. Play this game in the corner of the court or where errant kicks won't go too far.

Step 6: For balance, coordination, and cooldown (2 minutes): Perform the following yoga *asanas,* which are great for enhancing balance, coordination, and stability. Always remember to focus on your breathing.

- **The T pose.** With your hands behind your back, inhale and then exhale, bending at the waist and raising one leg straight behind you. As you balance on one leg, you form a T. Release and inhale, then repeat with the other leg.
- **The tree pose.** Balancing on one leg, place your arms with palms together above your head and lift your leg, placing your right foot on your inner left thigh. Pick a spot ahead of you to focus on with your eyes, and hold the position, breathing deeply. Release and switch to the other leg.
- **The skater's spin.** Squat down and extend one leg in front of you, maintaining your balance. Try to keep your supporting foot flat on the ground.

Workout 20-2

Step 1: For warm-up (2 minutes): Move around the court in a hollow run, (alternating a short jog followed by a sprint) practicing ground strokes, volleys, smashes, and running shots. Do a dynamic stretch of your choice, then continue jogging, sprinting, moving laterally, then backward. This will get you warm quickly.

Step 2: For injury prevention (5 minutes), do the following exercises:

- **Cat-stretch push-up.** These are great for the shoulders and lower arms. Get on all fours (hands and feet) and assume a normal push-up position. Lower yourself most of the way, but don't let your chest or chin touch the ground. Now, just as if you're licking ice cream off the ground, shift your weight forward and then move back into your push-up-ready position. Do 10 to 12 reps and then change your rotation slightly: from the extended push-up position move forward, down (to "lick the ice cream"), then back along the ground, but not touching. Do 10 to 12 reps like this.

- **Crunches.** Perform 3 × 20 crunches (one set each with legs up, legs bent, and legs extended).
- **Windmill.** Standing, swing your arms in large circles to loosen your shoulders. Do 4 × 25 reps rotating arms both forward and backward.
- **Back extension.** Lie face down on the floor with your arms extended over your head. Lift your upper body off the floor slowly and return to the starting position. Do 4 × 25.

Step 3: Power/drop sprints (1.5 minutes): Stand on a box, stair, or curb and jump to the ground, sprinting 20 yards and jogging back. Do this nine times. After dropping to the ground, explode forward, alternating the leg with which you take your first step.

Step 4: Power/stair exercises (2 minutes): Facing a step, step up and down as quickly as possible for 15 seconds. Turn sideways to the step and do the same thing, stepping up and down laterally, and repeat on your opposite side. Finally, jump onto the step with both legs and down again, for 15 seconds.

Step 5: For speed (about 5 minutes): Run from the baseline to the net as fast as possible, 6 times, with 10 seconds between sprints. When you're moving back to the baseline, shuffle sideways to avoid tripping. Use a crossover shuffle to move to the sideline and back, 4 times with 10 seconds between. Use pivot sprints to run to the sideline and back, 4 times with 10 seconds between. Finally sprint from the baseline to the net and back for 30 seconds.

Step 6: For agility (2 minutes), the hot-potato drill: Stand at the baseline with a partner at the service line. Your partner rolls tennis balls one at a time to your left and right. Shuffle to each ball, pick it up with both hands, and roll it back to your partner. To make this drill tougher, have her roll the ball short and long and at different paces.

Step 7: For balance (2.5 minutes): Get out on a pair of good-quality in-line skates and enjoy yourself. This is a great way to enhance your balance and get you comfortable moving from foot to foot. Remember to wear your wrist guards and elbow and knee protection.

10-Minute Workouts

The 10-minute workouts are designed to improve your cardiovascular fitness while developing the energy systems you need to play tennis and building power in your legs for explosive movements off the ground. Do the following workouts only after having warmed up and stretched.

Workout 10-1

Sit on a Lifecycle and start pedaling. Choose the manual program and start pedaling on level 1 for about 25 seconds. Now increase the difficulty level as high as you can go for the next 30 seconds. Downshift and pedal at level 1 for about 25 seconds. (It usually takes about 5 seconds to shift completely.) Then repeat for the entire 10 minutes. (For this workout I recommend the Lifecycle; you might adapt the specifics to another type of exercise bike.)

Workout 10-2

Use a stepper for this workout, which is similar to the previous one. Enter your relevant information, choosing the manual program and 10 minutes. Start slowly and, after about 25 seconds, turn up to the highest level possible. Go back and forth this way, about a half-minute at a time. For balance, try not to hold on to the rails. You also can conduct this workout on a flight of stairs in a hotel.

Workout 10-3

This workout develops the energy systems you use on the court as well as speed endurance, which is your ability to repeatedly sprint with recovery. Perform each set of these sprints on a tennis court:

7 × 100 yards; 25-second recovery

5 3 40 yards; 15-second recovery

12 × 10 yards; 10-second recovery

Workout 10-4

This workout puts a lot of bounce in your step and prepares you for a strong explosive interaction between your legs and the ground (especially important on your swinging strokes).

Step 1: Jump rope for 15 seconds as fast as you can, with 15 seconds of recovery. Do this 10 times (5 minutes).

Step 2: Set out eight plastic cones or empty milk containers in a straight line with about two feet between each one. Now take eight passes through the cones, running around or jumping over the containers. The first two passes will focus on the importance of loading your foot to prepare it for a strong push-off. So as your lead foot passes over the cone, keep your toes up. As you step down, you will extend your foot from this loaded position when the ball of your foot hits the ground. Many people who step down on the ball of their foot with their ankle extended simply absorb the energy buildup, which could be used to propel them to the ball. Start slow for the first two passes but gradually build up until you can go faster. On passes 3 and 4, focus on the arms, too. Work them simultaneously with what your feet are doing, but keeping them moving forward. On passes 5 and 6, try jumping over every other cone, working your arms and feet together. On passes 7 and 8, use lateral movements, so you're running through the cones in a slalom fashion.

5-Minute Workouts

If you only have five minutes to work out on a given day, then pick up your jump rope. It works your whole body and in my opinion is the best plyometric exercise there is. For example, try jumping rope as fast as you can for 15 seconds, then recover for 15 seconds. Repeat 10 times. (The next time you do this workout try double jumps!)

Another good 5-minute partner workout is to stand on the baseline facing your partner, who's standing on the other baseline. Through this whole workout, mirror the movements your partner makes for 15 seconds, rest 15 seconds, then have your partner mirror you for 15 seconds, and rest 15 seconds. Repeat this cycle four more times.

Be sure you and your partner's movements include the following:

- Rapid directional changes
- Up-and-back sprinting to the net, using a crossover step to move backward
- Shuffling, then pivot sprinting to the sideline
- Dipping, that is, touching the ground with both hands
- Starting with easy-to-follow movements, but then trying to fake each other out

Maximizing Your Nutrition

Conditioning is crucial, but you also need to fuel your body properly. Even players in great condition often tell me they're running out of energy late in their matches. What can they do?

Tennis demands a lot from your body, and often players don't replenish their bodies the way they should, because they're traveling a lot or they don't know what to eat or they don't have good food available. You might assume that the best players have this nutrition thing figured out. Guess again. Jeff Tirango, a notorious "bad boy" of tennis, told me that once before playing a match he ate a Big Mac and a couple of pieces of pizza. After you eat that, you should just go home and take a nap, because it doesn't make sense to try to train or play at your optimal level with that in your system.

Pat Etcheberry, strength and conditioning coach for Pete Sampras and Jim Courier, shares this story: "One year Pete Sampras beat Jim Courier in the Wimbledon finals and I said to him later, 'Listen, Pete, I know you were ready, but your energy looked low.' 'I didn't eat anything before the match,' he replied.

" 'How can you go out and play a five-set match with no food?' I wondered. 'Well,' he said, 'I was nervous.' "

Here's a guy ranked number one in the world who didn't know that he had to fuel up before a rigorous match. So if you're a recreational player or a weekend warrior and you're not sure what to eat, you're in good company. But proper nutrition is one of the easiest ways to improve your performance. And lack of proper nutrition will hurt you. No fueling!

There are foods that definitely help a player's concentration. We know now that you don't need just a high-carbohydrate diet but also more protein than was thought in the past. But be careful how you take your protein. For example, eating a big steak before a match is not the best way. You don't want your body wasting valuable energy on digesting heavy food when it should be preparing to play. Eat your steak (or other heavy protein) the night before, but keep your eating light right before a match.

The key is to be *intentional* about your intake. Don't just grab whatever's in the refrigerator. Plan your diet around your important matches and fuel up properly. If you take supplements, take them regularly and properly, in conjunction with your workouts. (And of course, make sure you're taking approved supplements.) It's probably a good idea to take some vitamin and mineral supplements. But take a look at your diet and see what vitamins and minerals might be lacking. Note that even vitamin-rich foods lose many nutrients in the cooking process.

Andre Agassi recognizes that proper nutrituion is crucial to top tennis performance.

Nutrition Assignment: On the Menu

Keep track of what you eat.

For one week, keep a food diary in your training notebook. Write down everything you eat, and when you eat it. Then, at several intervals during the day, note how you're feeling. Energetic or sluggish? Jittery or calm? Happy or depressed? Focused or scattered?

At the end of the week, go back through those notes and analyze the effect of certain foods on your mind and body. Do you see any patterns? Based on your findings, what foods should you eat before a big match? Before a training session?

Now go back and pick out six foods of which you ate the most. Give yourself the appropriate number of points for every choice you consumed from table 7.1.

Table 7.1—Nutrition Points					
5 points	**4 points**	**3 points**	**2 points**	**1 point**	**0 points**
Nonfat milk	1% milk	2% milk	Whole milk	Half and half	Nondairy
Nonfat yogurt	Buttermilk	Light ice cream	Whole milk	Yogurt bars	creamer
Nonfat cottage	Ice milk	Reduced fat	yogurt	Ice cream with	Cream cheese
cheese	Low fat	cheese	Evaporated	nuts	Sour cream
Fat-free cream	cottage cheese	Fruit or	milk	Light cream	Whipped
cheese	Vegeburger	vegetable juice	Eggnog	cheese	cream
Fruits	Grits	Dried fruit	Ice cream	Light sour cream	Vegetable oils
Vegetables	Oatmeal	Waffles	Vegetables in	Cheese	Salad
High fiber	Barley	Pancakes	cream or	Olives	dressings
cereal	Whole wheat	White bread	butter	Avocados	Margarine
Whole grain	pasta	White rice	Tortilla chips	Cream- and nut-	French-fried
bread	Brown or	English muffins	Crackers	filled cookies	foods
Dried beans	wild rice	Pasta	Breakfast bars	Garlic bread	Pesto
Egg whites	Pretzels	Bagel	Cake	Peanut butter	Candy
Shrimp	Wild meats	Sugar cereal	Fruit pie	Corn chips	Sardines in
	White meat	Granola	Cookies	Potato chips	oil
	poultry	Soybeans	Brownies	Cheesecake	Pork chops
	(skinned)	Salmon	Veal	Cream pie	Lunch meats
	Most fish	Liver	Lean ground	Croissants	Hot dogs
	Crab	Lean pork	beef	Eggs	Pepperoni
		Lamb	Trimmed beef	Nuts and seeds	Bacon/
		Dark meat	Ham	Herring	Sausage
		poultry	Poultry with	Untrimmed beef	Donuts
		Beef (chuck,	skin	Regular ground	
		flank, round		beef	
		or sirloin)		Tofu	
				Tuna in oil	

If you scored 25 points or more: You eat very well and probably have plenty of energy to do whatever you want to do.

20-24 points: Good job! You're making a lot of good food choices, you're just not so fanatical about nutrition. There's no need to change your eating habits.

15-19 points: You're eating some good foods but others that aren't so healthy. Watch out for enriched products (such as white bread) that seem to offer extra nutrition but actually strip the natural nutrients to ensure longer shelf life.

10-14 points: You probably are having your ups and downs with energy and concentration.

0-9 points: Are you still alive? It's time for some serious changes, or you're heading out to pasture.

Active Recovery and Rehabilitation

No question about it: a vigorous tennis match, or even a solid practice, takes a lot out of you. Even after your cool-down period and post-tennis stretch, you'll need to take good care of yourself for a while, letting your body recover, heal, and rest up for your next encounter on the court. Let me suggest some simple courses of rehabilitation for the most common recovery problems.

Muscle Stiffness

Try to jog for 10 to 15 minutes to loosen up, or lay in a warm bath or whirlpool or with hot-water bottles for 20 minutes.

Fatigue

To improve energy, look at what you're eating and drinking. Be sure you're getting foods that give you plenty of energy and sufficient fluids, such as fresh fruit or vegetable juices, especially those loaded with vitamin C. There are also some very good sport drinks such as Basica-Sport, which replace electrolytes that may have been sweated out during exercise. These drinks can be diluted with water and drunk during a match. But never drink a sugary soft drink directly after a match or practice. Sometimes a player will drink a cola toward the end of a match to get an energy boost, but there's absolutely no value and there is potential harm in loading up with sugar after you finish playing.

There are various "energy boosters" on the market, but treat these with caution. And their ingredients should be checked against the International Olympic Committee's list of banned substances no matter how much they promise to enhance performance. Only take other supplements with the support of a certified professional. While both creatine and amino acids are legal and may be purchased over the counter, a balanced diet is the best way to increase your energy. A nutritionist can help you to find the best combinations of foods for your individual needs.

Muscle Swelling

Say you've rolled your ankle during play or injured your wrist or shoulder. You were able to play through it, but now that you're cooling down, it's beginning to swell. You must act quickly, elevating the injured area (so the blood can flow back easily to your heart) and applying ice.

It's a good idea to have a plastic bag and a bandage with you, and know where to get ice nearby. Never place ice directly on the skin; it will burn. Every 20 minutes, remove the ice to allow circulation to return to normal for another 20 minutes. Repeat this process for about two hours. Stop if you see that the skin is starting to become extremely red. While some experts now are questioning the value of icing for muscle swelling, the accepted wisdom still favors it. If you have questions about it, consult your doctor.

The Rehabilitation Center Montag in Oberhaching, Germany has developed another method for treating muscle injury and swelling. Physiotherapist wrap the injured area with a bandage and then send the player on a walk in a swimming pool for 15 to 20 minutes. It seems the water pressure squeezes the fluid of the swollen area up into the lymph system, which then gets rid of the fluid, freeing the injured area for greater movement.

Sickness

When you're sick, the best policy is not to play; rest up and get better. Playing only weakens your body. With medication, you might feel well enough to play, but even this is a risk as you're just delaying your needed rest. If you try to play through it, you'll most likely get sicker.

There are a few exceptions. Say you have a muscle injury and, even though you're not 100 percent, you still can play with a bandage. That's fine, if you're careful. But illness requires bed rest, and there's not much you can do about that. In 1996, Boris Becker kept trying to play through an illness. He eventually had to take three weeks off to recover. Who knows? If he had rested immediately, his down time might have been only three days.

Sleep

To maintain your concentration on the court, we've already established that you need to eat right, but you also need to sleep well. These are the basic preparatory mechanisms of the human body and can't be ignored. There are many myths out there regarding sleep. Some think that everyone needs seven or eight hours a night. Others say that afternoon naps just make you more tired. But these ideas aren't necessarily true. However the effectiveness of sleep depends not so much on how many hours you get, but on how deep you sleep.

Brain research has shown that we go through five stages of sleep, and we cycle through these stages four or five times a night, with each cycle lasting 60 to 90 minutes. The first two stages—light sleep—make up nearly half of the total sleep time. Muscles relax, brain waves slow down, and blood pressure and body temperature drop. In this stage we are awakened easily.

Our sleep deepens as we reach stages 3 and 4. (Dr. James Loehr calls this the "good night's sleep.") In these stages our brain waves slow even more, our muscles relax totally, and our metabolic rate drops to its lowest level. Not only does this give us a well-rested feeling, but researchers also are noting the benefit of these sleep stages in fighting infections, repairing tissue, and effecting other aspects of physical healing. The body's growth hormone also is released during this time.

Stage 5—REM (rapid eye movement) sleep—takes up 20 to 50 percent of sleep. The first REM cycle typically starts 90 to 100 minutes after falling into sleep. Heart rate and blood pressure fluctuate considerably during this period. Breathing quickens and brain waves pulsate faster than during other phases. REM sleep is the period when dreams occur (dreams appear important for both learning and cognitive function). REM cycles become larger and more intense at the end of the night. Interruption of sleep during this stage can be disruptive to the learning process.

So let's bring all this research onto the tennis court. You're about to face a great opponent in the biggest match of your life. You have tossed and turned all night, in anxiety and excitement. Is your lack of sleep going to hurt you?

One sleepless night may have minimal effect, but sustained sleepless nights can "reduce thinking efficiency, cause a wide range of concentration problems, and negatively affect coordination and reaction time," according to Dr. Loehr. "Many people become irritable and feel stressed when normal sleep cycles are disrupted. People also report more headaches, pain, and illness during periods of sleep deprivation. Anxiety and poor self-image are also reported. . . . The result is less efficiency and less productivity. Chronic sleep deprivation also impacts life expectancy. People getting optimum sleep (and following other healthful habits) live longer."

How much sleep do you need? Everyone is different when it comes to sleep. Loehr recommends that you sleep and wake naturally without an alarm for five consecutive days. That will give you an idea of how much sleep your body naturally needs. If you've slept less than eight hours and you still feel tired upon awakening, you need more sleep. Most people sleep anywhere from 7 to 12 hours.

Tips for Quality Sleep

- In the evenings, avoid drinking or eating foods that contain caffeine.

- Don't drink too much (especially alcohol) late at night. If you have to get up at night to go to the bathroom, that will disrupt your sleep.

- Large, high-fat dinners require extended digestion time and interfere with sleep cycles. Eat smaller meals in the evening.

- Adhere to a regular sleep schedule every night and try to maintain it on the weekends. If you stay out late on the weekend, still get up the same time the following morning, but try to take a short nap (30 minutes to an hour) between 1 P.M. and 3 P.M. A midafternoon nap is primarily deep sleep, which is most refreshing. Naps are proven to help reduce fatigue, increase alertness, and improve certain aspects of job performance.

- If you can't get to sleep in the afternoon, merely lying down and resting could be as restorative as napping.

- Exercise in the late afternoon or early evening when muscle strength and flexibility are at their best. Working out during these times can help you sleep better.

- Rituals such as reading, prayer, yoga, meditation, and soft music can help you relax from a tough day and therefore enable you to enter sleep more easily.

- Sleep on a firm mattress that supports your entire body. You should not experience back pain or shoulder pain when you awake in the morning.

- Do not turn your bedroom into a place of activity such as eating or working. It should be used only for sleeping.

- If you can't sleep one night, don't try to solve the problem with medication. Instead get up, read, or stretch, taking deep breaths. Or go to another room for a while, relax, and then return to bed.

It's up to you to manage your body for optimum athletic performance. It makes no sense to spend hours on the practice court and working out if you're just going to sabotage your efforts with poor habits of sleep and nutrition. Learn to take care of yourself. These are preparatory skills that not only will enhance your tennis game but also will lead to a more healthy and vibrant life.

Using Stress to Your Advantage

A large part of the rewards of tennis includes the intrinsic joy of mastering a particular shot that you've been working on, or the grin on your face after you slice an ace wide, or the full-body satisfaction as you sit in the locker room after winning a third-set tiebreaker. These treasures of tennis can't be purchased.

Of course, tennis also can turn grown adults into sniveling babies. At some point, you play someone who insists on lobbing every ball halfway to Jupiter, or a lucky opponent who has lousy form but manages to return every shot you send at him. Or an "easy sitter" floats over the net as you set up for a satisfying smash—but you frame the ball and shank it straight into the bottom of the net. Some days you play great, other days you have to work harder to play great, and some days you wish you were somewhere else. This is trying stuff to deal with for anyone.

How do you handle the ups and downs, the stresses and victories? Your mental skills take on a greater importance as you move through the mileage phase of your development into the fine-tuning phase. By sharpening your mental skills you can learn how to bounce back, perform at your best by managing your stress even on the bad days, and fall in love with tennis again and again even when it seems the game has betrayed you.

Mental Skill Progression 1: Loving the Game

Remember why it's worth it.

Step 1: List five reasons why you're lucky to play tennis.

Step 2: List five things you love about tennis. The game of tennis can teach you a lot about how you live other parts of your life. If you develop a well-rounded game, integrating its mental and physical aspects, you can integrate the skills and tasks you do in your everyday life in the same way. It works the opposite way, too. As you develop a well-rounded life, with mental, emotional, spiritual, and physical dimensions all in balance, your game also will likely improve.

Achieving balance is the assumption behind the complete player approach. Just focusing on one aspect of athletics is shortsighted. We need to focus on the athlete as a whole. The more a coach or program embraces the whole athlete, the better the chances that the coach or program has a lasting impact on the athlete. John Wooden, the legendary UCLA basketball coach, and many other coaches with long traditions of success have known this. It's not just about the mechanics of the game. These coaches have connected with the whole person, engaging the spirit of each player—not just as an athlete but as a human being.

What does this mean to you and your game of tennis? Just that technique and tactics are only parts of the game. You need to condition and train your attitude, too. Learn to roll with the ups and downs of the game. Don't let your own passions defeat you. Leave your losses on the court, but take your victories wherever you go. Learn to love tennis as one great part of a wonderful life. That's how you become a complete player.

In the process, you'll develop life skills, inner processes that help you succeed in both tennis and life. These skills teach you how to ride the bucking bronco of stress. The eminent sport psychologist Dr. James Loehr identifies three such skills: welcoming stress, recovering from stress, and making waves.

What Is Stress?

Stress is basically energy expenditure, a biochemical event. You're probably familiar with some of the chemistry of muscle development. As you expend energy, working the muscle, it produces chemicals that result in growth. But, with the use of new brain-scanning techniques, scientists are realizing that every thought is a movement of energy. So, when you visualize a perfect serve, you're expending energy. There is a physical, biochemical event! Apparently mental and physical stress are more similar than we once thought. Some people think of mental training as unreal, just part of a fantasy world. But, just as with physical training, actual energy is being expended.

Stress comes from different sources and affects us in different ways. As you understand the types of stress that plague you, you'll be able to develop an effective stress-management strategy.

Welcoming Stress

Dr. James Loehr

Sport psychologist

The term "stress for success" may seem odd at first. Stress drags us down, doesn't it? It wears us out, distracts us, and keeps us from performing as well as we can. Right?

Only when we don't know how to handle it. Stress is actually a vehicle for growth. The more you want to grow, the more you have to expose yourself to stress. People talk about growing pains and utter the platitude "no pain, no gain." What are they talking about? The connection between stress and growth. Work your muscles to the point of pain, and you're causing stress. Do it right and you also are causing growth. If you want to grow physically and get faster and more explosive, with more endurance, then you have to stress yourself in those specific areas. If you want to get stronger emotionally, then you have to take emotional risks. No stress, no growth.

If you avoid stress, which is instinctive for most of us, you'll be shutting yourself off from your dreams. You have to develop a new relationship to stress, embracing it and using it to bring out the best in you. Don't rely on a coach or anyone else to push you into stress, seek it out yourself. Expose yourself to higher-intensity workouts on the court, pushing yourself at the proper moments, and you'll learn to grow through this mental and physical stress.

Physical Stress

Physical stress is the most obvious type of stress. Your heart beats faster, your breath gets shorter, your hands and feet may seem heavy. These conditions occur in the course of a normal tennis match, especially if your opponent is running you a lot or if you're in less than ideal shape (see chapter 7 for more on conditioning).

Mental Stress

Mental stress comes from a little voice I call an intercranial communicator, which loudly evaluates, criticizes, and judges your performance. In *Inner Tennis*, Tim Gallwey refers to this little voice as Self One (Self Two being the advanced self that controls your breathing, heartbeat, and tennis stroke). Your intercranial communicator just sits on the sidelines and screams, "You idiot! You loser! What made you ever think you could play this game?" When this little rascal is active, it seems that you're facing two opponents: the other player and your own brain. If you don't control this feedback, Self One really can wreck your game.

Preparing for stressful situations can help you deal with them more effectively and use the stress to your advantage.

Situational Stress

Situational stress comes from the challenging realities of, say, a tough opponent, a strong wind, or poor court conditions. These are all valid stress inducers, but when this outside stress combines with the mental stress of our intercranial communicator, we can defeat ourselves before we start, with such self-talk as, "How can I even presume to be on the same court with this person? There's no way I can win!" Great players rise to such challenges by using their situational stress to spark new energy.

Self-inflicted situational stress (distress), on the other hand, is a matter of poor preparation. If you go on court with no warmup, no review of goals, and only one racquet, you're asking for trouble. The situation itself usually is challenging enough, without you adding extra stress. Take time to map out in as much detail as possible what things you do to prepare for and play your best tennis. This offers you a blueprint to follow in order to reproduce successful performances. Carry your blueprint onto the court and look at it on the changeovers if necessary.

Life Stress

Life stress includes those concerns you bring onto the court from your off-court life. If you're getting a divorce or losing your job or worried about your kids, these things will affect your play. In the soap opera of professional tennis in recent years, we've learned a lot about the life stress of star players—financial troubles, estrangement from parents and partners. Some players understandably seem weakened by these struggles, but others find a way to leave this stress in the locker room, focusing fully on the match at hand.

Mental Skill Progression 2: Forms of Stress

Evaluate different stresses in your game and how you react to them.

Step 1: After playing a match, rate yourself in the following matters on a scale of 1 to 10 (1 being low stress, 10 high):

1. I experienced physical stress such as shortness of breath, a pounding heartbeat, sweating palms, and butterflies in my stomach. _____
2. A voice inside my mind criticized, second-guessed, and hurt my game. _____
3. I perceived the situation as threatening. _____
4. I was well prepared, arrived early enough, warmed up, stretched, had extra grips and racquets, was dressed correctly for the conditions, etc. _____   (1 = better, 10 = worse)
5. My play was affected by outside concerns of my life._____

Step 2: Based on your answers to these questions, rank the types of stress in order of how much they affect your game:

Physical stress _____   Mental stress _____   Situational stress _____
Self-inflicted situational stress _____   Life stress _____

Step 3: Now, as you read the tips later in this chapter for managing stress, pay special attention to those that will help you in your area of greatest stress.

Learn to push yourself physically and mentally. Concentrate on your game, during play and immediately before and after it. This may make you mentally weary, but extending beyond your comfort zone takes you to the heart of the growth process and allows you to handle stress more effectively to improve your game. Competition is your best form of exposure.

Recovering From Stress

Dr. James Loehr
Sport psychologist

Whenever you expose yourself to massive stress, you have to have equally massive recovery to balance it. Stress is the stimulus for growth, but recovery is when growth actually takes place. Recovery time is a crucial part of any training regime, because that's when you heal.

You need both a physical and mental recovery period. Active recovery, such as cross training with sports other than tennis, is one way to give your mind and body a break from the game while remaining physically active. Sometimes, though, if you are physically exhausted, you're better off taking a break from all activities. You need to determine what types of recovery are best for you.

Sleep, nutrition, your time alone, time to be free—all these become enormously important in the whole sequence of things. Young athletes spend a lot of time on the court, stressing themselves to achieve growth in their game, and they should. But there also must be time for healing. In addition, pushy parents, demanding teachers, and neglected friends may put even more pressure on young athletes. That's why they need to work especially hard to balance times of work and rest. Go to bed early, take naps when you need them, eat regularly and healthily, and go out for walks every so often. Tennis is an important part of your life, but not your whole life. Get your game in sync with all the other forces in your life. To get to the highest level of performance, you must find a harmony among the different elements of your life. Of course, this is just as true for older players. The pressures may be different—work, family, finding time to train, sleep, or eat healthily. But the fact remains, you must balance the stress of tennis training with times of recovery.

Stress is like taking money out of a bank account. You are spending energy, just as if you're writing a check. Every time you expend energy you take a little more out of your account of neurotransmitters, seratonin, and glycogen. But your times of recovery basically put deposits back in the bank. And if you're a world-class spender, you have to make world-class deposits. This is where many athletes fail, even at the professional level—not because they don't have the talent to win, but because they don't allow sufficient time for healing. When these players take time off, they often think of themselves as lazy. But if they don't take the time, they eventually break—mentally, physically, or emotionally.

Beating Stress

How do you avoid this physical, emotional, or mental breakdown? Periodization. This is basically a matter of picking your spots. You simply cannot have peak performance 12 months out of the year. Periodization establishes cycles of rest and activity, maintaining a steady ratio of stress and recovery. Proper periodization takes into account the physical training of the athlete, her age, school or work pressures, emotional strength, and family needs. Once you get a sense of a healthy cycle of scheduling, then consider the available playing opportunities—league matches or tournaments. You'll probably have to say no to some of them in order to maintain balance in your life and effective play on the court.

Periodization is built in at the scholastic level. There is a tennis season, with regular matches and constant practices, but this usually lasts only three or four months. Most student players can handle that with no problem. But beware of the coach who insists on year-round practices, pushing the players to put out maximum energy in season and out. You need time to rest. And while I don't recommend that you drop your racquet entirely for eight months of the year, you could ease up on your practice schedule for a few weeks in between periods of training that you have planned to help you peak for important tournaments. To keep your timing, you need to hit a few strokes even in your off-periods, but you don't need to go through heavy-duty workouts every day of the year. In fact, occasional rest will do you good, refreshing you mentally as well as physically.

Tennis experts usually talk about periodization in ranges of weeks and months, but a form of it also applies on a daily basis. Some players need to concentrate totally on an upcoming match in the preceding 24 hours, or 48 hours, or the whole week. Others practice and take a laid-back attitude toward their preparation. Different players have different mental, emotional, and physical rhythms. You should find your best period of time before a match to start focusing on it. But if you want to go out to a movie the night before, that's fine (just don't stay out too late if you have an early-morning match). Keep your life in balance, and find the proper period of time to get psyched for the match.

Making Waves

Dr. James Loehr
Sport psychologist

The first two life skills that tennis will teach you are accepting stress and allowing recovery. The third is making waves. This is really just balancing the stress and recovery. If you have constant stress, it's just push, push, push until you break. But if you have nothing but recovery, it's just relax, relax, relax until you're a motionless blob. The key is learning how to cycle between episodes of stress and recovery by making waves.

When playing, imagine the waves of an ocean. One wave comes crashing in, unleashing tons of energy on the battered shore. It's loud, it's furious, it breaks surfboards in half. But then what? The water pulls back. There's a calm before the next wave. That's what we're talking about in your tennis game. In practice or while playing a match point by point, there is expenditure followed by recovery.

Making waves is what I want for you as a tennis player, but not just physically. I want you to gear up for an important point—mentally and emotionally as well as physically—and recover in 20 or 25 seconds for the next point. You don't have time to beat yourself up over an unforced error. Learn from your mistake and move on. Speedy recovery, mentally and emotionally, is the best marker of confidence and the best way to perform at your best.

Evaluating Your On-Court Stress

Stress happens. As I advised earlier, welcome stress and manage it when it happens. You may not be able to control the amount of stress that happens to you, but you certainly can decide how to manage it. To make your stress work for you, you need to understand it and to understand yourself. If you get a handle on your situation, you'll be able to plan your times of stress and recovery, making waves for maximum performance.

Sometimes you just have a day when it is difficult to feel the ball. And other days, everything you touch turns to gold. You can help yourself mentally if you learn to identify what kind of day you're having. If a day starts out bad, it doesn't have to stay that way. But if you fail to recognize the day, you may keep from taking advantage of a good day, or you may make a bad day worse.

I've identified five types of days on the tennis court, according to the "feel" you have for the ball:

1. **A King Midas day.** You remember the mythical king with the golden touch? That's you. Everything you hit goes in. Don't analyze what you're doing, just enjoy it. Keep your positive outlook, which should be pretty easy since everything's going in. Don't change your play radically, but you should be able to take some chances on a day like this.

2. **A great day.** This is a day when you're playing well with maybe one or two breaks in your concentration. Ignore comments from your opponent, who may try to break the spell by saying, "Wow, I have never seen you play so well" (in other words, "You're not really this good"). Just smile and continue to follow your rituals on the court, recreating the movements and tactics that allow you to play the way you are.

3. **A so-so day.** This can go either way. If you keep yourself moving and focus in on your goals, then you push yourself into making it a great day on the court. But if you don't make the effort, your game can go downhill very quickly. Use positive imagery. Shake off your mistakes; each point is a new one. Don't panic. Just keep working, and before the end of the match you may find your feel and end up having a great match.

4. **A just-get-it-in day.** Your best shots aren't working. So focus on playing the percentages; lower your expectations of what you know you can do. In other words, the aces you were hitting with power a few days ago aren't going to happen for you today. So work on the placement of your shots. Stay away from fancy stuff. Too often players beat themselves on just-get-it-in days by going for too much.

5. **A no-feel day.** It doesn't matter what level you are—every player has experienced this. It may last for a game or two, or you might go into a slump for a week. The key here is to stimulate yourself. Wrap a new grip on your racquet, restring your racket, practice on a different court, play a different style, put on a fresh shirt, or even turn your hat backward. Whatever works for you . . . just bust out of your patterns.

Mental Skill Progression 3: Have a Good Day

Making it a better day.

Identify your feel and try to raise your game at least one level. Say you're having a so-so day because you're a little tired. Then focus on moving between points and really trying to get into position on every shot. Before you know it, you'll be having a great day or even a King Midas day.

Choosing Your Stress-Management Tools

If you're a golfer, you know that success or failure often rides on a simple decision: which club will I use? You have a bag of weapons at your disposal, but your situation calls for this wedge or that iron. The same kind of thing occurs with stress. You'll adopt different strategies depending on the type of stress you're facing and perhaps on the kind of day you're having.

Breathing

We tend to take breathing for granted. For most of us, it's been a pretty steady companion ever since that first spank from the doctor. But we can get lazy about our breathing, drawing our air in shallow, inefficient ways. It's obvious that physical exertion taxes our breathing abilities, but mental stress also can affect our breathing.

On the other hand, proper breathing does a great deal to relax us and to keep us balanced, physically, mentally, and emotionally. When we breathe properly, our brains release endorphins, which make us feel good—just as if we're eating chocolate (but with fewer calories).

Picture a three-year-old who suddenly gets scared. Dad is there to comfort him, but the crying continues. The loud sound is forgotten, but the crying goes on. The child struggles for breath, and that's scary, too. Everything is out of whack for this child, and now he's crying because he's crying. The smart father urges the child to take a breath, a couple of deep breaths. It's not easy with all the sobbing, but the child does so. Suddenly everything falls into place. The child feels better, more in control. The fears have flown.

Monica Seles is known for grunting loudly with each hit she makes. This vocal exhalation helps her keep her breathing rhythm steady.

In the same way, stress makes good breathing difficult, but good breathing helps to manage stress. Your best tool in working with the stress of a tennis match is good, sound breathing. If you work at developing good breathing habits, eventually they will become second nature.

Many people take breaths that are too shallow—their chest expands, their shoulders rise, and their gut remains sucked in. This may look impressive, but it's not effective breathing. Rather, breathing deeply and slowly, drawing the air all the way down to your abdomen, is a more effective way to breathe. When you inhale, imagine you're trying to blow up a balloon in your abdomen using your diaphragm muscle, what people refer to as their stomach, which ought to be expanding when you inhale. Watch a baby breathe and you'll see this good breathing form.

After you've played a point, when you're walking back to the baseline, take a few deep abdominal breaths. It's best to inhale deeply through the nose and exhale through the mouth. This good breathing will give you new energy and restore a sense of balance and control, relieving tension, anger, impatience, or nervousness.

Even during play, proper breathing can help you achieve a rhythm. I encourage students to time their breathing on two cues: (a) when the ball bounces, and (b) when you make contact. Start to exhale when the ball bounces, and don't inhale until after you make contact.

One way to get in the habit of this two-cue breathing is to practice saying a two-syllable phrase. When the ball bounces, say "bounce," and when you hit it, say "hit." Or you could try "can't . . . miss" or even "ten . . . nis." Just don't take a breath between the syllables. It's one long exhalation.

Once players can do the two-cue breath, I try to get them to elongate their breathing. Here I use cue words such as "yesssssssss," or "tennnissssss," or "can't missssssss." Elongation of the exhalation results in a long swing outward and upward toward the desired target.

A strong exhalation is necessary for maximum power, but the two cues are the same. This exhalation helps you to focus your energy, as it does in karate (the *kiai*). Prudish tennis fans were startled when Monica Seles burst on the scene, loudly grunting with each shot—but she has the right idea. Her breathing is united with her body movement, resulting in a sharp exhalation (and a grunt) when she unleashes her energy on the ball. Just remember that these outbursts of energy are all part of a steady breathing rhythm that continues throughout each point.

Mental Skill Progression 4: Gut-Level Breathing

Develop your abdominal breathing.

Lie on the floor and place your hands on your abdomen. Then inhale through your nose on a four-count, filling up your lungs all the way down to your abdomen. Exhale slowly on a count of five, letting the air flow out your mouth. Try this for 8 to 10 breaths. Now go out on the court and try the same thing as you are walking back to the baseline between points.

Mental Skill Progression 5: Can't Miss

Enhance your rhythm and timing using a two-part breath.

Step 1: Establish a rhythm while you practice your ground strokes. Say "bounce" each time the approaching ball bounces and "hit" when you make contact. Then try saying other words—"ten . . . nis" or "can't . . . miss."

Step 2: Try one steady exhalation from the time the ball bounces until you make contact. Use the "s" sound in "tennissssssssssss" or "can't missssssssssss."

Step 3: Try the same thing without the words. Begin a long exhalation when the ball bounces and continue it until you make contact.

Imagery

Imagine the smell of a new tennis ball. Do it right now—put the book down and savor that unique smell. I'll wait. . . .

That's imagery. It's not just imagining smells, of course. It might involve picturing the stroke of a favorite player or remembering how it felt when you hit a winning shot. In many sports, coaches have talked about visualization—seeing in your mind's eye what you want to happen. Imagery starts there but expands through all your senses. Feel the stroke you need to make, hear the "plock" of the ball against your racquet, and find some way to savor the sweet smell of success.

Imagery is another tool you can use to focus your playing, to make tennis stress work for you and not against you. As you develop your ability to use imagery, you'll accelerate your rate of improvement in all aspects of the game.

Imagery can be internal or external and both can be helpful. Internal imagery previews the scene from the inside looking out—seeing, hearing, and feeling your perfect match. External imagery sets up your mind's eye outside of yourself. You see yourself playing, and you sense everything as if you're on the sideline watching the match. (In fact, watching a videotape of your own play can be a good way to develop external imagery. That way you can lock in clear images of yourself making things happen on the court.)

It's very important to have a collection of images in your mind upon which you can draw when you need it.

Imagery has been a part of Tommy Haas's training from an early age.

Besides images of yourself, collect images of your favorite players, especially as they exhibit qualities or skills you admire. Certainly we're all biomechanically different. You may not be able to copy all your heroes' shots, nor should you. But you still can benefit from imagining the form, balance, rhythm, or rotation of the top players. And look for the intangible qualities, too. Maybe you admire the grit of Thomas Muster or the confidence of Martina Hingis. Then get a mental picture of these players and use it.

Peter Haas, father and coach of Tommy Haas, instilled in his son from an early age strong images of certain players: Ivan Lendl's backhand, Muster's determination, etc. By just thinking their names, the younger Haas could activate hundreds of mental images he had collected from watching those qualities.

It will take patience and practice to get good at controlling your images. In general, imagery should lead your mind forward and upward. That is, you're always imagining your next shot, not critiquing your last one. Don't let that external camera put you in a self-critical mode. Imagine how you will succeed from here on. And when your mood is dragging—you're angry at the linesman, frustrated with your own errors, or just depressed about your bad luck—let your imagery inspire you to shake off the problems and be a champion.

Mental Skill Progression 6: What You See Is . . .

Gather positive images.

Step 1: List two or three professional players and aspects of their game that you admire.

Step 2: Take some old tennis magazines and cut out pictures of these players, making a collage that you can put up and look at frequently throughout the day.

Step 3: Watch and videotape these same players playing matches.

Step 4: Close your eyes; now in your mind, recreate the images you have collected on these players.

While good imagery can help your game, poor imagery can wreck it. I bet this has happened to you. On a second serve, you imagine yourself hitting the ball into the net for a double fault—and you do. You're trying so hard not to do it that your mind focuses on it, and this negative image becomes reality. Negative imagery also can cause problems such as lack of commitment, confused shot selection, increased frustration, and low self-confidence.

Mental Skill Progression 7: No-Fault Service

Use imagery to improve your second serve.

Step 1: Hit a successful second serve.

Step 2: Imagine repeating your performance.

Step 3: Repeat the performance.

Sometimes you'll see pro players miss a stroke and then take a few extra swings before setting up for the next point. What are they doing? Erasing the image of the missed stroke and replacing it with a proper stroke. This "shadow swing" helps put them in the groove the next time they need that stroke, and it immediately rebuilds their confidence.

Mental Skill Progression 8: The Shadow Knows

Use shadow swings as positive imagery.

Practice taking a correct shadow swing after hitting a great shot or making a mistake.

Imagery also can help you anticipate what will happen in your match. Just as skilled chess players can think through the game several moves in advance, smart tennis players usually can imagine three to five shots ahead. This helps them plan winning strategy. They're not just playing the current shot, they're setting up their opponent for a putaway 20 seconds from now.

This isn't all that difficult. As you understand where your shots go and how your opponent is likely to return them, you can trace some probable scenarios yourself. In fact, this is a great way to prepare for a match. Take a few minutes in the locker room or while driving to the site to rehearse in your mind. Imagine the likely scenarios: you strongly return a hard serve, he runs you right, but you're ready with a strong shot down the line; his backhand is weak, so you rush the net and deposit a winning crosscourt smash. This imagery will boost your confidence, relax you, and also prepare you to play out that scene on the court.

Mental Skill Progression 9: Writing Your Script

Use detailed imagery of different playing scenarios.

Imagine the match in advance. Write down a scenario depicting where each shot goes for the first point that you serve and another for the first point your opponent serves. Then read through your scenarios several times, trying to see this happening in your mind's eye.

You might ask a friend to videotape those points when you are playing or at least to chart how those points went. Later, see how accurate your predictions were. Even if they weren't exactly right for the first points, they probably resembled some points in the match, and so you were better prepared to play them.

Mental Skill Progression 10: Highlight Reel

Use postmatch imagery to learn and improve.

Record your experiences. After the match take the time to review what has taken place. Accurately record in your match book which images you want to hold on to. Describe them as vividly as possible—this is a great way to lock in and reinforce your positive images.

Energy Management

Energy levels can fluctuate on a tennis court for a variety of reasons, physical or mental. Maybe you've eaten something that's draining your energy, maybe you're sick, or maybe you haven't slept well for a couple of nights. Possibly you're just stiff and aching from playing a lot. Or you might just be bored because you feel your opponent is too weak. Maybe you've played so much tennis that you get sloppy, forgetting what you're trying to accomplish on the court. Whatever the reason, your energy is fluctuating. How do you handle it effectively and still play your best?

It's important, first, to get an idea of the kind of energy problem you're having. Energy fluctuation can be a matter of quantity or quality. It's not just a question of whether you physically have high energy or low energy, it's also whether your mental energy is positive or negative. When we put these two scales together, we get four possible energy situations:

High positive   Low positive

High negative   Low negative

If your energy is high positive, everything is going great. You're probably experiencing a King Midas day in which everything you hit turns to gold—net rollers, balls on the lines, and winners. Mentally you are in the zone. When you're in this ideal performance state (as Dr. Loehr calls it), you don't want to think too much—just let it flow. And observe it. Collect images you can use later when things aren't going so well. After a high-positive match, write out how it felt in your notebook.

What if your energy is low positive? That means you're feeling good, but tired. So you need to keep moving between points and focus on your exhalation. Be careful not to allow negative thoughts to creep into your mind. When your energy's low, you easily can slide from positive to negative. Keep your confidence up and your thoughts positive and focus on the areas of your game that you need to improve.

In a low-negative situation you're feeling physically drained, and your mind just isn't into it. You're probably feeling overmatched or undermatched, terrified or bored. In a case like this, get your mind in the game by focusing on the basics. Think about your breathing or how you're moving your feet. Play percentage tennis; this is probably a just-get-it-in day, so work at keeping the ball in play.

Also keep your goals in the front of your mind. Remind yourself why you're playing. And then challenge yourself to do better by setting performance standards such as 75 percent first serves, serve-and-volley on the first serve, etc. If you feel you're far better than your opponent, these mini-goals can keep you from getting bored, and you can use the match as a practice. If you feel your opponent is far better than you, these mini-goals can give you some satisfaction and keep your confidence from being totally squashed.

On a high-negative day, you're probably tired, angry, sick, fatigued, or everything all together. I'm talking high mental stress. You're worked up and ready to explode. Physically, you're pumped, maybe too much so. But your mind is all over the place. Maybe you're frustrated that your opponent is trouncing you, or maybe you're convinced that the linesmen are conspiring against you. Whatever the problem, you need to grab control. Walk slower, breathe after every point, take a bit longer on changeovers. Slow yourself down and find your best playing rhythm. You also might want to do something wacky just to break your own tension. After all, this is a game.

Mental Skill Progression 11: Go With the Flow

Manage your energy.

Step 1: Identify your energy level—high or low, positive or negative.

Step 2: Keep track of your energy level for five consecutive playing days. After each day, list three things that may have contributed to your energy level for that day.

Step 3: For the next five playing days, manage your energy by following the recommendations mentioned above.

Goal Setting

I've worked with many players who have focused on outcome goals, such as winning the club tournament, improving their ranking, or beating a player they've never beaten before. Unfortunately, a player doesn't have total control over these objectives. You may run into an awesome opponent, adverse playing conditions, or just bad luck. It's better to start by setting reachable goals based on your preparation and performance, not on the outcome of your matches.

Work backward. Pick the outcome(s) you would like to achieve, then choose medium- and short-range performance goals of which you are in control. These shorter-range goals will be stepping-stones to achieving your long-term goals.

Short-term performance goals are immediate as to what you want to accomplish in your practice, your practice match, or even a tournament. You might set a goal of warming up for a certain period of time, or of working on specific SMARTS skills for 15 minutes each. You might even set goals for your mental game, such as breathing between points to control your stress.

Medium-range performance goals are what you are working on for the next four to six weeks. For instance, you might be working on particular shots that you're trying to master—returning up the middle or serve-and-volley. You might set a medium-range goal of practicing these shots enough so you can perform them effectively in the tournament next month. Note that you're still not saying you'll win the match, or even the point, just that you'll perform the shot effectively in game situations.

Long-range outcome goals are what you hope to be able to do with your game in six months—say, winning the club championship or defeating a pesky friend.

Set goals by assessing what you want to achieve and then determining what smaller steps you need to take to achieve the bigger outcome.

Mental Skill Progression 12: Go for the Goal

Set short-term and medium-range performance goals.

Step 1: Jot down in your notebook what your short-term goals will be in each of your practice sessions this week. Later check off the ones you have achieved.

Step 2: Consider one medium-range performance goal, perhaps an area of your game that needs improvement. Set a time four to six weeks from now when you can test your progress. Of course, this will influence your short-term practice goals.

Step 3: If you like, set an outcome goal for six months to a year from now. Is there an opponent you'd like to defeat, a tournament you'd like to win? Be reasonable; don't shoot for the moon. And understand that outcome goals are far less in your control than the short- or medium-range performance goals.

Self-Talk

Some people think you have to be crazy to talk to yourself, but it can help keep you focused when you're playing tennis. Still, you want to make sure your self-talk is effective. I generally see two extremes: Some players desperately announce their superiority when the score proves otherwise, and others use sarcasm to berate themselves for poor play—"Another double fault. Real good, ace."

Self-talk must be constructive to have positive impact on your performance, but it also should face up to the realities of the situation. Use it not just to bolster your confidence but mainly to focus you on the task at hand. You're not the best player in the world, and it won't help to tell yourself that you are. At ad-in, facing a wicked serve, your world ranking is irrelevant. What you do need to tell yourself is that you can strongly return this serve, by seeing it well, timing your split step to stay on your toes, rotating, and so on.

Throughout this book, I give you certain cues—short phrases to help you remember key aspects of your game. For instance, by saying (or thinking) "low to high," you are giving yourself a reminder as to how to put topspin on the ball. "Load and explode" is a reminder to rotate powerfully on a base you have created for yourself. Using cues such as "spin to win," you can remind yourself to make effective shots while staying aggressive. Use these and other cues in your self-talk to coach yourself as you play, paying attention to the specifics of your game.

You don't need to keep telling yourself how good you are; that may backfire. In fact, it's best not to worry about such categories as "good" and "bad." Focus your attention on this shot, this serve, this recovery, this approach. You can do this. And if you ever will defeat the best player in the world, you'll have to do it one shot at a time.

Mental Skill Progression 13: Talking to Yourself

Develop effective self-talk using cues.

Step 1: Practice your ground stroke, saying a cue out loud each time you hit the ball. You might use the cue "turn . . . finish" or "low to high" or something else that fits your particular needs. (See the specific cues suggested in chapter 3.)

Step 2: Begin using spoken cues on other shots, especially those you want to improve.

Practice your mental skills daily with the same perseverance as you give to the other skill groups of stroking, playing, and preparation. You will start to see instantaneous and dramatic improvements over time.

Performing Under Pressure

Tennis can be frustrating. You carefully practice all your strokes, making sure you have proper form. But when you play a match, you find yourself scrambling to reach the ball, improvising your rotation and transfer, doing whatever it takes to get the ball over the net. And, of course, lots of times you miss. It's hard to stick with the good form you've learned in the heat of an actual match. You need to practice like you play and play like you practice.

Blending Strokes

Take your strokes out of the laboratory of the practice court and into the real world of match play. This will involve a process I call blending strokes. You need to merge your routine strokes with your improvised strokes to find a pattern of play that works under pressure.

You take routine strokes when you have the time and position to swing freely at the ball. In lessons and practice, you get a lot of easy balls to handle, and you can load up and let loose. You take improvised strokes when your position is less than ideal and the ball is coming at you quickly. With the improvised shot, the end justifies the means. Whenever you're more concerned with winning the point than with practicing good form, you'll use improvised strokes if you have to.

Now it's time to put these together so that you can respond in different phases of play by being able to execute both routine strokes and improvised strokes when rallying, challenging, attacking, counterattacking, and defending. We need to work on consistency, placement, pace, height and depth, spins, and taking the ball on the rise. Proper patterns must get so ingrained in your muscles that these are the moves you use when the going gets tough. Now you are at the beginning of the mileage phase of your development. You tend to perform better in practice than you do in a match (see introduction, page vii). Now you are working to become a better player in the heat of the match.

Players in this phase should spend 25 percent of their time on stroking skills or technical development, getting instruction from a teacher or coach; 25 percent on drills that blend stroking skills with playing skills; and 50 percent on match play. I recommend playing three to five sets a week. Everything else you want to do for your game—be it conditioning, mental training, or extra lessons—is secondary to playing sets against different opponents.

But be careful in choosing the people with whom you play; choose players of varying levels. You want to have variety and a high rate of success. Sure, it's good to test yourself once in a while, but you're still trying to learn how to win, and you can't do that if you're chasing missiles all day. So as you select opponents, sometimes test your skills against the neighborhood rocket-launchers and other times test yourself against a pusher.

Serves

When you started playing tennis, you just wanted to get a serve in. If you were lucky, it was the first serve. Now it's time to start placing your serve, varying the spins and pace you are putting on the ball. By being able to vary your serve, you will make it increasingly difficult for your opponent to return your serve and therefore break you.

Stroking Skill Progression 1: Made Service

Blend consistency, height, placement, depth, spins, and pace.

Step 1: Around the world (for consistency): Serve five times from each of six different spots (see figure 9.1)—the normal position on both the deuce and ad sides of the court, halfway between the service line and the baseline on both sides, and the service line on both sides. How many of those 30 serves can you make?

Step 2: The Monica Seles service drill (for height): Seles practices serving from three to four feet behind the baseline. Serve half a basket of balls to each service box to get the feeling of hitting up on the ball.

Step 3: Hit the spot (for placement and depth): Place three cones (or large racquet bags or tennis ball cans) deep in the service box, not on the service line but about half a foot inside. Try to hit them all with your serve.

Step 4: The spin cycle (for spins). Try to hit those same spots with three different spins (flat, slice, and topspin).

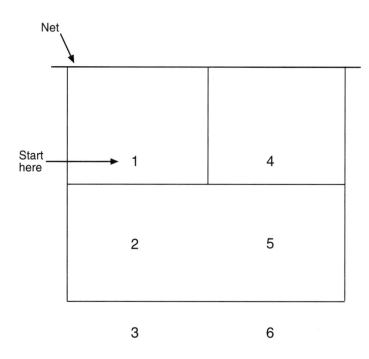

Net

Start here → 1 | 4

2 | 5

3 | 6

Figure 9.1—Six spots on the court to play "around the world."

Step 5: Follow your calling (for blending skills): Aim for the same three spots in the service boxes and name them; "one" might be wide, "two" middle, and "three" up the service T. Have a friend call out one of the spots just before you serve, and serve it there. Do this on both the ad and deuce sides. Once you have control over your placement, then try to add a little extra pace to the different spots. Next goal, try different types of serves (slice, flat, and kick). Have your friend call out the spot and the spin: "Two, flat!" Or, "Three, kick!"

Step 6: Second the motion (for differentiating between first and second serves): Take 12 pairs of balls and practice serving both first and second serves to the deuce and ad sides. See how many pairs you successfully serve to the spot for which you're aiming.

Step 7: Self-serve (for working on your second serve): Raphael Font De Mora, former assistant to Jose Higueras, has his students play a second-service game with one ball in the hand at a time (to re-create the second-serve situation). Play a game against yourself. If you make the serve, the score is 15-love; and if you miss it, love-15.

Step 8: Serve-and-volley, stay back (for blending shots): This is a tricky blend of shots to practice. Your serve should propel you into the court somewhat, and that may set you up for a volley. But then you don't need to approach the net (your momentum would carry you). Often it's best to stay back and rally if your opponent's returning well. So practice a pattern of serve-and-volley, then stay back and rally. With your partner returning, repeat this pattern six times.

Step 9: Stan's Fan Plan (for varying serves): According to tennis great Stan Smith, you can create a large variety of serves by changing your serve location. Fan out to six different spots along the baseline and try slice, kick, and flat serves from all of them. See where the ball goes.

Returns

As a beginner, you tried to anticipate your opponent's serve, setting up in an appropriate spot, timing your movement, and adjusting to the incoming ball. When your opponent was kind enough to give you an easy serve, you were able to line up, take your backswing, and execute a solid return deep in her court. But if you were receiving cannonball serves, you just stuck your racquet out and hoped for the best. Am I right?

At the mileage level, to be honest, you'll still have trouble with cannonball serves. (Even pros get aced by superior firepower.) But you should learn to make your returns more offensive than defensive—not just returning what you get but hitting a shot that gives you the advantage. This is not necessarily with pace. You may direct the return well to get your opponent running.

Stroking Skill Progression 2: Many Happy Returns

Return serves with consistency and placement from behind the baseline, on the baseline, and well inside it.

Step 1: The center-court drill (for consistency): The first area that you should be able to return to is the center of the court. I call this neutralizing. Have a friend hit you all kinds of serves, and try to return them all to runway A.

Step 2: Second serves to center: Have a friend hit you some weaker second serves, but putting them at various heights and in different parts of the service box. Hit them to runway A. When necessary, practice moving around these balls to hit your forehand. Work on these skills until they become second nature.

Step 3: Hit the corners (for depth): Now that you can place the return up the middle of the court, practice hitting to the corners to make the server run. Use slice, topspin, and flat hit to do this.

Step 4: Second-service return: Your opponent gets one serve. You should practice moving in and taking the ball on the rise, putting pressure on your opponent by running him or coming to the net.

Ground Strokes

As a beginner, you tried to neutralize balls by hitting deep up the middle in your opponent's court. If you could keep the other player in zone 5 most of the time, you'd have a distinct advantage. Now it's time to fan out your shots. Deep shots are still good, but you should start hitting the corners, too, opening the court widthwise. Vary your shots to keep the other player guessing and running, and learn to hit to your opponent's weaknesses.

Just as a boxer works on combinations of punches, you should work on combinations of shots. Blend together your deep ground strokes with angles, lobs, and drop shots.

Stroking Skill Progression 3: Open for Business

Open the court with your ground stroke.

Step 1: Four-square: Divide each court into four squares (imagine the center line extending), and play a game of four-square, in which you're not allowed to hit to the same square twice in a row. But don't just vary your placement; try varying the type of shot as well. You can do four things with the ball: hit short; hit deep; hit with height; or drive balls that go low over the net. Rotate these four shots, trying both forehands and backhands and eventually adding some changes of pace with spin and slice.

Step 2: All the angles: When you're consistently hitting deep, making the ball bounce over your opponent's baseline, you're hitting through the court. Now work on opening the court widthwise by placing angle shots and drives crosscourt that land in the court and then bounce over the singles sidelines. Angles require the same swing path as the basic ground stroke. Open the court with an angle and then drive the ball through the court (or vice versa) to make your opponent run.

Step 3: Hitting the weak spots: Imagine three weaknesses your opponent might have—perhaps backhand, short balls, and balls hit directly at her. (These may or may not be the actual weaknesses of the friend with whom you're hitting. Work on a range of possibilities.) Work at placing the ball precisely within those weak areas.

Step 4: On the rise: Stand inside the baseline with your partner at the net. As your partner volleys to you, practice stepping forward to hit the ball on the rise.

Step 5: Adding spin: To hit angles requires spin. So as you blend your shots, the logical progression from the angle, then, is to the topspin lob. The two shots require the same preparation, with a similar swing path, but with the lob you hit the ball higher over the net with an acceleration of the racquet head and upward swing path. So, as you drill these two strokes, stand at the center of your court with your partner at the net, but to one side. Hit an angle to your partner, who will then volley back to you. Then hit a topspin lob.

Step 6: Slice: Ground strokes, angles, and topspin lobs fit well together and can be combined easily when practicing. On the backhand side you have the option of hitting with slice through the court (deep), or slicing an angle shot and opening the court (especially effective against a two-handed player), and following with a slice drop shot.

Punching Strokes

Once you can hit slice, slice lob, volley, and drop shots, then you're ready for angle volleys and drop volleys (see chapter 4). These punching shots can make you or break you. It's not that hard to hit a volley from zone 1 or 2 into the opposing court. But you need to put that volley somewhere to make full use of your position and to put your opponent on the defensive.

Boris Becker moves into position for the volley.

Stroking Skill Progression 4: Punch It

Vary your punching strokes.

Step 1: With a friend feeding you easy balls, practice the following blend: volley, smash, then recover. Repeat until your friend gets tired of chasing the balls you smash.

Step 2: Practice the following progression: volley hit deep through the court, angle volley opening the court, and drop volley.

Transition Shots

Transition shots are among the most difficult to do well and the last ones most people learn. And yet the transition game is one of your most effective tactical weapons. If you can move smoothly from defense to offense, or answer your opponent's attack with a counterattack, you can take control of the game.

So blending from the backcourt to the forecourt is the assignment here. Measure your backswing according to your court position and blend your stroking skills of transfer, rotation, and swing. Either place it somewhere that helps you get a better position or go for an outright winner.

Stroking Skill Progression 5: In Between

Blend your transition shots.

Start a ground-stroking game with a friend in runway A. After a few warm-up strokes, begin an approach—but only take two steps between shots. Adjust to the balls with your hands and feet as needed. Hit a half volley if you need to catch the ball on a short hop, then keep volleying as you move toward the net.

Stroking Skill Progression 6: Putting It All in the Blender

Blend your strokes into a workable game plan.

This is probably best done with a coach or instructor who can feed you a basketful of balls. Vary the height, depth, direction, pace, and spin. Hit a couple of ground strokes, an approach, a first volley, second volley, second volley angle, and then a smash followed by a drop volley. As you become more confident, add to your transition shots the swinging volley, which has the same mechanics as a ground stroke.

Now that you have your arsenal of shots, and can blend them as needed, when should you hit which shot? Some of it depends on how well you're positioned. If you have the proper distance to the ball and it is in a strike zone that you like, swing fully through the shot. However, if you're close to the ball or it is low and you are in trouble, then take some of the speed off the ball with a slice or by just getting the ball back.

Phases of Play

I've discussed the different phases of play, based on court location and type of ball received, in chapter 5. Now you need to make your shot selection based on your phase of play. Let's review what your shot intention should be in the different phases of play.

Defensive

In the defensive phase of play, you want to get the ball over one more time, hoping that you can improve your situation or that your opponent makes a mistake. You want to hit with height over the net if you are deep in the court. If the ball is really low and you are near the net, get the ball over the net by opening your racquet face and aiming over the lowest part of the net. Use any variety of spins including topspin, underspin, or slice. Ideally, if you use a slice, try to keep it low over the net so your opponent receives a difficult ball with which to put you away. Place the ball up the middle if your opponent stays back, so you don't give her an angle to create off of your shot. If she comes in, then go crosscourt with a ball that dips to her feet with topspin or goes right at her. If you need to lob, choose a topspin or a slice, but give the topspin lob more height. Slice lobs with backspin naturally give the ball some lift. If the ball is low, then hit crosscourt to get it over the lowest part of the net.

Rally

In the rally phase you want to do whatever you do best as often as possible. Practice running around your backhand to hit your forehand if it's your better stroke. Some players (such as Todd Martin, Serena Williams, and Malivai Washington) like to do just the opposite—hitting backhands when they have a choice. I prefer my students run around and hit with their forehands as they can get away with being late on the forehand side easier than they can on the backhand.

If the approaching ball is too fast for you to do much with, it's not bad to hold your ground and hit a slice. Eventually you can gain an advantage by varying your shots: short, long, angles.

Challenge

In the challenge phase your intention is to take the ball early by catching it on the rise and placing the ball closer to the lines. Try to draw a short ball from your opponent that you can then attack, hitting an outright winner or challenge again, gaining better position on the court. You can challenge by hitting the ball deep through the court, opening the court up with angles, or hitting angle volleys, drop shots, or drop volleys. You may lob the ball up to your opponent's backhand and sneak in to the net looking to put the ball away.

Attack

In the attack phase you are going for the jugular. You are stepping down hard on the accelerator and trying to hit a winner or force your opponent into an error. Your individual tools for attacking really depend on your strengths and weaknesses within your particular style of play. Maybe you have a really big serve, so you go for a big first serve waiting for your opponent to return the ball short, which you then run around and attack or challenge with your forehand. Or maybe your weapon is your net game and you create opportunities to come forward.

Yevgeny Kafelnikov attacking his serve.

Combinations

Boxers have them. Football and basketball teams call them plays. I'm referring to combinations—not just one perfect move, but a series of actions that create a desired effect. In tennis, combinations of shots are useful to get the ball where you want it. With the right combinations, you can unlock your opponent's game and put him where you want him. Now that you've mastered the individual shots, you need to add combinations to your arsenal. Combinations are the directional component of your tactics that can help you to defeat your opponent's particular style.

Some players have their favorite shots, spots on the court where they like to send the ball using the ball controls of height, spin, depth, direction, and pace. In the right situations, these shots can be winners. But you can't always hit that shot. Considering where you and your opponent are and what type of ball you're receiving, your best shot may not be available to you. If you try too hard to force it, you'll hit a low-percentage shot and probably lose the point.

You need to be able to hit to specific spots on the court, anticipating certain responses, which you then will direct to move your opponent or to open up an attack opportunity for yourself. Combinations employ all your tricks—running your opponent, opening the court, creating wrong footing, and attacking your opponent's weakness. The key is that you're running the show. You're limiting your opponent's options, anticipating what response you'll get, and setting up your winners. Your opponent may surprise you sometimes (or you may hit a weak setup shot), but then you just counterattack, rally, or go on the defensive until you can start a new combination.

There are eight spots in your opponent's court to which you can hit the ball and be reasonably sure where the ball will be returned (see figure 9.2). Of course there are also different ball controls you can match up against your opponent's characteristics (his body type, grips, shot preferences, speed, anticipation, etc.). Practice sending different shots to different spots, and see what you get in return.

Knowing your strengths and weaknesses and identifying patterns of play from your opponent (as well as her style of play) can help you to formulate different strategies. But don't let that distract you. "Sometimes players get so caught up in what the other player is doing that they forget to play their own game," warns Bobby Banck (coach to Jimmy Arias, Aaron Krickstein, Justin Gimblestob, and Mary Joe Fernandez).

You can execute combinations from the baseline, in transition, or at the net, using different ball controls. When learning the combinations, work on each skill progression for two weeks to one month. In the exercises below, I have listed two- and three-shot combinations, but it's common when playing to a person's weakness to see lengthy combinations of shots, such as an 0-3 (three balls to the backhand in a row) or a 1-4 (one ball hit to the forehand side and four hit to the backhand).

The most basic combination is simply 1-1, sometimes called the run-run or the run-and-gun. With a 1-1 combination, you hit to one side of the court and then the other. On serve, for example, you serve wide and then try to take your opponent's return and challenge, rally, or attack to the opposite corner. If you are challenging or rallying the ball, then you're making your opponent run, but if you're going for the outright winner (attack), then you're gunning the ball to the corner.

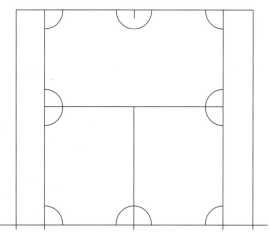

Figure 9.2—Eight spots in your opponent's court to which you can hit to and anticipate where the ball will be returned.

Combination Skill Progression 1

Practice developing your out-wide serve, getting your opponent off the court. If you do this well, his return should go down the line or come up the center of the court. Practice hitting your opponent's return deep crosscourt (into the open court), making him run.

Combination Skill Progression 2

On the deuce side, practice serving a three-quarter-pace slice serve that lands high up on the singles sideline. If you catch your opponent by surprise and she hits short, rally or challenge the return by opening the court with an angle. Hit an angle, for example, to the other side (angle 1-1). Work on doing the same on the ad side, using the kick serve to get the opponent off the court.

Combination Skill Progression 3

Serve out wide but now, when the opportunity presents itself, challenge with a drop shot.

The 1-2 combination: Hit one shot to your opponent's forehand and two shots to the backhand. It might go something like this:

- *You return a second serve from the deuce side crosscourt to your opponent's forehand that he rallies to your backhand.*
- *You run to hit your reply, taking it crosscourt and causing him to hit defensively.*
- *You now can challenge the ball, hitting it behind him, placing it, or attacking the ball (going for an outright winner).*

Combination Skill Progression 4

Serving the ball up the T, you should expect the ball to come up the middle of the court. Practice challenging or attacking the return—trying to wrong-foot your opponent on her backhand side, hitting first with depth, then angles, then drop shots.

The 2-1 combination: When rallying, hit two shots to the forehand, then one shot to the backhand. This is especially useful if your opponent has an outstanding backhand or is an attacking baseliner who likes to stay in the backhand side of the court and hit winners.

Combination Skill Progression 5

When counterattacking, the success of the combination depends on how well you are able to set up your opponent. Say, for example that your opponent attacks to your backhand and comes in. When you're under attack and you have a choice as to where you will hit your pass, start by hitting the passing shot crosscourt. It is a high-percentage play. Try to hit the ball crosscourt, low, and down on your opponent's feet. If you are successful at doing this, then you move in anticipating that she may volley or half-volley short, at which time you can then pass, lob, or hit directly at her.

Passing shots: Any number of combinations can be executed with the pass, including crosscourt, crosscourt angle, middle, lob, and down the line.

Combination Skill Progression 6

When you can do all the above, try hitting with as much pace as you can muster right up the middle of the court. If your opponent doesn't adjust well to balls hit directly at him, he then will be jammed by the approaching ball, volleying his response short. Move forward and hit the winning passing shot.

Combination Skill Progression 7

Try the lob now, hitting with height and depth over your opponent, who may be closing too tight on the net. After hitting a good lob over your opponent, get to the net yourself.

Combination Skill Progression 8

Finally, practice hitting your passes down the line, first deep and then short, hitting the service line. On those short shots, if you get the ball to dip as it goes over the net, you'll force your opponent to stretch on the volley or half volley, and his shot probably will go short in your court. Then you can move forward and hit the winning passing shot.

Serve and volley (1-1, 1-2, 2-1): Practice hitting your volleys deep, angled, and drop. Generally your first volley will be deep in the court (though I know some pro players such as Pat Rafter who close so quickly that they can hit an angled first volley away for a winner). If your opponent lobs, you'll need to smash his lob away. Directing a smash where you want it to go also will take some practice.

Mark Philippoussis builds his game by serving big and ripping the short return.

Combination Skill Progression 9

Hit the serve in to your opponent's body on the side of his weaker stroke (jamming him), then approach the net and volley into the open court (1-1 volley).

Combination Skill Progression 10

Now on the deuce side, serve again in to the body but hit the first volley behind the returner on the forehand side. Then take his next response and volley or smash it into the open court (2-1 combo).

Combination Skill Progression 11

Now serving on the ad side, go behind your opponent with the first volley on the backhand side, and then volley or smash into the open court (1-2 combo).

Returns: The 1-1, 1-2, and 2-1 combinations also can be practiced by hitting your return to specific parts of the court and then trying to rally, challenge, or attack the ball in the desired direction while varying the ball controls of depth, height, spin, and pace.

Combination Skill Progression 12

For ground-stroke combinations beginning with a return, start off by hitting the following returns: middle, crosscourt, down-the-line, angle, and big forehand. Then try to execute a 1-1, 1-2, or 2-1.

> *Transition **return combination**: This starts with a serve that can be challenged or attacked, followed by a first volley, maybe a second volley, and possibly a smash. You also can work on variations of your transition game, such as hit-and-charge, angle, chip-and-charge, big forehand, and drop shot.*

Combination Skill Progression 13

For defining your game, follow these steps:

Step 1: Recall how you prioritized your different playing styles.

Step 2: Define your best game plan within your preferred style of play, based on your strengths and weaknesses. Say you like the style of being an attacking baseliner and have a very good serve out wide on the deuce side, but you have trouble directing your backhand to where you want it to go. So to execute a 1-1 you might serve wide and run around your opponent's response, hitting your forehand to the opposite corner of the court.

Step 3: Now try to come up with three or four combinations at which you're really good. List them and practice them.

> *These different combinations sometimes make up predictable patterns of play that you may start to observe in your opponent. Let's say you notice that when your opponent is facing a break point on the ad side, he always serves up the T and tries to serve-and-volley. Recognizing your opponent's patterns of play can then help you to make an educated guess as to where he might hit his shots on big points. Of course this will help you hit winning responses. But beware, because your opponent may be noticing some of your patterns of play, too. So sometimes it's fun to try some surprises—for example, hitting a lob when he's beginning to move early for your crosscourt pass.*

If you play the same opponents frequently, you'll get to know their patterns. Why not keep track of their favorite plays in a notebook? "Drew likes to pass crosscourt on his forehand on the run." Or, "Susan doesn't like low slice to her forehand." Ivan Lendl kept a very detailed log of shot patterns on all of his opponents.

Try to use all of your senses. We already have discussed how to be visually sensitive to what is going on in the whole court, and using soft focus, but you need to start using other sensations too, such as touch and hearing. Some players seem to have a sixth sense about how and where the next ball is coming. This is not ESP; they're just very good at gathering cues from all of their senses and instinctively analyzing the probabilities of their opponent's shots.

Say that you feel you have just connected well with the ball, really launching it to your opponent's side of the court. You have felt the strong connection of ball against racquet and you have heard the solid "thwump" of that contact. You see the trajectory of the ball and your opponent moving toward it. All of this tells you that your opponent will be defensive and you can expect a floater or an easy putaway. This expectation is confirmed as you see your opponent lunging for the ball or swinging desperately. You may even hear a different kind of "thwump" (or a clunk) from your opponent's racquet. In any case, don't just stand there admiring your shot—go in behind it to put added pressure on your opponent to make a good shot.

Good anticipation can raise your game to a new level. And you can feed your anticipation skills by using all of your senses on the court.

What to Expect

Combinations are based on reasonable expectations of how your opponent will respond to certain shots. If you learn to anticipate returns, you can develop your own combinations to defeat just about any foe.

Two years ago I asked Mark Philipoussis how he had beaten Mark Woodforde at the Open. He answered matter-of-factly, "Well, mate, I hit my serve as hard as I could and then ripped the next ball with my forehand deep to the corner and came in."

Philipoussis knew what his strengths were (his serve and big forehand), and he played his game against this formidable opponent. Certainly he was using his tennis experience to anticipate the kind of shots Woodforde would send him, and he realized that Woodforde would be forced to counterattack the pace and depth of shots. So he formulated his game plan and then focused on his own play.

The analysis involved in tennis may seem intricate at times, but it basically comes down to doing what works. In this case, Philipoussis served and ripped and that worked for him. So he kept serving and ripping . . . and he won the match.

All of this may seem difficult to remember, especially in the heat of play. But remember, you're not just learning a catalog of responses. You're developing a feel for your particular situation. You'll build your own repertoire of favorite challenge or attack shots, and you'll learn what shots can turn a defensive situation into a more positive one for you. So don't be overwhelmed by all the options. Just follow the basic strategies, and build your game from there.

Table 9.1—What to Expect

Ball sent	Ball recived
Any shot deep to the corners with pace that puts your opponent on defense.	Short return or easy floater that you can volley.
Any deep shot to the corners with an angle, causing your opponent to step outside the singles court.	If he gets to the ball quickly, expect a return down the line, crosscourt, or to the middle. But if he's late and stretching for the ball, expect it down the line.
Any shot (or serve) with depth and pace up the middle of the court which jams your opponent or forces him to back up.	If a right-handed opponent is jammed backhand, the ball should go to your right as you approach the net. If your opponent is jammed on the forehand, the ball should go to your left. (Reverse this for lefties.) When your opponent is on their back foot and hits a slice, try to attack the next ball possible, because his ball is going to float.
To spot 3 or 5 by any stroke.	If opponent is there with time, the ball could go anywhere. But if the ball is low, the oponent will probably take the ball crosscourt or up the middle, playing the percentage.
To spot 2 or 5.	It depends on the height of the ball you hit. If it's low, the return will probably be more to the center.
To spot 7 or 8.	If your opponent reaches the ball early, he will try to beat you down the line or rip crosscourt or directly at you for the lob, drop, or crosscourt flick.
Net roller, a ball that catches the tape and rolls over the net.	Depends on where your opponent is standing, but if they're around the baseline, move in quickly, because their response will be defensive, popping the ball up.
Shanked shot.	Hard to say what kind of shot your opponent will hit, but he might be adjusting to the weird spin that you may have imparted on the ball, so go to the net and give him even more to worry about. Note: Your opponent will sometime mis-hit shots too. When this occurs, move forward, anticipating the ball to be shorter in the court.
Serve out wide.	If your opponent's late getting to the ball, then the return will be down the line. But if he's waiting for the serve, he'll take it crosscourt.
Serve up the T.	On the deuce side, if your opponent is late, then the ball will be returned to the middle of the court on your forehand side. If he's early, he may hit to the middle of the court or down the line to your backhand. On the ad side, if he's late, then the ball will be hit left of center. If he's early, then he can go middle or down the line.

Analyzing Your Opposition

10

Did you ever play the rock-paper-scissors game? Each of those objects had superiority over only one of the others. Scissors cuts paper. Paper covers rock. Rock smashes scissors. Sometimes in tennis, styles of play are like that. You can have mastery over some opponents and have trouble with others, all because of the differences in your opponent's style and your own.

You're going to encounter many different playing styles among your opponents. Your own playing style will match up favorably with some of these. With others, you'll have to try special tactics to get the upper hand. Tailoring your game to your opponent's strengths and weaknesses takes keen analysis, which I discuss in this chapter.

Opponent's Skill Level

Your opponent will play better than you, worse than you, or about the same as you. That's your first consideration as you analyze your opponent's game.

Better Than You

If your opponent is better than you, I call this an A-level player. When playing someone beyond your skill level, stick with the basic skills; don't get fancy. Hit your basic ground strokes over and over. Aim to keep the ball in play at least three to six times on each point. Do whatever it takes to keep A-level players on defense or rallying the ball. Prevent them from going on offense by keeping the ball deep. This will put tremendous amounts of pressure on your opponent to come up with the goods to put you away.

Against A-level opponents, take the defensive position—it's actually an easier job! If you hold that position tenaciously, consistently hitting solid strokes deep in the court, your opponent may get frustrated and start improvising. That's when unforced errors occur.

The Same as You

If your opponent is the same as you, this is a B-level player. On both sides, you'll see routine strokes combined with improvised strokes when under pressure. The goal is to keep balls in play 6 to 10 times per point. You probably will ebb and flow through defensive, rally, challenge, and attack phases. Don't hesitate to seize opportunities to challenge or attack, but don't rush things either.

Worse Than You

If your opponent is worse than you, this player is at C level. In many cases, good players play *down* to the level of lesser opponents. Why is this? Well, one reason is the slower pace of play. It can throw off the rhythm of a better player, who feels forced to generate power on the swing. This is a tough temptation. The ball comes in slowly, giving you more time to adjust to it—and more time to mess up your swing. Be careful about this. Prepare and execute your SMARTS on the ball just as quickly as you would against an A-level player.

Beating a C-level player requires that you psyche yourself up to hit the ball at least eight times over the net per point (pick a higher number if you like). That requires some patience, but it will keep you from making foolish errors. Against C-level players, some try to push the action, killing the ball on every stroke or trying low-percentage putaways. This action results in unforced aggressive and tactical errors and the weaker player coming out on top.

The reason you are a better player is, first of all, that you're more consistent at executing your strokes in all phases of play. You also can place them better, using your ball controls of height, depth, spin, and pace. You can put away a short or easy ball and hit to your opponent's weakness. Most of this has to do with control rather than power. When you try to push the action on court, creating opportunities where none exist, you lose the control aspect of your game. So stay in control! Your opponent will give you opportunities to challenge and attack, so wait for these. And if you have to settle for a long series of crosscourt rallies, so be it. Chances are, your C-level opponent will make a mistake before you do.

Analysis Progression 1: Previewing the Situation

Develop a broad game plan according to your opponent's level.

Step 1: Before a match, find out as much about your opponent as possible, especially her skill level and her strengths and weaknesses. Do this by asking others who have played your opponent what her strengths and weaknesses are or by watching her play.

Step 2: Decide whether your opponent is an A-, B-, or C-level player in relation to your own ability and draw up an appropriate game plan. Will you try to out-rally your opponent, just trying to get the ball over the net one more time? Will you play a controlled but somewhat aggressive game? Or will you just ebb and flow through the phases as opportunities arise? Based on what you know of your opponent's strengths and weaknesses, what kind of balls and where in the court will you try to hit?

Opponent's Style

Tennis players have many different styles. Style has to do with

- where you feel comfortable on the court,
- what kinds of ball you like to hit, and
- what strategies you employ.

There are defensive baseliners, attacking baseliners, attackers, all-court players, and variations of each of these categories. Most players get into certain patterns that you can figure out after watching them for a while. If you learn to recognize your opponent's style, you'll be able to guess where he likes to play and how he'll hit the ball—and prepare accordingly.

Defensive Baseliners

I divide defensive baseliners into three types: counterpunching baseliners, who can act by counterattacking; moonballers, who wait for your mistake; and junkballers, who give you varied paces and depths of shots.

Counterpunching Baseliners

Counterpunching baseliners respond to your attacks with great passing shots and lobs. They tend to be fit, mentally tough, and aware of where their opponents are on the court. They move well, hitting good ground strokes, returns, passing shots, and topspin lobs. They'll pounce on you if you start getting tentative. Their weapons are consistency and placement. They wait for you to beat yourself. Usually they possess a so-so serve, but if you attack it, they almost always have a great passing shot and topspin lob. Most defensive baseliners also run well laterally.

Tactic: *Be aggressive and commit to attacking repeatedly when the opportunity presents itself.* Mentally focus on your cues and don't second-guess yourself. Look for a weak second serve or a short ball off of one side or the other. Approach up the middle

Counterpunching baseliners like Michael Chang excel at counterattacking and making very few unforced errors.

sometimes, forcing them to hit a lob. Intentionally hit short shots or angles, since counterpunchers don't venture to the net by choice. Their net game can be suspect. Over the years counterpunchers can become good all-around players if they spend the time to improve their serve and coming to the net. This type of player is as steady as a backboard and doesn't make many unforced errors. Mentally you have to prepare for long points, so bring your towel and energy bars and drink lots of water. Michael Chang and Arantxa Sanchez Vicario are good examples of counter-punching baseline players. They play themselves into the match, moving the ball around and remaining steady.

Moonballers

Moonballers keep the ball high over the net and deep in your court. They lack the ability to attack, but they still can beat you by forcing you to play their game, leading you to make mistakes.

Tactic: *Hit high and deep down the middle and sneak in.* If your opponent hits a shot that doesn't bounce above your shoulder, then try running her up and back. (Hit short and then deep; or if she comes in, hit right at her or over her head.) You'll be tempted to overhit, trying to show the moonballer you can blow her off the court. But that would just make you beat yourself with unforced errors. To avoid this temptation, commit to rallying the ball 8 to 10 times before trying to put your opponent away. If the opportunity presents itself sooner, then challenge or attack. On the pro tour, this type of player has become extinct.

Junkballers

Junkballers give you little or no rhythm. They hit short drop shots, drawing you to the net, and then have a big smile on their face as they lob the ball over you. It is not uncommon for them to hit the ball with pace and then to massage your reply, sending it short with a deftness of touch.

Tactic: *Attack.* The junkballer is going to bring you to the net regardless, so you should initiate the attack first. Do not let him be the puppeteer and you the puppet. Karsten Braasch is a good example of a professional junkballer on the pro tour.

Braasch exemplifies the junkballer type of defensive baseliner. His play relies on varying the paces and depths of shots.

Attacking Baseliners

I make a distinction among three types of attacking baseliners: big-forehand baseliners, heavy-topspin baseliners, and pure ball strikers.

Big-Forehand Baseliners

Big-forehand baseliners are able to run around their backhand and hit winning forehands from anywhere on the court. They dictate rather than react. They're usually quite strong, hitting with power from the backcourt, forcing their opponents to make errors. They usually have big serves, too, and some have strong backhands. They always are looking for a short ball to attack, but they usually prefer to win the point with their forehand from deeper in the court. They'll often camp out in the backhand corner of the court and try to control the game from there. Steffi Graf, Ivan Lendl, Jim Courier, Andre Agassi, and Tommy Haas all fit this profile.

Tactic: *Keep this player on the move.* Don't hit to the same corner repeatedly, or your opponent will get into a groove. Play short or long to her or hit side to side. Plan on running a lot and hitting into the open court, be it crosscourt or down the line. The down-the-line backhand will be important to keep this style of player honest (it runs her to her forehand side, opening up an attack on her backhand). Try to keep her on defense by hitting balls deep in the court that are difficult to attack. Or go on the attack yourself, forcing her to counterattack or play defensively.

Keep big-forehand baseliners, like Steffi Graf, on the move.

Heavy-Topspin Baseliners

Heavy-topspin baseliners use topspin for lift and placement. The ball rises as it goes over the net and then dips down sharply. These players run you all over the court. They're usually consistent and fit, so the longer the point lasts the more they're favored. They're especially comfortable on clay. Arantxa Sanchez Vicario, Frederick Pioline, Alex Corretja, Sergi Bruguera, and Carlos Moya are examples of this type of player.

Tactic: *Apply the pressure quickly by trying to attack first with serve-and-volley, coming in off the first short ball or attacking the serve.* Try to get your opponent in trouble so he doesn't have time to get into a groove and run you.

Pure Ball Strikers

Pure ball strikers hit hard and flat to the corners with very clean strokes. This is as close to a living ball machine as you can get. You might wonder how to break down this type of player. Change the pace and height of the ball by hitting high balls, hard flat balls, and low balls such as slice, and look to attack the short ball or come in. Mary Joe Fernandez, Mary Pierce, Yevgeny Kafelnikov, Jimmy Connors, and Chris Evert are all pure ball strikers.

Tactic: *Keep the ball moving up or down in the varying strike zones.* Play high balls, then low balls. Vary your serve using wide, with your body up the service-T, and high and low.

The clean strokes of Mary Pierce classify her as a pure ball striker.

Attackers

Attackers rely on five basic strokes: serve, volley, return of serve, approach shot, and overhead. I divide this group into two categories: the big-serve attacker and the net crusher.

Big-Serve Attackers

Big-serve attackers build their game around holding serve by hitting aces or big first serves and ripping the short return away. They only need to break serve once. Goran Ivanisevic, Mark Philippoussis, and Brenda Schulz are like this.

Tactic: *Change position on the first serve by moving inside the baseline* (or backing up like Thomas Muster does). Give your opponent different looks as you set up for the return, hoping she'll miss her first serve. Keep track of where she serves her big bombs—maybe she can serve well to only one spot! If you do manage to return the serve, be patient, keeping the ball in play. A player like this has a quick mentality. She usually wants the points to end quickly. Physically she tends to be big and strong, so attack her movement and keep the ball low. You must hold serve yourself, but be on guard for a go-for-broke style from your opponent. (With such a great serve, your opponent may only need to break yours once.) If you can hold serve and break her once, the pressure pushes onto her.

Big-servers, such as Goran Ivanisevic, only need to break serve once each set.

Net Crushers

Net crushers get to the net by serving and volley-ing or by coming in off of second serves and short balls. It's hard to get anything past them when they're at the net. They tend to possess a strong first and second serve and they excel at placing approach shots and getting into position. Pro net crushers include Patrick Rafter, Stefan Edberg, Martina Navratilova, Greg Rusedski, and John McEnroe.

Tactic: *Take the ball on the rise as much as possible and avoid hitting balls up the middle in baseline exchanges.* Serve the ball out wide if your opponent starts coming in behind his return. This opens the court for you to pass. You can beat an attacking player by counterpunching if you're a good counterpuncher. If not, then try to attack first or pin him on the baseline. Keep attacking players pinned to the baseline by moving them from side to side, hitting wide serves and trying to angle them off the court, which forces them to attack from outside the sidelines. Long points from the baseline are not what attacking players like, so they usually try to come in on the first short ball. Choose your spots on the return, tak-ing the ball early to give them less time.

It's difficult to get anything by a net crusher such as Patrick Rafter once he is at the net.

All-Court Players

Some players can do all the above. Facing them, you have to figure out what they *don't* do so well or maybe something you can do to bother them. Watch them closely after winning points to look at their body language for signs that they're beginning to crack. With all-court players you have to notice which parts of their game are not matching up well with yours. Or look for other factors such as body type. For instance, a tall opponent who plays well from the baseline may not like to get low to the ball. Your slice may disrupt his baseline game and force him to start attacking. That's all right if you are an excellent counterpuncher with great passing shots. Pete Sampras, Martina Hingis, Venus Williams, and Serena Williams are excellent models of the all-court player.

Tactic: *Pick whatever is winning you the most points and stay with it.* All-around players can do it all, so it might take a couple spins of the dial before you unlock their game. They can stay back, rallying the ball, or they can come in and finish points at the net. So try a lot of different things in order to see what works. Your best bet is to wait for your opportunity (second serves, short balls) and attack as soon as possible, trying to put them on defense.

Analysis Progression 2: Playing With Style

Identify your style and that of your toughest opponents.

Step 1: From the nine styles listed above, pick four that are most like your game.

Step 2: List four styles that give you the most trouble when playing against them.

Opponent's Temperament

Playing style has a lot to do with a player's temperament. As I've been saying all along, tennis is not just a physical game—it's also mental and emotional. Players' temperaments often dictate the choices they make. A type-A personality, someone who is controlling and driven, possibly with a short fuse and hot temper, usually will be an attacker. On the other hand, those whose temperaments are even, controlled, and patient tend to be the best defensive baseliners. If you learn to read your opponent's temperament (and control your own), you may be able to control the game.

I saw an example of this in the U.S. Open in which two players with completely different temperaments were playing one another. One was a hotshot, a notorious "bad boy" on the circuit. He routinely yelled at the judges, threw his racquets, and showed up his opponents. The other was straitlaced, clean-cut, calm, and controlled. You couldn't find two players more varied.

In one game, the hotshot was being especially dramatic, hitting a succession of drop-volley and half-volley winners, and it was beginning to bother the other player, but he seemed to stay in control. On one tough short ball, the clean-cut player made a tremendous shot, moving far to his left to hit a crosscourt angle. The hotshot just made it to that ball and only could launch a half volley to where his opponent was playing.

This was an ideal green-light situation. The clean-cut player had two-thirds of the court wide open. He was in zone 3, with time to set up for a winner. He ripped a return straight down the line, and it tailed out of bounds. He lost the easy point.

I'm guessing here, but I think this was a clash of temperaments. I think the clean-cut player had lost patience with the hotshot's antics and he wanted to show him up. Remember: he had just hit one great angle to take the offensive on this point. Now he wanted to put the hotshot away with a perfect down-the-line winner. Except that was a low-percentage shot. He could have dropped the ball anywhere on that side and won the point, but he wanted to make a statement—and so he lost.

The fact is that most of the famous bad boys of pro tennis—John McEnroe, Goran Ivanisevic, Ilie Nastasie, etc.—have known exactly what they were doing. Their feisty temperaments fit with their attacking style, allowing them to take control of the game. On the other hand, many great players have been known for their cool, collected demeanor. They play a measured, careful game, often on the defensive until their opponents make mistakes.

Common Temperaments

Defensive baseliners: consistent, patient, and relaxed

Attackers: type A, driven, impatient, and controlling

All-around players: patient, self-driven, calculating, and studious

So if you know your temperament is naturally impatient, make that work for you by developing your attacking skills. You know you'll never be satisfied with an endless ground-stroke game, so you might as well learn to attack properly. But if you're a calmer sort, work at consistency in your defensive game.

And as you evaluate your opponent, see how his temperament matches his style. If the player has a patient temperament and a defensive style, what's the best way for you to respond? If you're a defensive player yourself, you could try to outlast your opponent. But if you're more comfortable attacking, you can take control of the game—just be smart about it. Your opponent's defensive tendency to stand back three to five feet from the baseline should allow you to add some short balls and angled balls to your repertoire. Normally these would invite the other player to challenge or attack, but your patient opponent may go right back on defense.

If your opponent has a driven temperament and an attacking style, you can try to force low-percentage attacks. Keep the player on the run and deep in the court, but be ready with a lob or passing shot when necessary.

Also be alert to situations where a player's temperament doesn't match his or her style. An impatient player may be trying to play defensively—so a lot of shots to zone 3 (the zone of decision) will drive that player nuts. Or a player may try to attack but not really have the guts for it. Such players hedge their bets, resulting in attack shots that are easy to return. If you spot these tendencies early, capitalize on them.

Make your opponent's temperament work for you.

Analysis Progression 3: Taking Your Temperament

Identify your temperament and how it affects your play.

Step 1: Which type of temperament would you say you have?

Step 2: Does it fit the way you like to play?

Step 3: If not, which should you change—your temperament or your playing style? How will you change this?

Developing Your Style

There are definite advantages and disadvantages to each style of play. A defensive baseliner keeps balls in play and is precise. As a result, such players are successful in the core and mileage stages because they are hitting more balls in the court. Their opponents are beating themselves with unforced errors and aggressive errors. The patient mentality of defensive baseliners also is to be commended because they play themselves into good tennis—that is, by playing more strokes per point, they get into a good rhythm and naturally can correct any mistakes in their form.

At the intermediate level, attacking baseliners and attackers make more errors because their style is more difficult. In ice-skating a routine with a quad is more difficult to execute than a triple and therefore earns a higher score from the judges. Unfortunately in tennis you don't get extra points for degree of difficulty. But as your skills advance to the fine-tuning stage, the difficult shots begin to pay off.

Recently I ran into Chuck Gambill, whose family is from my hometown in Spokane, Washington. His son, Jan Michael, is an aggressive baseliner with a big serve who hits two-handed off the backhand and forehand. He recently had beaten a string of great players including Philippoussis and Agassi. When I asked Chuck about his son's sudden success, he said, "Jan Michael is still playing the same game he always has, hitting the ball hard to the corners." He then paused briefly and added, "The only difference is that he is not making as many errors." Jan Michael Gambill has worked long and hard on his attacking style and his best tennis is yet to come.

Attacking players need time, lots of practice, and reassurance. Fitness is key to the attacking player who relies on explosive movements (see chapter 7, page 125). Tennis fundamentals need to be stressed with emphasis placed on shot selection. For example, attacking baseliners should not try to hit winners from six feet behind the baseline or off the first ball that bounces deep in the court. Believe me, they will try.

The all-around or all-court player can evolve in a variety of ways. Some are defensive baseliners who learn how to attack and start doing so successfully at the fine-tuning stage. Others are attacking baseliners who learn to come in behind their weapons and also become good at counterattacking and playing good defense. Still others are attacking players who always want to come to the net, but eventually they improve their ground strokes to the point that they can rally and hit winners from the baseline.

Usually styles evolve in the mileage stage, as players are encouraged to do what they don't do best. Say you are an offensive baseliner and you're leading 30-0 in a game on serve. You have improved your volley and serve in practice, so why not try serving and volleying to put additional pressure on your opponent just by coming in?

Martina Hingis is an outstanding all-court player.

I've seen another scenario from players working on their long-term development. They're trying to become all-around players who can rally, come in, hit winners, and do whatever it takes to win. That's a great goal, but often they lose in the mileage or early fine-tuning stages because they try too many things. Such players need to set their priorities, like a last-place team in the last month of the season. Is it more important to win today or to develop for the future? If the game must be won, these all-around-players-in-the-making need to play "according to the score." When a game's on the line, execute the shots you're sure of, but you can experiment a bit on the early points. Those experimental shots may be hit-or-miss today, but next month they'll be winners.

Analysis Progression 4: Style Evolution

Plot your course as you develop into the player you want to become.

Step 1: Identify your style of play.

Step 2: Is this the style you want?

Step 3: If not, then which style must you practice more?

Step 4: Practice your chosen style when leading by two or more points.

Step 5: Select two drills from the weapons development lists.

Developing Your Weapons

Before playing your next practice set, try a couple of drills from the following lists, which will help you finish points in ways that fit your style of play.

Aggressive-Baseliner Drills

Big forehand and come in. Play games to four points and award two points for a winning volley or smash.

Back up and hit forehand. Your partner feeds a high, deep ball to your forehand, and then the point begins.

Big forehand, three-quarter court. Place a cone at the net, three feet from the sideline on your backhand side. Hit every ball to the right (forehand side) of that cone with your forehand; on the other side, hit backhand. Play to four points.

Second-serve game. Play to seven points, having your opponent do only second serves, which you challenge or attack.

Two-point lead on return with big forehand. Start games leading 30-0.

Rally ball comes back, run around big forehand. Play to four points with your opponent taking your three-quarter-pace serve and returning it up the middle of the court. Run around the return and hit your forehand.

First strike player after your return or serve. Use this game to develop anticipation and court positioning. Try to strike first, taking the offensive and putting your opponent under pressure. Do this off the serve if possible, or off your opponent's return of serve. (On any ball that is even remotely "yellow" or "green," you should challenge or attack.) Score three points for an outright winner, two for a forced error, one for anything else. Play to seven points.

Inside the court. Both you and your partner stand inside the court and play a ground-stroking game to 11 points. This develops your ability to challenge and attack balls by giving your opponent less time to respond.

Mini-tennis big forehand. Your opponent stands in either the forehand or backhand corner of the court behind the baseline and only can hit the ball back to you in the service boxes. You must run around and hit forehands from both boxes. Play to seven points.

Defensive-Baseliner Drills

Ground-stroke game. Play the first three balls deep to your opponent's forehand corner (try backhand later), then start playing the point. Play to 11 points.

Over the service line. Play a baseline game to 11 points, but each ball has to be over the service line or you lose the point.

Second serve and return, opponent comes in. In this game the server is on defense. The returner challenges or attacks the ball off the easy serve, by chipping the ball with underspin or hitting over the ball with topspin and approaching the net.

Change of direction. Rally crosscourt with your opponent until she hits the ball down the line, which starts the game. You can then play open court. This game also can be practiced by first hitting down the line and having the point begin with a crosscourt shot.

Four-square. Divide the court into four squares (by imagining the center line extending back to the baseline). Then play games of four-square in which you cannot hit to the same square twice in a row. Play games to four points.

Attacking-Player Drills

Serve-and-volley. Practice having your opponent return your three-quarter-pace serve back to you. The return can be at your feet or with pace. The point then begins when you volley into the open court.

Serve-and-volley on first and second serves. Play tiebreakers, with the server playing a serve-and-volley every time and the returner putting the ball anywhere in the court.

Chip and charge. Your opponent hits a second serve and you come in. Play a game to seven points.

Hit and come in. Do the same as chip and charge, but you're hitting topspin.

Serve and sneak. Start with a serve and then rally the ball to your opponent's weakness, hitting the ball slightly higher than normal and sneaking in to the net to volley your opponent's response. Instead of the high balls, try sneaking in after an angle/deep shot combination.

Navratilova drill. Your opponent stands inside the baseline with a basket and feeds balls at you while you are on the net defending yourself with volleys. Use caution to avoid injury.

Five-ball drill. Your opponent feeds balls to you from the basket and you hit an approach, volley, smash, angle volley, and drop volley. Each time you execute all five shots without an error, you get a point. Play a game until you have reached seven points or made three errors.

Up and back. You are on the net, volleying into the right or left half of the court. Your opponent can lob, pass you, or put the ball on your feet. You constantly must be adjusting up and back. Play to seven points.

Jim Grabb half-volley game. Start with a ground-stroking game, but on one of the first three ground strokes step in and take the ball on the rise with a half volley. Then follow your shot to the net and play out the point. Play to 11 points.

All-Around-Player Drills

First return, come to the net. After returning your opponent's first serve, come to the net.

Short-long drill. Play a game of two-square, dividing your opponent's court into two squares (imagine the extension of the center line). You're not allowed to hit into the same square twice in a row. Use just the right or left side of the court and alternating short and long shots. Play to five points.

Michael Chang drill. One player stands at the net on one side and is permitted to hit placement volleys and overheads at three-quarter pace anywhere in the court but no winners. The other player must hit to the side where the volleyer is standing, hitting lobs or trying to hit through (or past) the net player, forcing a mistake. Play to 11 points. The loser does 20 jumping jacks.

Serve-and-volley game. Server hits a three-quarter-pace serve and goes to the net. The other player returns to the approaching server, who then volleys the return into the open court. The returner then launches a lob or hits a passing shot and the point is played out.

Ground-stroke game. Players are awarded three points for winning volleys or smashes. Play to 11 points.

Petr Korda game. You're at the net, with your opponent at the baseline. See if you can hit 10 volleys or smashes without missing. Your opponent will make this difficult for you by directing you side to side and deep in the court.

Limiting Unforced Errors

No question about it: you're going to make mistakes on the tennis court. There will be days when you can't seem to do anything right. There will be matches when your opponent seems to be hitting all your weak spots. There will be times when you're doing great—until the game is on the line, and then you choke. There will be points when you get a perfect floater, something you could put away in your sleep, and you shank it into the net.

I'm all for successful thinking and positive imagery (see chapter 8), but you can't deny the fact that mistakes will occur. The question is: *what are you going to do about them?* Mistakes bring out the mental toughness in true tennis players. Sometimes they make you want to curl up and die, but you have to drag yourself back up, learn from your errors, and improve your game. The further you get in your tennis development, the more of a factor your mental game will be. As you get better, your opponents will get better, too. You each will be able to execute just about any shot you set your mind to. So, which shots are you setting your mind to? That's where the big difference will occur. As an advanced player, your success or failure will be based about 80 to 90 percent on your mental decisions.

We've already discussed shot selection (chapter 5), and we've covered the ways of analyzing your opponent's style, the conditions, and the game situation (chapter 10). Now we need to focus on an even tougher subject: analyzing your mistakes, preventing them, and learning to overcome them when they occur.

The Points Against You

How does your opponent win points against you? First of all, *by hitting winners!* That's pretty obvious, but every winner by your opponent is a learning opportunity for you. Pay attention to what her weapons are and how you played into those weapons. What kind of ball did you send, enabling your opponent to rip that unhittable shot? Obviously, you want to avoid doing that again. Even if you're getting aced, take a look at where your opponent is tossing the ball. That should give you a clue about where to set up for the return.

Second, your opponent forces you to make errors *by hitting shots that you reach but cannot return over the net.* Analyze these points the same way. How are you setting up these shots? Is your opponent telegraphing where the shot is going? Can you anticipate the location and get into place sooner? Are there certain spots on the court to which you always have trouble getting? Do you need to adjust your positioning?

Third, your opponent scores points *on your unforced errors.* This is when you are in position to play the ball over the net but don't. The following are the most common types of unforced errors and how you can correct them:

- **Execution errors:** Technically you are not executing properly.

  Solution: Review your SMARTS to figure out why you did not execute. Sometimes a player's swinging skills will break down, but execution errors also occur with seeing, movement, adjusting, rotation, and transfer skills. Work especially hard on any shots that consistently break down in your game. Go back to the basics. For instance, if you have a weak smash, make it a point to get help on your smash (chapter 3), slow down, work on your form, get your rhythm, and practice as often as possible.

- **Aggressive errors:** You tried to do too much. For instance, you went after the high sitter in the middle of the court and just hit it long.

Steffi Graf learned from the aggressive errors she made as a junior player.

Solution: Look to repeat the shot again but give yourself a greater margin of error. For example, don't try to paint the baseline—aim just past the service line. If you're still hitting it long, then try stringing your racquet a bit tighter. That can help you gain more control over your aggressive errors. Mentally speaking, these are the best kind of errors to have. They mean you're in the game and trying hard. As a junior player, Steffi Graf had an unforced error rate of over 27 percent, most of those aggressive in nature (Jacobson 1993) So don't despair; you're in good company.

- **Pressure errors:** You respond to the pressure of a game situation, an easy shot, or off-court circumstances by failing to execute basic shots. For example, your opponent is off the court and has fallen down, but you're at the net and miss the easy volley.

Solution: Pressure errors come down to your perception of the situation. On easy shots, you actually can be distracted by an out-of-place opponent or the wide range of options open to you. Redirect your attention to your execution of the shot or your tactic of placing the shot. To use the above example, you might use hard focus, keeping your dominant eye on the approaching ball while your peripheral vision is aware that your opponent is on the court, or focusing on the tactical cue of *play into the open court*. Lack of mental focus is the problem when you're dealing with the pressure of game, set, match, and even setup points. Most pressure errors occur on the first shot of a point, before a player's body settles into the rhythm of the game (Jacobson 1993). You'll see double faults and missed returns when players allow negative imagery to throw off their normal performance. Focus your mind on what you're trying to accomplish. Take it step by step.

- **Strategic errors:** These are bad choices you make that play into an opponent's strengths rather than weaknesses. Say you're attempting to get to the net as often as possible, but your opponent is a very good counterpuncher who really enjoys playing against an attacker. Oops.

Solution: Knowledge of various playing styles is your best way to eliminate poor strategic decisions. This will come with experience (see also chapter 10). Prepare as thoroughly as possible for a match by learning about your opponent's style. Formulate a game plan that targets your opponent's weaknesses. But if that doesn't work, switch to plan B. If you don't have a plan B, make one up, once you decide that plan A isn't working. Your strategy is ultimately judged by your execution and the outcome. If you are winning important points such as setup, game, set, and match points, keep your strategy. If not, consider changing it.

- **Tactical errors:** Certain shots and combinations that make up your strategy are consistently failing. For example, you're serving and volleying—which is a good strategy against an opponent who doesn't like to be attacked—but you repeatedly try to finish the point with a cute drop volley (wrong tactic) instead of punching the ball into the open court. Bill Jacobson, founder and president of Sports Software, Inc., said that Boris Becker used to have trouble against Andre Agassi because Becker had a low percentage of first serves in play and frequently served and volleyed on his second serve. Agassi loved to take the ball early on those points, which resulted in lots of Becker volley errors.

Solution: Review your arsenal of shots according to your ability to execute them and your opponent's ability to handle them. Be willing to limit or remove shots that aren't working with this opponent. In the example mentioned, Becker's best

Taking deep abdominal breaths throughout your match can help you offset fatigue late in the match.

play was to stay back on second serves and work his way in to the net—when he received a ball that he felt he could challenge or attack—or make more first serves. Normally serve-and-volley on the second serve was a great way for Becker to put pressure on his opponent—but it didn't work with Agassi. Becker had to choose other tactics.

- **Fatigue errors:** You fail to execute properly because you're weary. This happens late in matches, on long points, and on hot days.

  Solution: You may need to work on your overall fitness (see chapter 7), but also consider your breathing. How do you breathe when you're tired? Try taking deep abdominal breaths throughout the match. Work hard on your conditioning. The point *after* a long point often yields fatigue errors. Players such as Thomas Muster intentionally play faster after a long point because they know that they have the stamina to outlast the competition.

Mental Skill Progression 1: Something in the Err

Learn to evaluate your mistakes.

Step 1: Ask someone who knows tennis to chart your next match. Be sure she notes the type of error, the shot, and the game score.

Step 2: What types of errors did you make? Based on the charting data, what portion of your errors were execution, aggressive, pressure, strategic, tactical, or fatigue related?

Step 3: On what specific shots did you make the most errors? Based on these data, plan an extra 15-minute practice period to work on the shots that gave you the most trouble.

Court Surfaces and Unforced Errors

Different court surfaces tend to bring out certain types of unforced errors. Table 11.1 shows unforced errors published by the United States Tennis Association (USTA 1993). Frequency is defined as high (Hi), medium (Med), and low (Lo). So if you're playing on a hard court, be especially careful about aggressive and tactical errors, since these are more common. On clay, look out for pressure, tactical, and fatigue errors.

Table 11.1—Unforced Errors			
Type of unforced error	Grass	Hard	Clay
Execution	Hi	Lo	Med
Aggressive	Hi	Med	Med
Pressure	Hi	Lo	Hi
Tactical[1]	Lo	Med	Hi
Fatigue	Hi	Lo	Hi
[1]The USTA groups what I'm calling strategic errors with tactical errors.			

Also of interest is the statistic comparing forced errors versus unforced errors on different surfaces (see table 11.2). The faster surfaces of grass and hard court make it easier to force your opponent into errors. The slipperiness of clay and its effect on the ball yield more unforced errors.

Table 11.2—Errors on Different Surfaces		
	Percent of unforced errors	Percent of points won forcing
Grass	13.0	36.3
Hard	16.9	32.7
Clay	19.6	29.7

Error Clusters

Errors are part of the game of tennis. However, errors often can lead to more errors. In your club, at school, or among your friends, watch how players perform after making an error. Frequently you'll see them lose clusters of points. Of course this leads to frustration, loss of concentration, and sometimes tanking the match.

These error clusters go way beyond the physical, though they may look like problems in technique or execution. And they're not mental errors of strategy or tactics; rather they're *emotional* in nature. The players' emotions are affecting everything else in their game, resulting in clusters of lost points.

Let's say Wendy is going up against a very good serve-and-volley player, one of the best in her club. In a couple of previous matches with this player, Wendy has lost badly, but she's determined to do better this time. She has worked hard to develop the tactics she will use against this serve-and-volley style. So Wendy comes into this match confident that she can win. And she performs well for a while, holding serve in the first set to 4-4. But then Wendy makes a dumb mistake. She loses concentration and makes another unforced error. Her opponent breaks serve, and Wendy suddenly loses hope. Her commitment to try to play better is waning. She thought she could beat this player, but apparently she can't. Flooded with sudden self-doubt, Wendy loses intensity. Or she gets angry at herself for making these mistakes and begins to focus on herself rather than her opponent.

In any case, she has made the situation far worse than necessary because she made her errors bigger than they were. Let's rewind to that first "dumb mistake" at four games all. What was Wendy saying to herself at that moment? Probably something like, "Oh, no, here I go again. I knew this was too good to last. I thought I could beat this player, but I guess I can't." Or, "I am so stupid. I had a chance to win this set, maybe the match, but now I've gone and ruined it all. How could I be so stupid?"

Notice that she is seeing this mistake as more than just one lost point. It's the ruination of the whole match, an indication of her true inferiority, the beginning of the end. And, as we've seen, that approach can become a self-fulfilling prophecy.

But what if she minimized the mistake? What if she told herself something like this? "Oops. That was dumb. But it's only a point. I have a great feel today, so I should be able to make up for that—if I bear down and keep playing well." It may not guarantee a victory. She might still lose the set and the match, but she wouldn't see a cluster of errors due to lack of focus. She wouldn't talk herself into losing.

You've been there, haven't you? You've blown some easy shots and walked away mad at yourself. You have called yourself every name in the book, haven't you? You've shaken your head and stomped the court and thrown your racquet—and thoroughly botched the next three points.

Errors happen. But error clusters don't have to. Keep your composure and play one point at a time. Don't make one mistake into a federal case. Shake it off and start anew.

Mental Skill Progression 2: Handling Your Mistakes

Stay in control after making errors.

Step 1: Develop a posterror ritual. Instead of ranting and raving, send your energy in a more positive direction. Try quickly turning your back on your opponent and walking back to the baseline, while taking a few deep abdominal breaths to help you recover. This may seem strange, and it's not for everyone, but you might want to create a simple "sorry" movement—something like a hand to your head or hair, tapping the racquet, or closing your eyes—by which you tell yourself that you goofed and you'll try to do better. Some would say that players subconsciously punish themselves by making more errors after a particularly bad mistake. This ritual is a way of removing the need to do that.

Step 2: Do a quick posterror analysis. What type of error was it? Forced or unforced? Aggressive, pressure, tactical, or what? What went wrong? Keep a mental file and after the match jot down your observations in a notebook on how many times you've made this error. If a particular shot hasn't worked three times, make a mental note to change it. Stay away from it in this match, and work on it in your next practice.

Step 3: Improve your imagery. Instead of rehashing the mistake you made, imagine yourself making the same shot properly. Take a practice swing the way it should have been done.

Step 4: Forget all of that and prepare for your next point. Get in place, in a ready position, seeing everything you need to see, planning your return. Or get ready to serve, visualizing where you're sending the ball.

Dealing with Pressure

Dr. James Loehr
Sport psychologist

In training for any sport, there are three essential elements. One is the issue of *talent,* which is predetermined but clearly a factor in athletic performance. Then there are the *acquired skills*—biomechanical skills, level of fitness, and any other abilities that are required for you to be in a sport. The other factor is *the ability to summon all of that talent and skill in a competitive arena.*

What are the skills, tools, and acquired learning that enable players to bring to life their talent, skill, and genius *under pressure*—and to do so consistently over time? That is an acquired set of skills, to be sure. Even though parents and environmental influences play a very important role early on, there is no evidence to suggest that this is an inherent ability. Great coaches always have had an instinct about how to motivate performance under pressure; this is an important aspect of great coaching.

To identify the factors that contribute most fundamentally to pressure performance, I have over the years developed my own toughening model. I started out looking at *mental* toughening, but then as it all began to boil down, I started to realize that the most important concept is really the whole issue of emotions.

What we are trying to deal with here is stress, and as discussed in chapter 8, stress is a biochemical event. It's also very much an emotional event. Stress is the way you respond to a particular stressor in your environment. So emotions will pretty much determine how you *perform* in that environment. I view emotions then as the link between the mind and body. That is how they're being treated in many other areas of research.

There are two tools for controlling emotions. One is mental or cognitive; we would call it *mental training.* The body also can play a profound role in altering the chemistry of emotion and the physiology involved in an emotional response. We know that emotions such as anger and fear generally complicate an athlete's ability to summon his best in competition. But athletes have a unique response to the pressures of competition that generally produces brilliance or consistently high performance. Every athlete has his own psychophysical state of arousal in which he performs his best. In the early years of my training, I heard different athletes using similar words over and over again in a wide variety of sports to describe what it felt like when they were performing at their best.

Ideal Performance State

What does this state of arousal feel like? They were so unanimous in their descriptions that I began to talk about a universal state, eventually referring to it as an *ideal performance state* (IPS). The feeling most commonly reported is one of relaxation, the sense that there is no pressure, which is quite surprising. There is a state of high energy. It is a wonderful, quiet energy that leaves you with a sense of optimism and spirit, of wanting to be there, of being automatic, instinctive, and confident. There is a sense of intense focus and concentration, a sense of effortlessness, a sense of being in control. This is how athletes repeatedly described their finest hours.

If I were to use one word to describe that emotional response, the word would be *challenge*. They are challenged by whatever they face, with a sense of optimism and present focus. That is, the athlete tends to be preoccupied with the present moment, as opposed to the past or future, and she is very aware of where she is, in tune with what is happening at that very minute. The more anchored these athletes are to the past, the more likely they will become connected to negative emotions and feelings of anger. If they become too occupied with the future, then they get caught up with nerves. This ideal performance state is a very much present-centered phenomenon.

The next challenge was to see how we could accelerate control over this special stress response. Two broad categories have emerged as the most important dimensions in this type of training: performer skills and acting skills.

Performer Skills

Performer skills are designed to move emotions and physiology in targeted directions on demand. What are some of the tools you can use to harness your emotions when a bad line call occurs or you have tremendous pressure to perform, or you lose your ranking, or you have parents leaning on you? How can we control this cascade of chemistry that is occurring inside us?

One of the best ways to control your physiology is to build a ritual around it. Whether you're dealing with public speaking, jet lag, or going crazy in traffic, if you want to get control of yourself, build a ritual around the activity. Professional athletes have built rituals around serving, returning serve, walking on court, and packing their bags! It's a way of maintaining control.

There are so many things in tennis that are beyond our control. Rituals give you some control, even if it's just taking a deep breath before serving or bouncing the ball a few times. Having a regimented, sequential routine is very much like what NASA does when launching a sophisticated spacecraft. You will never hear mission control just say, "Let her rip!" or, "Wing it!" Yet the launching of an IPS state is more complex than any missile ever launched by mission control. There are so many complex systems that have to be synchronized and harmonized in this event that the rituals really serve to create a sense of rhythm and control, anchoring these complex mechanisms to specific events.

The most important moments in tennis come *between points*. That is where I have done most of my work, seeking ways of thinking and acting that will produce the greatest likelihood that IPS will occur at the start of the point. It's important to ritualize that whole time. But if a ritual turns into a superstition, then it becomes a problem. It can become a false belief, and that takes away your control. Yet rituals have proven themselves to performers in every arena—from Olympic athletes to high-stress surgeons going into the operating room to pilots going through preflight checklists. Anyone in a high-stress arena basically has learned that this is the best way to deal with it.

There are good rituals and bad rituals. Everybody has responses for how they handle mistakes. You can see it in how they walk when they feel cheated or disappointed. These responses get to be habitual. Yet many of them are not contributing to an IPS state but actually taking you in another direction. Some rituals are dead because they don't really summon the sense of belief, accuracy, and precision with focus. So what I'm trying to do is to bring to life the emotions and physiology that make things happen on demand. Sometimes rituals become old and outdated. Rituals cannot be things that you think about; they have to be automatic and instinctive. They have to truly summon the focus, the right look—and all of this has to be sequentially anchored.

Acting Skills

The next area is *acting skills;* yes, just like actors in Hollywood. Good actors summon real emotions and the appropriate physiology on demand. They use images and thoughts to drive their emotions in a very precise way, and then they act with their body in a certain way to bring the script to life. The script in tennis and other sports is IPS. We have learned that images are very powerful stimulators for driving physiology and emotions. We even know that the muscles in the face can powerfully trigger autonomic reactors that help to summon a particular emotional response. So you need to imagine things that drive the emotions.

That's what I have been trying to accomplish with players. It's not to hold in emotion or to choke out emotion, but to summon the emotions and make them real. If players are carrying anger, that may hurt their game, but they can benefit if they genuinely convert this anger to a fighting sense of challenge and actually use whatever mechanisms they need to make that happen.

All of this time I've been an acting coach! I didn't realize it at first because I always thought that acting was phony. But then I learned that the best actors stir real emotions within themselves. *Bad* actors produce false emotions, and we have a lot of bad actors in sports. They're bad actors because (a) they don't follow the script and (b) they cannot bring to life real emotions of fun, enjoyment, and confidence. They need practice! Just as a Hollywood actor needs practice summoning a particular emotion on demand, so must tennis players practice achieving IPS. That involves working with your face, your walk, even the way you carry your head and shoulders in the heat of battle.

Four Stages

As I intensively studied all the best players, I identified four distinct phases between points. One is a very strong sense of presence immediately after the point is over, refusing to allow a contaminating emotion to enter during the first 25 seconds. This is the *positive physical response* stage.

For about 6 to10 seconds there's a period of relaxation in which a player mentally goes away and skillfully summons a *relaxation response*. His eyes go to the strings and he walks with presence and really settles down. The greater the stress of the preceding point, the longer he takes in this stage.

Third, the players take three to five seconds to *prepare for what they want to do in the next point*. They get a picture of what they want to happen, based on the score.

Then comes the *ritual state*. Of course, the whole thing is a ritual, but this is where they go into an automatic state, bouncing the ball or whatever. It's the launch of IPS in a purely instinctive way. They're summoning their confidence, focus, and intensity.

Putting It on the Line

I know, you don't have a lot of time to spend on the mental aspect of your game. In the mileage level, you're trying to play three to five sets a week with different opponents. And as you continue to work on the physical aspects of your game, it's easy to overlook mental skills. But don't. I'll give you three reasons.

First, these mental skills will help you in every aspect of your life. What do you do when you're not playing tennis? Working in an office, going to school, or taking care of a family? Whatever you do for a living, it involves performance of some kind. If you learn to achieve an ideal performance state on demand, it will improve any kind of performance you do. It will help you focus on your work and help you deal with stress.

Second, good mental skills multiply your tennis potential. They're not just an add-on, something you tack on to your other tennis skills. No, they enhance every other aspect of your game. Your mental focus will improve your serve, your return, your passing shots, and your smashes. You name it, it gets better when you bring your mind to the court with you. Ten plus 10 is 20, and as you've developed different shots, you've added onto your tennis ability . . . 10 plus 10, plus another 10. But 10 *times* 10 is 100, and every time you apply your mental focus to a shot, it gets multiplied. Don't underestimate the value of mental skills!

Third, it really doesn't take much time and effort to develop your mental game. Once you develop your rituals, they will become habitual. Take some time—even riding to or from the court—to think up helpful images that will focus your emotions on the court. Perhaps you might memorize some lines to tell yourself in certain situations.

And go back through Dr. Loehr's four-phase ritual between points: stonewalling, relaxing, preparing, and bouncing (or whatever you do in your ritual). Make it your own, and use it as you play.

Marcelo Rios prepares to return serve.

Mental Skill Progression 3: The Way the Ball Bounces

Develop a between-point ritual.

Step 1: Go out on an empty court and pretend you're playing a match. Take a real racquet and ball with you. Practice the first part of Dr. Loehr's four-stage ritual—25 seconds of *positive physical response*.

Pretend you've just hit a winner. Now walk back to position with a sense of control. Be glad, but not prideful—there is more work to be done. Essentially, during this period of 25 seconds, you're shielding yourself from strong emotions—positive or negative—that would throw off your game. Practice a strong, relaxed walk.

Now pretend you've just outlasted your opponent in a long ground-stroke point. Your opponent just hit it into the net. You're tired, glad to win the point, but you have to get ready for the next point. Practice your 25-second walk.

Now pretend you've just tried a passing shot that went out. Nice try, but a narrow miss. Practice your walk back into position, shaking off the error, staying in control.

Now pretend you just made an awful shot, missing an easy smash, putting it in the net. Practice your walk.

Pretend you're down 40-love and it's match point. Pretend you're up 40-love at match point. Pretend you've just been aced with a 100-mile-per-hour serve. Pretend your opponent just faked you out with a drop shot. Pretend you just got a bad call against you.

Step 2: Work on your 6-to-10-second *relaxation response*. Look at your racquet, imagine a peaceful scene, take a deep breath or two, hum a tune to yourself. This is the moment when you can feel the joy, pain, or anger of the preceding point—and do something with it. Let any negative feelings sail away with your breath.

Go back through some of the "pretend" scenarios from step 1, adding these extra seconds of relaxation.

Step 3: Now add *preparation*. Pretend you're serving, and "see" the ball landing in precise spots in the service box. Imagine a two- or three-shot point, employing different tactics. Pretend you're returning serve. Where will you put the return? Then what?

Here is where you would take a practice swing if you need it.

Step 4: You already may have a ritual you follow before you serve or return. If not, here's the time to develop one. Bounce the ball, look at the service court, and go into your toss. Or take a few split steps in a ready position as you await a serve. Find some movements that can become second nature to you.

Now, set up different scenarios for yourself —score, opponent, serving or returning, how the point goes. Play it out on your side of the court, moving as if you were actually playing those points. After each "point," go through the four steps of your ritual—walking back, relaxing, preparing, and going into your serve or return.

We tend to learn more from the matches we lose than those we win, simply because we want to try and stop losing. However, win or lose, analyze the mistakes you made, what your opponent did well, and what you would do differently. Ask yourself if you made unforced errors or if your opponent forced you to make mistakes. Maybe your strategy wasn't correct or fatigue caught up with you late in the third set. Maybe you just couldn't win the pressure points or your execution was off, or perhaps you were just too aggressive. Think of your game as a high-performance Formula One race car. With each lap you tighten nuts and bolts and add parts that you need for peak performance and to win the race.

Adjusting to Tough Conditions

You always are making choices in the game of tennis. Where will you hit the ball? Crosscourt? Down the line? Short in the court or deep? How will you hit the ball? With topspin or slice? With pace or height? Will you step forward, taking the ball on the rise and following your shot to the net? Or will you stay on the defensive?

Your mental computer always is churning the possibilities and calculating the percentages. As you become more experienced, you get a better idea of what works for you and what doesn't. You develop a feel for what shots to use in which situations. You program your mental computer by constantly reading data on the court, including your opponent's temperament and style of play (see chapter 10). As you evaluate your opponent, you're better able to anticipate what kinds of balls she will send your way as well as your most effective response. I've also discussed red, yellow, and green balls—how placement and ball characteristics affect your shot tactics (see chapter 5). If tennis were played in a controlled environment, like a scientific lab, that data might be all you'd need. But you'll be looking up at different skies, hitting into different winds, bouncing the ball on different court surfaces; all of these factors change the dynamics of the game.

I have discussed how environmental conditions affect *your* play. That's pretty basic stuff—hit harder into a headwind, change your stance or toss so you don't stare into the sun. But now here's a new wrinkle: How do the playing conditions affect *your opponent's* game? Wind, sun, rain, and court surface all will make a difference—you can bank on that. If you learn to analyze the conditions and how they change your opponent's game, then you can take advantage of the situation. It's like having an extra player on your team.

Wind

How strong is the wind? From which direction is it blowing? That's your raw data. Will you have to shorten your backswing, lower your toss, or let overheads bounce? Will you need to hit more balls to one side of the court? Does the wind reduce your margin of error on winners or passing shots? Naturally you'll be making these adjustments in your own play. But your opponent also will have to make those adjustments. How will that change his style of play?

Tune in to your opponent's weaknesses, but pay special attention to any weaknesses created or exaggerated by the conditions. Use the SMARTS system to evaluate what's happening.

Opponent Playing Into a Strong Wind

Can your opponent keep the ball deep to you when hitting into a strong (10-mph-or-higher) wind? If not, then expect to receive some short balls. Move inside the baseline, even when returning serves, but resist the temptation to approach the net quickly unless this is your style of play. It's better to wear your opponent out by placing your ground strokes side to side.

Run your opponent for a while; you can take advantage of a short ball to hit a well-placed approach shot (placement will help you more than pace) and move forward for a potential putaway.

Hit your first serves so they bounce wide, again forcing your opponent to run. Remember that your serve will be wind-aided, so you can reduce pace and add spin. The running tactics should cause fatigue, since the other player has to work extra hard to hit the ball deep. But be careful that you don't hit the ball out. Use topspin and aim for the service line.

Seeing. Does your opponent seem to recognize the wind conditions? Some players get so focused on their game that they don't adapt to the wind until later in the match.

Movement. Is your opponent getting near your shots? Is he working more with his legs to get into position to hit into the wind? Is he lunging at the ball? If you're succeeding in wearing him out, keep running him. If not, then you may need to use those short balls to challenge or attack.

Adjusting. Is your opponent getting to the ball well balanced and achieving proper distance to the ball? Is he adjusting well to balls that bounce high or low? If so, then keep running him until he tires—or until *you* tire, in which case you could go for a more aggressive approach. Has your opponent made the most important adjustment with the hand—to open the racquet face slightly at contact and to aim higher over the net? If not, then you can expect the ball to be short.

Rotation. Is the increased ball speed from your shots forcing your opponent to hit from a more open stance, with less rotation? If so, then he will hit weaker shots and possibly spray his shots wide.

Transfer. Is your opponent lunging at balls? Then you can expect weaker shots that are shorter in the court.

Swing. Has your opponent shortened his backswing to compensate for the increased ball speed of your approaching shot? If not, then you can expect him to shank balls, miss by a large margin, or hit short.

Opponent Playing With a Strong Tailwind

Some players don't adjust well to a strong (10-mph-or-higher) tailwind, and maybe your opponent is one of those. See whether she moves inside the baseline and goes far enough forward to meet the balls you send. Does she add more spin and aim shorter in the court? If she continues to stand tall and hit the ball strong and flat, you can expect the ball to go out.

Take note of how your opponent plays with a tailwind and work to gain an offensive position early.

But if your opponent does adapt to the wind, you've got your work cut out for you. You can expect to receive balls fast and deep in the court. You need to hit these back *hard*, with height and less spin. Open the racquet face to add height. You need all the power you can muster. Bobby Banck, coach of Mary Joe Fernandez, urges all his players to work harder and expend more energy when playing into the wind. Your opponent should try to run you, so keep your legs moving. Work hard and fast to get into position to hit solid strokes.

With all this effort, you probably won't survive a drawn-out ground-stroke game. You want to gain an offensive position pretty early, but the wind will keep pushing you back to defense. Take any opportunity you find. If you're playing a player who hits flat, then go to the net. The wind will push her passing shots and lobs right out of the court.

Seeing. Again, see if your opponent is aware of the wind and is adjusting to it.

Movement. Is your opponent lunging forward to hit the ball because it's dropping shorter than she expects (with the wind knocking it down)? That's a good sign for you, because it results in a weaker shot, or an error. You could take advantage by intentionally hitting short, but use an angle or disguise a drop shot. If you set it up properly, your opponent should be in trouble.

Adjusting. Has your opponent adjusted to the wind and moved inside the baseline, staying low, with flexed legs? If so, she's ready to put spin on the ball. If not, the ball may sail out.

Rotation. Is she taking a shorter backswing, since she's closer to the net? If not, that's more free points for you. Too large of a backswing will put too much power in the shot, sending it out.

Transfer. Your best hope is that your opponent is putting too much power into the ball and hitting it out. Is she stepping strongly into her shots, especially transition shots? If so, you may be watching the ball go past you.

Swing. A controlled, measured swing that imparts topspin on the part of your opponent is bad news for you. But if she's swinging wildly, that's good news. Let her play. Put the ball low in front of her and let her take her wild swings; she will give you the game on her errors. It's not a bad idea to come to the net against a big swinger (or one with no spin). Chances are, her passing shots and lobs will float long.

Crosswinds

If there's a strong crosswind, you want to keep the ball on the side of the court from which the wind is blowing (the upwind side). That way, the wind will blow the ball in to your opponent's body, jamming him. You also hope to see him hit balls wide (on the downwind side), blown out by the wind.

If your opponent receives the ball on the upwind side and gets jammed, expect him to hit down the line and short. If he manages to adjust well, running around the ball to get a full swing, expect a return with pace, crosscourt, aided by the wind.

If your opponent has to run downwind for the ball, possibly requiring an extra stretch, expect the ball down the line. It will be hard for your opponent to run, set, and rotate for a strong crosscourt return.

Use the wind on your own shots. When serving to the downwind side, kick or slice balls out wide so they're difficult to return. Serving toward the wind, aim directly at your opponent, going for the jam. In regular play, hit angles and inside-outs to the downwind side. "Hitting winners with the wind going to the open court is a great way to draw a weaker response and gain court position," states Andrew Finn, former director of the Hitting Hot Program at Ivan Lendl's tennis center in Connecticut. "When hitting with the crosswind, you should expect a weaker response from your opponent, which is an ideal time to come to the net. From the baseline you want to mix it up, setting up your points by hitting into the wind (upwind side) and then hitting to the windward (downwind) side when attacking. Once you have moved in and taken position on the net, then it is easier to hit a winner into the windward (downwind) side."

Seeing. Does your opponent seem to be aware of the crosswind?

Movement. Movements around the ball are required to achieve proper distance and to take advantage of the crosswind. If you hit to the downwind side and then into the open court, you'll force your opponent out of position.

Adjusting. You already have mastered the backward **C** and **C** patterns (see chapter 1) required to run around your backhand, thus preventing the wind from blowing the ball in to your body. Now it's your turn to see if your opponent can do the same. Understand that you have a much greater contact range with a forehand than you do with a backhand (which requires a more exact point of contact). If your opponent doesn't know this, you can take advantage.

- *If the wind is blowing toward your opponent's forehand side,* you could hit to the upwind (backhand) side and jam him, or you could hit downwind at a distance from him, because the wind will carry your ball even farther, requiring a lunge.

- *If the wind is blowing toward your opponent's backhand side,* try hitting right at him, or slightly to the backhand or forehand sides. These shots around the body require minor adjustments that your opponent may not be able to make.

Rotation and transfer. These factors hinge on the player's ability to adjust to the crosswind. Obviously, if he gets jammed, full rotation and transfer are not occurring, and that creates a weak shot. If a player has to lunge for a windblown ball, there's usually some rotation and transfer, but not enough to send the ball crosscourt.

Swing. Two-handed players have an advantage when the ball is blown in to their backhand. They still can generate some power, even with last-second adjustments.

Sun

The sun sometimes can be your worst enemy on the tennis court or actually help you to win matches. Do not underestimate the effects that the sun can have, not just on being able to see the ball but also the effect it can have physically. Heatstroke is a condition that can occur during competitive tennis matches if you don't take proper precautions and stay well hydrated and protected against the sun.

You're Facing a Bright Sun

The only two ways to cope with a bright sun are (a) to block it or (b) to look away from it, changing your angles of play so you're not staring into the sun. I recommend that players warm up on sunny days in the court facing the sun. This has two purposes: First, you can get the feel for the different angles you'll need, given the position of the sun. Second, you deprive your opponent of the chance to do that, so she will have to do her adjusting during the match.

Seeing. To block the sun, wear a visor, cap, and sunglasses. Get in the habit of using your nondominant hand to shade your eyes on high balls.

Movement. Let lobs bounce and wait for high bouncers to drop into your strike zone. You may need to run around some balls to get a less sun-blinded angle.

Adjusting. As you serve you may need to adjust your toss to one side of the sun or the other.

Rotation. You will need to rotate according to your toss.

Transfer. If blinded by the sun while serving, do not attempt to serve-and-volley. Let your eyes clear or put on some sunglasses.

Swing. Position yourself to take your normal swing.

Opponent Is Facing a Bright Sun

What are you looking for? An opponent who has not prepared well—no hat or sunglasses. Or one who's not comfortable using a free hand to shade his eyes when serving into the sun or hitting smashes. If your opponent fails to adjust to the sun as well as you do, you have a clear advantage.

If you can, make a left-hander serve into the sun for the first game of a match. Be sure on the spin of the racquet to exercise your fourth option, which is to give your opponent the choice of deciding whether to serve, return, or take side. Whatever he chooses, you can arrange it so his first service is into the sun. Yes, at some point you'll have to serve into the sun, too, but you presumably know what to do—adjusting your toss and using your free hand to block the sun. Also, remember on changeovers to place your chair in any shade possible.

Anticipate receiving serves with spin, if your opponent adjusts the toss. Serves may come out wide with slice or kick. Send balls right back at your opponent. It will be hard to pick up your return right away after looking toward the sun.

Seeing. Where is your opponent having trouble seeing the ball? What's the angle of the sun? Can you put the ball in those trouble spots? Is he temporarily blinded after hitting a serve or smash? Then move into the court and take his patty-cake serve or defensive smash on the rise, putting him under pressure.

Movement. Your opponent may work hard to move out of normal positioning, if that normal spot is in the sun's glare. That adds a few steps, which may throw off his timing. Take advantage of this by varying the pace or spins of your shots, to throw off your opponent's timing even more.

Adjusting. If your opponent is not adjusting the toss on a serve, then you will see double faults. Even with the adjusting of the toss, he may feel uncomfortable with the change in rhythm or form and hit the serve with less pace or meaningless spin, or he may just launch a push serve that lands short in the service box, inviting you to attack. On a smash, if your opponent doesn't adjust by using his free hand to block the sun, then the shot will be tentative, offering you a chance to go on the offensive.

Rotation. Both on the smash and the serve, your opponent should be able to make solid contact by rotating out of the direct path of the sun. This should result in more of an angle on the serve, with topspin on the ad side and slice on the deuce. Be ready for this. But if you observe that the player is not rotating like that, then move in, because you probably will receive weaker serves.

Transfer and swing. These factors will directly be affected by your opponent's ability to rotate his head and body to avoid looking into the sun. This forces him to meet the ball at a different point of contact. Usually this results in weaker shots, since he's unfamiliar with this point of contact, and his timing may be off. On occasion, however, he supplies *more* rotation and transfer than usual, creating a more powerful shot. In any case, your opponent will be playing outside of his comfort zone, and that may mean less control over his shots.

Heat and Humidity

On a hot and humid day, you are hoping to see an opponent who's not as well prepared as you are with your extra white shirts, towels, grips, hats, and wristbands. If your opponent has one shirt, no towel, no extra grips, no hat or wristbands . . . *perfect!*

Anticipate receiving short balls as your opponent becomes fatigued. As the heat and humidity take effect, ill-prepared players start losing their grip (mentally and physically). Keep sending balls that require your opponent to run.

If you've come to play in the heat you'll have an advantage over a less well-prepared player.

When It's Hot, You're Hot: Five Tips for Playing in Heat

1. Keep your hands dry. Wear wristbands, and use sawdust, chalk, or a towel to keep your grip.

2. Keep your eyes clear. Wear a hat or headband if sweat tends to drip into your eyes. Take a towel or two and use it between points.

3. Keep your body hydrated. Take a drink on the court with you. Water's good, but a performance drink such as GNC's Hydrofuel is what many of the players on the tour are choosing to use.

4. Keep yourself fueled with foods that help your energy and concentration, such as celery, carrots, bananas, baked potatoes, and raisins for potassium; and salty foods or spaghetti with meat sauce for a great boost of energy.

5. Keep your opponent running. In heat, tennis becomes a game of endurance. Wear out the other player before you wear out.

Seeing. Heat and fatigue can play tricks with the eyes, so notice how your opponent is seeing the ball. Also, note whether there's sweat or hair in her eyes.

Movement. Make your opponent sweat even more. Run her as much as possible, whether you win or lose the point. (Seriously, if you're confident you can outlast your opponent, you may want to forgo an easy winner early in the match, just to keep her running a while longer. You probably will still win that point, and you're wearing her out for more important points later in the match.) Hit behind her to wrong-foot her, and sit back and watch her become sweat-soaked. Look for her to start stretching and squatting in the legs. Watch your opponent walk, between points: look to see if she's taking longer on rituals and changeovers. "The more time, the more you grind," states Andrew Finn. The more sweat-soaked your opponent becomes, the more potassium and sodium she loses, leading faster to fatigue. Granted, she may be drinking a sports drink loaded with sugar, which will give her a sugar boost—but keep her out there. You're even better fueled, with fruit and vegetable juices that provide sodium and potassium as well as fructose, which is a slower-burning energy booster, compared to a sugary sports drink.

Adjusting. When it's hot, those little moves become so much harder. Sheer momentum can get you to the vicinity of the ball, but those last few steps to move around the ball or line up on it—they are killers. Your legs feel like they weigh a ton each. Hopefully, that's how your opponent starts to feel on a hot day long before you do. The result is a lack of precision: your opponent's ball goes out or into the net, rather than exactly where aimed. At this point, you can try to force your opponent into low-percentage shots. Late in the match, you may be able to approach the net and put away shots that don't quite have the sting on them as they did earlier in the match.

Rotation and transfer. As your opponent starts to fade, she'll start to hit with a more open stance, too tired to go into a full rotation. She'll hit later, losing control, spraying the ball more.

Swing. Your opponent may go for the putaway earlier, using bigger, sloppier swings.

She just wants to get this over with, so she may take chances on low-percentage shots. Be ready for drop shots from deep in the court or kamikaze charges on the net—and keep your cool! She'll win a few of these points, but in the long run she'll make more costly errors.

Be Cruel to Be Kind? Ruthlessness in a Friendly Sport

All of this talk about running your opponent may seem pretty cruel. What about tennis as a civilized, polite sport? Aren't you supposed to show good sportsmanship?

Well, yes. If you just want to hit the ball around with a friend, you can be kind about it. Don't hit the ball high into the sun or run your friend all over the court on a sweltering day, and you can hope your friend will be just as considerate toward you.

But if you're involved in competitive tennis, you're playing to win. If you're better prepared for heat or sun, if you're in better shape, if you have fueled your body better for the rigors of tennis—that's all part of the game. There's nothing wrong with taking advantage of those factors. In fact, you're actually helping your opponent to play better and prepare better in the future.

Be courteous on the court. Treat your opponent with all the honor you'd show to any other human being. Show respect at changeovers and shake hands at the end of the match. And if you're playing with a friend, enjoy the competition thoroughly. But play to win.

Cold Weather

Warming up is crucial on cold days (10 degrees Celcius [50 degrees Fahrenheit] or lower). Leave your sweats on until you start to perspire. If you don't like the feel of heavy sweat tops, then the classic tennis vest also will work.

Watch your opponent warm up, too. See if he shirks any part of the warm-up. Pay attention to how your opponent moves forward to short balls. When it's really cold, blood tends to desert the hands and feet and move toward the vital organs. For this reason, an opponent who likes to play with a lot of feel or power may become frustrated on a cold day because the ball does not respond as it normally does.

So, during play, expect to receive balls that land short in the court—since the cold may restrict parts of your opponent's rotation, transfer, and swing. Send balls that vary in depth; try hitting deep for a while and then intentionally hitting short.

Seeing. If a player wears contact lenses, they may dry out in cold weather, causing discomfort, distraction, and poor vision.

Movement. See how your opponent moves forward into the court. Sometimes the cold makes it hard to get moving. You can intentionally try to hit short because the ball will stay low.

Adjusting. Does your opponent move back inside the baseline after you hit the ball deep? If not, hit deep and then intentionally hit short. Even getting to the ball, your opponent has to adjust the racquet face by opening it—otherwise the ball will go into the net. Those minor adjustments of the hands and feet are especially difficult in cold weather, so the precision of shots will be affected.

Rotation. More rotation is necessary because of the lack of energy from the cold balls and strings. Balls will bounce flat. If your opponent does not add rotation, expect shorter shots.

Transfer. Sometimes in cold weather a player can look stiff when trying to transfer weight into his volleys. He's not smoothly blending rotation and transfer, resulting in erratic shots. You can add to his difficulty by hitting balls with slice or topspin at his feet if he's coming to the net.

Swing. If your opponent is not lifting the ball up with a good margin of safety, then start to move him back by hitting deep, or move him out wide. With the deadness of the ball and racquet, you want to force him to hit the ball far. He may not be aware of how much extra force he has to use to clear the net. For your own swing, it's a good idea to string your racquet a few pounds looser, according to expert stringer Tom Parry.

Rain

Sometines environmental conditions change suddenly and to various degrees, as in the case of rain. Water will affect the performance of your equipment. That's why you need to bring towels and keep drying your grip and strings as well as your shoes (especially if you're playing on clay). If your opponent fails to do this, you will have a distinct advantage.

You can anticipate varying ball depth, depending how wet and dirty the ball is. Also, your opponent may be having trouble setting up properly, resulting in some weak shots. Your best tactic is to send balls that force your opponent to move. If you take the offensive, forcing your opponent on defense, you can limit your own running while running your opponent. If the court is slippery at all, this is a critical factor.

Seeing. Rain can hinder visibility. Is your opponent having trouble seeing the ball? Sometimes rain makes it tough to look up at lobs or high bouncers. So send a few high ones and see how your opponent handles them.

Movement. Keep the other player moving. Force as many stops and turns as you can. Wrong-foot your opponent; hit short balls, then long balls; serve wide and then hit to the opposite corner. Because the balls are getting wet and heavy, they are staying lower. For this reason your opponent should be moving inside the baseline and opening the racquet face on low balls. If not, you can make her pay by hitting short. The low balls make it important to play crosscourt as often as possible, hitting over the lowest part of the net. Beware of trying to hit angles or drop shots, since the ball is too heavy to get a touch shot over the net with precision.

Adjusting. Rain affects the primary adjusters, your feet and hands, at their primary contact points—the feet can slip on the ground and the hand can slip on the racquet. You need to do everything possible to make sure these connections are clean, dry, and solid. Your opponent should, too. For instance, does she take a wider stance for a greater base of support? If not, then her rotation, transfer, and swing will be affected and she will not be able to generate as much power.

Rotation, transfer, and swing. If your opponent is slipping at all, the timing of the rotation and transfer will suffer, resulting in some wild shots out of play, but even good shots will probably have less power. You won't get many well-placed touch shots, but you may get some short "mistakes." To keep your stability, get your shoes clean after each point or two by giving them a good whack with your racquet. If you expect inclement weather, then string your racquet with a synthetic string and a few pounds looser.

High Altitude

In high altitude (at least 2,500 feet above sea level), the air is thinner and therefore the ball travels faster than at sea level. Ball control, including the use of various spins, becomes essential. Ideally, you'll be playing against someone who likes to hit the ball flat. Such a player will hit the ball out of the park a few times and then get tentative. Mix up your shots, testing your opponent by hitting high balls with topspin or slice and adding in some flat serves or slice backhands to force him to lower his center of mass. You can expect an erratic game, with balls hit with differing heights and speeds. It's important to keep a controlled style.

Seeing. Is your opponent picking up your spins? If not, you can gain quite an advantage by varying your spins to keep your opponent guessing.

Movement. Another feature of high altitude is that it's harder to breathe the thinner air. For that reason, keep your opponent running while controlling the center, limiting your own exertion. Hit side to side, varying depth and spin. Also, watch your opponent's knees.

Adjusting. High altitude requires a great deal of adjusting with flexion and extension—bending and reaching. You need flexion for the low shots and extension for the high-kicking balls off of topspin serves or ground strokes. Test your opponent in both of these areas. Hard, low balls tend to bounce fast and low in high altitude, forcing you to bend low to get them. See if he's widening his base to lower his center of mass. If not, keep the ball low with underspin. If he's not flexing well, mix in some slice or underspin.

Rotation. Thinner air requires a measured stroke, with a shortened backswing. If your opponent keeps swinging for the fences, especially early in the match, hit some easy ground strokes and watch him clobber them.

Transfer. If your opponent appears to be shortening the swing and blocking balls back to you, then hit heavy topspin if you can. Or just hit higher over the net. Watch out for the player who steps forward with a short backswing and takes the ball on the rise. This will be a fast-paced game—be ready for it.

Big servers at high altitude have an advantage.

Swing. Is your opponent able to shorten the swing? Can he adjust to varying heights of balls? Can he put spin on the ball to keep it in the court? If the answer is "no" to any of these questions, then he'll start to get tentative and push the ball, or he'll get frustrated and play wildly. Lower yourself and accelerate your racquet swings upward and outward, imparting spin on your ground strokes and returns. Is your opponent good at taking the ball on the rise? Put him to the test until you find a ball height that drives him crazy. Remember to start deeper in the court on your ground strokes and then move inside the baseline until you find your rhythm and timing. Uli Kuehnel, stringer for Boris Becker, also suggests that you string your racquet a few pounds tighter.

Difficult Seeing Conditions

Difficult seeing conditions—changing light or flat light due to clouds, dusk, smoke—will require you to maintain a still head and to track the ball with your dominant eye. Reflection off water or surrounding mountains or canyons can be helped by wearing glasses or a hat or both can help you during these times.

You can anticipate receiving balls that land short in the court, with excessive spin, or balls served out wide. If your opponent is having difficulty seeing, you want to send balls with pace but variations of height, spin, and placement—and an occasional change of pace. These tactics will keep the pressure on your opponent to see the ball and respond quickly.

Seeing. Look for cues that your opponent is having a tough time seeing—double faults, mishits, being badly out of position. Take advantage of this by messing with her sense of timing or by putting the ball where she doesn't expect it. Be especially alert to moments when she's just been looking up—a serve or a smash. Even if the sun is not blinding, the changing light can be a problem—looking into a bright sky and then a dark court.

Movement. If your opponent is moving late for the ball, making sudden, jerky movements, hit the ball right at her. This is an especially good tactic if she seems to be blinded by the sun or sky, attempting to serve or smash.

Adjusting. Your opponent may have difficulty adjusting the toss while serving. This may result in double faults or tentative serves that are short and easy. Be ready to take advantage of this.

Rotation, transfer, and swing. These elements all will be affected by the ability to see the ball. Your opponent's normal timing will be thrown off, and she may start taking shortcuts just to get the ball over the net. So you can expect some balls short in the court or hit erratically. On such short balls, shorten up your backswing to make contact easier (since you may have trouble seeing the ball, too).

Indoors

Most players generally play better indoors because most of the environmental conditions are left outside. Players' accuracy tends to improve and therefore their confidence escalates.

However, indoor courts can pose certain challenges, too, such as lack of space behind the baseline and on the sides and a limited ceiling clearance. Courts tend to be faster indoors, and if this is combined with a higher altitude that you frequently find at indoor facilities in the mountains, you can have quite a challenging time.

Playing indoors, you can expect to see increased pace and precision from your opponent, and a lower-bouncing ball. Without all the variables of an outdoor environment, the game is much more accurate. You even hear the ball better, resulting in improved timing. You should plan to send balls back with a shortened swing and flatter strokes.

Seeing. Players often will double-fault or hit smashes in the net when they're playing indoors because they pull down too quick instead of reaching up fully for the ball. Somehow the lighting plays tricks. This also occurs outside at night under lights. Players moving in from the outdoors tend to be late on their shots until they shorten up their backswings. If you're lobbing, it's important to have a good sense of how high it needs to be. The ceiling and light indoors can fool you, and it can fool your opponent. So you may be able to pick off some lobs, and let others go long.

Movement. Movement indoors can be challenging for a variety of reasons. Indoor courts tend to be faster surfaces, requiring players to get into position sooner. And certain types of indoor court surfaces can be a little grabby on the feet. For this reason Bobby Banck, coach of Mary Joe Fernandez, suggests playing in slightly older, more worn shoes. Other obstructions such as dividing nets, benches, and screens too close to the court also can pose problems. If your opponent is relatively slow, take advantage of the fast bounces and grabby court by hitting side to side, short and deep. Make him run. With faster foes, you can use sharp angles and deep topspin bouncers to force them into side screens and back screens. Screens usually are pretty safe, but running your opponent into a side bench risks serious injury. Good sportsmanship won't allow that; move dangerous objects (i.e. teaching baskets, etc.) before play begins. Notice whether your

The Williams sisters warming up indoors.

opponent likes to take ground strokes deep behind the baseline, letting the ball drop into the strike zone rather than taking it on the rise. If so, you may be able to run him into the back screen. If he tries the same to you, just step in and take it on the rise or in the air.

Adjusting. Look to see if your opponent is lengthening his stride or lowering his center of mass. If not, then keep running him around the court, and he'll start hitting into the net. (With the lower bounce of the ball, he'll need to keep his legs flexed to get down low enough.)

Rotation. A shorter backswing is necessary if the ball is staying low and skidding off the court. If your opponent is using a big swing, try to keep your shots low. Use the sound of the ball hitting your opponent's strings to help time your rotation.

Transfer. On ground strokes, transfer occurs with a lengthening of the stride into the shot. That allows a player to stay low. If your opponent isn't getting low and lengthening stride, he just will be arming the ball and not getting too much on his shots. You should be able to take the offensive.

Swing. If your opponent has too large of a backswing and doesn't create a good base, you might see him getting tentative, blocking or pushing the ball back to you. Take advantage of this. Remember to lengthen your stride, line up, and accelerate your swing—don't decelerate.

Playing Outdoors After Being Indoors

Andrew Finn
Former director of the Hitting Hot Program, Ivan Lendl Tennis Center

Our kids play indoors almost seven months a year up here in Connecticut. When the kids do get outside, they tend to initially lose their timing on the serve and the smash because of the changing background on the toss. As a result there are more mistakes on serve and smashes. Indoors, the speed of the ball does a lot of the work for you. Outside you have to create the pace on the ball.

After playing indoors, players also tend to be less tolerant of weather conditions and easily frustrated by wind and temperature. You can count on things indoors, but outside, players can feel like fish out of water. (One player I coached put it this way: "I control any situation inside, but there is a slight doubt outside.")

If you're outside, and playing someone who's used to playing inside, you should anticipate seeing balls hit short, especially under adverse conditions. Send balls with spin and height deep into the court. Pay attention to the environmental conditions already discussed.

Outdoors

Seeing. Even a blue sky can be a tough backdrop when you're trying to find the ball and judge its depth. Your opponent may have problems picking up your lobs and high bouncers, especially early in the match.

Movement. Various factors outdoors make the ball move slower, so the points tend to be longer. Is your opponent ready to move that much? She may start to go for winners prematurely in an attempt to finish points quickly, as she would indoors. Physically put her to the test by making her run.

Adjusting. Outdoors, there's a lot to adjust to. You need a lot more action in your hands and feet to respond to windblown balls and unexpected bounces. You also need more margin for error. So clear the net a bit more and aim more inside the lines. If your opponent is a precision player indoors, she may become frustrated outdoors.

Rotation. Because the ball is coming slower, there's a bit more time to create a solid base and counter-rotate, creating more elasticity in the muscles for generating power. That means a power player will be able to add more power outdoors. Set yourself up accordingly.

Transfer. The extra time also allows for more transfer. "Make it a goal to hit off of your front foot as often as possible," suggests Petr Korda. When playing outside, players sometimes wait for the ball to come to them (as it did indoors), but it's far better to step forward and meet it. If your opponent is not stepping in to add transfer, try hitting short or with slice or underspin, so the ball catches her standing too deep.

Swing. Inside, players tend to hit flatter strokes with a shorter backswing. Outside, players should lengthen their swing. If your opponent is still taking an indoor-type swing, the ball may go short in the court, so be ready to move in and hit a winner. Or keep running her on the baseline and wait for her to hit the net or hit short to you. On your service games, watch out for harder returns. The shortened backswing your opponent has rehearsed indoors will result in a strong shot.

Playing on Different Surfaces

Are you playing on a hard court, on soft clay, on grass, or on some kind of indoor carpet? Each surface poses certain challenges.

Grass courts can be fast or slow, depending on the length and type of grass, the moisture content, and how well they're rolled. You can see this each year at Wimbledon: the ball stays lower the first week, but by the second week the court starts to play more like a clay court, with higher bounces. You can anticipate shorter rallies, lower bounces, and difficulty with the footing. Send balls with varying pace and spins. These will skid and stay low. If you reduce pace, the ball will die—which is useful for a drop shot or drop volley.

Clay courts have higher bounces and play slower. Conditioning will be a factor, as will patience. Send balls that clear the net with height and spin. Move your opponent back and forth. Observe whether he knows how to slide to balls. Or does he run as if he's on a hard court? If he's slipping a bit, out of control, take

Good conditioning is especially crucial when playing on clay.

advantage by wrong-footing him, hitting behind him, or hitting twice in a row to the same corner of the court.

Granulate courts, often found in Europe, play similar to clay because it's possible to slide on the small rubber pellets that make up the top surface of the court. If there are a lot of these rubber pellets on the court, then typically the court plays slower. So anticipate high bounces, as on clay. Apply pace to the first three shots you hit, to establish a first-strike advantage and to take advantage of a slow-moving opponent. Be sure to clean the lines on clay or granulate courts before you play. Those lines can get blurry, and you want to see the court's outline as clearly as possible.

Hard courts have the most predictable bounces and can be extremely fast or slow depending on how the last layer of surfacing is textured and swept. Anticipate a variety of ball heights and speeds, and send balls with the same variety.

Supreme and carpeted courts play very quick with even bounces, and the ball comes more toward you instead of sitting up (as on clay).

Wood courts and plastic courts tend to be the fastest, with the ball just skidding across the floor, staying very low. Send balls that are a little flatter on the faster courts.

Your ability to adapt to different surfaces is an excellent way to develop different styles of play and to fine-tune your own style of play by varying the surface on which you play. Enjoy each surface and the sensations that you receive while playing on it.

Winning Match Strategies

It's show time! All of your practice sessions fade into the background when it comes to playing an actual match. In practice, your objective was to learn the game, to develop your abilities, to get into a groove of shot selection and execution. But now you're playing for keeps. Your goal is simply to win.

If you're in some kind of tournament, it's quite exciting. You may be facing someone you don't know, just a name on a draw. Or maybe you're aware of your opponent's reputation. Perhaps you've played this same person a dozen times. In any case, it's an electrifying feeling. No more exercises—now it counts. And even if you're just playing with a friend, there's something magic about the moment you say, "All right, enough warm-up. Up or down?" This chapter highlights how to prepare for your match on match day and during the game and what you can learn evaluating your play after the match.

Prematch Routine

I want to bring all of the skills you have worked on thus far under one umbrella. As a complete player, your game strategy starts long before the first serve. You've been assessing your opponent, talking with other players who know her game, or watching her in a preceding round. What are your opponent's strengths and weaknesses? What style of player is she? Is she right-handed or left-handed? Where does she like to hit her shots under pressure?

Before Match Day

By the day before the match, you've had your racquets restrung and a stencil placed on the strings (looking professional never hurts). You've gone out to hit and have acquired your feel, playing maybe a set or two to get ready. At home you have laid out the clothes you want to wear and packed your equipment bag with

- spare racquets that recently have been strung;
- spare grips;
- wristbands;
- a towel;
- extra shirts, shorts, socks, and tennis shoes;
- extra contact lenses or glasses;
- a hat;
- sunscreen;
- sunglasses;
- bandages;
- energy supplements; and
- your notebook and a pen for jotting down your observations.

On Match Day

Follow this checklist to prepare yourself on match day:

- ☐ **Use imagery.** On your way to the court, use imagery to see yourself executing your best tactics. Devise your best strategies, reviewing what you expect your opponent to give you and figuring out how to respond. For example: "I hear she loves to go down the line, so I'll cover down the line when coming to the net." Or, "He's a serve-and-volley player, they tell me, so I'll just have to move into the court on return. . . ."

- ☐ **Evaluate the conditions.** Upon arrival at the event, walk to the courts and take a look at what the playing conditions will be for your match. On what surface are you playing? Is the wind or sun posing a challenge? Look up the conditions covered in chapter 12 to see if you can gain an advantage. Take a moment to include the weather and court surface in your imagery.

- ☐ **Warm up your body.** Find an area in the parking lot or on an adjacent court to conduct your warm-up. Once you're warm and stretched, you can hit against the wall if you like or with another player to warm up all your shots.

- ☐ **Check your equipment.** Check that your racquets are gripped properly and select the racquet with which you want to play. Most players I know check the tension by holding two racquets (one in each hand) and gently hitting the string bed with one and then the other. Mix up the favorite drink that you've brought. Now you're ready to check in at the tournament desk.

Preparing for Battle

Dr. James Loehr
Sport psychologist

What kinds of things can athletes mentally do before going onto the court to prepare for battle? Those skills clearly are important to being able to execute under pressure. Just as you have to work on your movement skills and your fitness, this is another area you have to work on—mental preparation. I have developed a routine that requires a several-step process.

Every time you go into competition, first think about why this match is important. Why have you gone to all this trouble, putting out a 100 percent effort? What is on the line here? A win is important for a ranking, but there's even more to

consider. Why is it important to try to do the things that are within your control, to try to be positive and optimistic, to deal with this pressure and not to surrender your spirit? Every battle brings a new challenge and demands something new from us. What I have found is that athletes don't really connect this to something really important in their lives. If you can't figure out why it is important to fight out there today, then you probably won't; you'll find a way out.

So anchor yourself before going on the court. Then you have a picture of how you want to respond to the forces of life today on that tennis court. If this were the last match you ever played, how would you want to be thought of as a competitor? What is the image you want to project to the world? Who are you, and what is your character?

Any technical coach demands that you be precise in setting up your forehand or backhand. A fitness coach is the same way in strength or resistance training. I just want the same kind of precision on the emotional side. This is a competitive arena, and your performance is emotional as well as physical.

Use a variety of tools, such as visualization. Experts have learned that the more surprised people are, the more trouble they have anticipating shots and developing a game plan. Use affirmations or self-talk, so that when you go on that court you put yourself 100 percent on the line—no excuses.

Complete Player Warm-up

Unfortunately, most players have no clue about what they're trying to accomplish in their warm-up periods. As a result, they can botch some early shots in a match simply because their bodies aren't yet ready to play. Or they risk injury by warming up ineffectively or improperly or by cooling off too quickly.

A good warm-up helps you start a match explosively. If you hold serve and break serve right at the start, you're already up 2-0 or even 3-0 before your opponent wakes up. That's a powerful advantage for you. On the other hand, if you go through a halfhearted warm-up before playing, you still will be getting ready while your opponent is going up 2-0, maybe 3-0. That'll be a tough hill for you to climb. Make it a priority to *warm up efficiently and effectively every time you play.*

On-Court Warm-Up

Once you are on the court prior to the match, your objective is to warm up all your responses of depth, spins, placement, height, taking the ball on the rise, and pace. You also want to tune up your concentration and start assessing your opponent. As the late great Arthur Ashe once said, if you don't miss a ball in the warm-up, you'll win the match 98 percent of the time.

Assess your opponent. If you haven't seen your opponent before, start sizing him up as he walks onto the court. Note first what his body type is—endomorph, mesomorph, or ectomorph.

- *Endomorphs* tend to have softer looking bodies, underdeveloped muscle tone and be more round-shaped. Endomorphs tend to do well with movement but can be prone to cramping and have difficulty with high balls. Reaching wide balls and high-bouncing balls can prove challenging because they have a shorter reach. Make them run by moving them short and long, bringing them to the net and then lobbing or stretching them on the pass. Or get them off the court with wide shots, running them back and forth or wrong-footing them. An endomorph with a one-handed backhand might have problems with high-bouncing balls such as kick serves, rally balls with heavy spin, and even moon balls that bounce up to strike zone A.

- *Mesomorphs* are characterized as having a more hard, muscular looking body that is more rectangular in shape. Mesomorphs usually are good all-court players. Being well proportioned, they tend to be well-balanced athletes who are difficult to get off-balance. Look for other areas of their game to exploit.

- *Ectomorphs* tend to be thin, tall, lightly muscled with a more delicate build than other types. Ectomorphs have a bit more difficulty getting their larger frames around the court, especially if the ball is low or right at them. Force them to adjust by hitting balls at their body or keeping the ball low. Ectomorphs can have trouble with balls that are in strike zone C, such as slice balls, slice serves, angles, and recovering drop shots.

Regardless of body type, however, remember that good players who execute SMARTS well can meet the ball at an optimum level.

As you start to warm up, look at your opponent's grips and mentally note that he is right-handed or left-handed. Notice the strike zones where he prefers to hit balls.

Generally players who have continental grips have difficulty with high balls and those with eastern grips will have more difficulty on low volleys. Semiwestern and full western grippers will have even a harder time with low balls from the baseline, so pay attention when you hit a few slices to them.

Review your play situation. Now review what you have observed so far: playing surface, conditions, body type, and grips. Are there any observations that overlap and could be challenging to your opponent? Say that you're on clay, playing an endomorph with a continental forehand. You definitely want to try hitting high balls to test his SMARTS. That's not to say he cannot hit high balls, but he'll have to work hard to do so—and maybe he'll give you a couple of free points.

Do a swinging warm-up. Start off swinging at a speed you can control, keeping the ball deep in the court. Then add spin, hitting topspin balls with height and depth in the court. Vary with backspin on the backhand and, after hitting some slice backhands, hit a drop shot or two. Keep in mind that with any specialty shots, you're not trying to anger or embarrass your opponent—you're just getting your feel for these shots!

Continue to rally with your opponent, observing his SMARTS and noting any errors off balls you are sending. Step up and hit a few balls on the rise. When your opponent hits a ball short, take the approach and try to keep it deep. Come in only as far as the service line and warm up your first volley, keeping the ball deep and hitting it with backspin. Move in, taking your second volley, and hit a drop or an angle volley to get your feel. Now take your normal smashes, then a few bounce smashes; move to your right (if you're right-handed) and take a couple of backhand smashes.

It's your opponent's turn to come forward. Watch how he volleys and from where. Does he warm up his first volley or move in immediately for the second volley? Roll a few balls with some spin and see if he bends to get the balls. Stand inside the baseline and make him volley deep to you, forcing you to retreat back a step. Can he do it? Without being obvious, speed up your swing for a couple of strokes while he is volleying to see how he reacts to increased pace. As your opponent takes smashes, get a good feel for opening your racquet face and lifting the ball.

Practice serves and returns. I recommend that you take serves and returns separately. When your opponent serves, hit the return back to him. Practice taking the return from different spots—deep behind the baseline, on the baseline, and inside. Don't put too much stock in where your opponent sends these practice serves. Sometimes players like to do all their serves up the T in the warm-up and then go for the ace out wide on the first point of their service game. Always expect the unexpected. On your serves, hit different spots with varying spins and pace. Use both the deuce and ad side; too often the ad side is neglected.

Playing the Match

You have four choices when winning the spin of the racquet: you can choose the side of the court from which you want to start, or whether you want to serve, receive, or make your opponent decide.

Hitting angle shots can help you take your opponent off the court.

If you win the toss, I encourage you to return first. At the very start, your opponent (or you) may be nervous, not warmed up enough, or both. This is one of your best chances to break serve, and that can be a great confidence boost for you in the first game of the match. By the time you're serving the second game, you're more warmed up and the butterflies in your stomach have flown away.

If the sun is an issue (see chapter 12), and if your opponent is left-handed, consider making her decide. You want her to have her first service game into the sun. So she elects to serve and you choose the side. This is not being dirty but taking advantage of environmental conditions to aid your chances for getting a break the first game of the set.

Should your opponent win the spin, play with the same hand as you do, and choose to serve first, that is fine for you. Choose the side where she is not facing into the sun because after the first service game is over, you have to switch sides. If your opponent has read this book too, and gives you the choice on a sunny day, choose to receive.

The First Few Games

Use your knowledge of SMARTS. Look at your opponent's strokes and observe how he responds in the differing phases of play to determine his weaknesses. Maybe you notice that he doesn't *move* well side to side or up and back. Maybe he is having difficulty *adjusting* to balls hit at him or up the middle of the court. If your opponent doesn't *rotate* enough on his backhand slice and just chops at the ball, causing it to float, this allows you to attack the reply.

In the first couple of games, what does your opponent do when he gets a short ball? Does he blend his rotation, transfer, and swing to hit a winner, or does he end up hitting a short ball? Does he only *transfer* weight into his shots from a closed stance? Hit balls that take your opponent off the court, such as wide serves or angles. You may get him to start lunging at balls by doing this.

Is your opponent in position on the *swing*—lined up with his hands and feet, displaying good body control, and balanced—or is he off-balance and flailing? Does your opponent play at a level he can sustain? Certain opponents come out swinging for the fences and blasting every ball, but if they really could keep that up for two sets they'd be on the tour, right? Be patient and make your opponent play until he cools off.

The first two games of each set should present you with different challenges. You're trying to get as much information about your opponent as possible. But you're also trying to get a leg up on him by quickly breaking serve and holding your own serve.

By the same token, how are you starting off the match? Everyone likes to start off differently. According to Bob Brett, Boris Becker's former coach, Becker always liked to play himself gradually into the match, while Goran Ivanisevic would go full speed off the first ball.

Preparing for Every Situation

Ideally, you've been preparing yourself for weeks. You should be sure of yourself, knowing you're ready to exploit every opportunity when it presents itself. But life isn't always ideal.

If you've had less time than you had planned to prepare, if you've been swamped at work, or busy with your family, a more cautious but confident approach is necessary. Your goal is to get your feel for the game while creating opportunities for yourself. You can do this by playing high-percentage tennis, swinging at a speed with enough spin on the ball to keep it in play until your opponent makes an error or you can go for the winner. Don't beat yourself with unforced errors.

As mentioned, Boris Becker was notorious for starting slow, getting his feel and working his way into the match. Michael Chang also works his way into his matches. But by the end of the first set, they both start to use all cylinders. Try working your way into the match this way, as opposed to throwing everything you have at your opponent and having only one way to go—down.

Your First Return Game

The first return game is statistically your best opportunity to break your opponent's serve. Remember, your opponent may not know your game well, and she could be nervous. If you've done your prematch preparation, you have an advantage.

Obviously, making returns is important. If you're nervous, start by going crosscourt or up the middle if your opponent is serving hard. View the second serve as an opportunity to send a message to your opponent that you're going to do something with her serve. Maybe you place it deep to the corner or you move in and attack the serve, then go to the net. If you have practiced your drop shot, this also can be a surprise, especially on a clay court.

The Changeover

When you sit down on the changeovers, it's more than a breather. Now is the time to evaluate what is happening on the court. Eat and drink something, and use imagery to replay some of the scenarios that already have occurred in the first game, solidifying your successes and rewriting the script for the points you lost.

Your First Service Game

Challenge yourself to make 80 percent first serves in the first game you serve. That doesn't mean you're rocketing aces through the court. You can ease up a bit on pace, as long as your serve is consistently to your opponent's weakness and deep in the box. This is enough to send a message to him. As your confidence grows, add pace to your placement. If you do have to hit a second serve, then try to send it to his weakness. If you miss it deep, no problem! But if you lay in an easy second serve, you're just serving up a nice fuzz sandwich that your opponent should kill! You deserve to be punished for that, and you probably will be. However, if you want to get better, really hit your second serve.

Setup Games

In *Winning Ugly*, Brad Gilbert and Steve Jamison define a setup game as "any game that can move a player to within one game of the set." So if you're leading in a set, four games to anything, the next game is a setup game. Gilbert and Jamison add that "the setup game at 4-4 or 5-5, when both players have a chance to move up to a position where the next game may result in the set or match being won, has tremendous dynamic value." At that stage of the set, if you break serve, you've practically won. Your opponent has to break your serve in the next game to keep from losing the set. If you hold serve in a setup game, your opponent must hold serve in the next game, and that can add substantial pressure.

First Two Games of the Second Set

Let's say you've won the first set. How does your opponent feel coming into the second? Will she be disheartened and basically roll over and die? Probably not. "More likely you'll have a Wounded Bear on your hands," say Gilbert and Jamison. "And a Wounded Bear is dangerous." Your opponent will have extra ferocity in this situation, with a sharpened focus and renewed motivation.

What's your response? Obviously you want to squash her comeback. She's not disheartened yet, but she will be if you capture the first two games of set two.

But what if your opponent wins the first set? Then, according to *Winning Ugly*, you're dealing with a Happy Camper, a player who is "relieved . . . pleased . . . satisfied." You hope, of course, that the Happy Camper lets down her guard, losing some intensity as the second set begins. So, if you've won the first set, don't appear to be a Happy Camper. Wounded Bears eat Happy Campers for breakfast. Keep your intensity up, knowing that your opponent probably will be extra fierce. If you grab these games, you can break your opponent's spirit and sail to a sure victory. But if you lose, it's a whole new match. Your opponent can see the way to even things up.

Rebreak Games

If your serve has been broken, obviously you must break back. The best time to do this is the very next game. You are hoping that your opponent gets that happy-camper mentality and plays loosely for a couple of points. Stay motivated and focus on getting returns back and attacking your opponent's weaknesses with your strengths.

Games for the Set or Match

If you're on the verge of victory, continue doing what put you into this position in the first place. Look for signs that your opponent is getting tight and keep the pressure on him. Don't let your opponent off the ropes by making unforced errors; he will fight like crazy to avoid losing. Strangely enough, at the intermediate level you sometimes see players put together two to three winners in a row—aces, ground-stroke winners, or whatever—and then bow out, giving you free points on unforced errors. Still, you can't count on those free points!

Break Between the Second and Third Sets

It's 1-1 and you're probably getting tired. If you won the second set, keep your momentum going by doing what you did to recover from losing the first set. If you lost the second, regroup. Remember, everything is even again, so go out, try to get a break, and keep on the pressure. Do not hold back now or try to get your feel. Go over in your mind or with a coach what you need to do; keep your plan simple and concise.

Momentum Points

Any time you put together two or more points, you are creating momentum. Of course, your opponent can do the same. Sometimes while charting matches I've seen players lose up to 20 points in a row. Stopping momentum requires first that you're aware of the challenge of winning or losing three points in a row. Once you learn to feel the momentum, you can begin to do something about it.

In your next practice, play the momentum game. It's really just another way to keep score. The game awards a momentum point to the player who can win three points in a row. Start off with one player serving, as in a normal match. Then alternate serve and return.

In your match, if you lose three or more points in a row, do something different! If you're staying back, come in. Or change some of your ball controls—pace, depth, height, or spin. You merely want to give your opponent something else to worry about, to break the rhythm, to stop the train.

If you're winning three or more points in a row, keep doing what's working. Now is not the time to overanalyze or worry that your opponent is catching on to you. She may be well aware of what you are doing but just doesn't have the skills to counter it. You're in a groove. Don't think about it, just do it.

If you've established momentum in the match, keep doing what is working.

Maintaining Continuity

Playing with continuity is what fine-tuning your game is about. Often on the pro tour the difference between a top-100 player and a player ranked only in the top 500 is not pace on the ball or technical skills, but continuity.

The top-100 player continuously can replicate successful performances. This is not to say that these players don't experience breaks in performance, but they know their own thought processes and the movement patterns that they must make to get themselves back on track.

To prevent your opponent from gaining momentum, focus on your own game and know what to do to get back on track. Store as much information as you can in your mind after each match by writing down what it was that you did well and how you did it. For example: "I warmed up my serve at three-quarters speed and followed my serve into the court. I continued to do this into the first game and held at love. As I started speeding up my serve, I continued to follow my serve into the court, stepping over the baseline and then recovering behind the baseline to start the rally."

Now when you are in trouble or need to serve well, you can reproduce the image of what you did and execute it on the court.

Consequent Actions

Between games on changeovers and between points it also is important to follow a set routine. Have your bag properly equipped, with something to eat and drink. Between points, have a special place picked out where you can go if you need a second to towel off or to take a deep breath. Your rituals should be as consistent as your execution. They will help you to handle the stress of the game.

Setup Points

Setup points are the same thing as setup games on a point level. The setup point puts you one point from winning the game. "For some pros (the ones not making any money) and most recreational players," says Brad Gilbert, coach of Andre Agassi, "there are two kinds of points—ad points and all the rest. Wrong. I treat the point that can get me or my opponent to an ad point as a major moment because it offers a major reward. That reward is the opportunity to win (or convert) a game."

So anytime you're at 30 or deuce, you're playing a setup point. If you can find a certain intensity for these points, similar to your game-point intensity, you'll get to play more game points, and you'll keep pressure on your opponent. (You also should recognize your opponent's setup points and play these with intensity, so you avoid the pressure of playing game points against you.)

If your opponent is serving and you are at break point, play your opponent's weaker side.

Game Points

Pressure is high when the game's on the line. At game point, many players beat themselves with unforced errors. These usually occur on the first shot, whether a return of serve or a serve. So when you're leading at game point, keep the pressure on your opponent by making a solid first serve or return. You don't need anything fancy here, just force your opponent to play. Avoid the temptation to go for the kill. See if she can come up with shots under pressure or if she chokes.

However, if your opponent seems unfazed by the pressure, and you start to question your ability to get this game, then turn the tables. Start to play as if you're trailing instead of leading. That may give you the intensity to grab the game from your opponent.

If you're trailing at game point, simply dig in. Keep yourself from visualizing the loss of the point. See yourself establishing momentum and getting out of trouble. Continue to attack your opponent's weaknesses, and play the best serves and shots you can. In stress situations like this, some players do best when focusing on themselves, that is, their hand speed, their footwork, their breathing, or the spin they're putting on the ball. Others focus attention on where they want to send the ball.

Break Points

If your opponent is serving and you're at break point, it may help you to imagine that you're trailing. Put yourself in his shoes for a moment. In danger of being broken, he'll be relying on his strengths, so quickly review in your mind where he has been serving and guess where he's most likely to serve in this situation. Play on his weakness and force him to defend himself by hitting his weakest shot.

Tiebreakers

Don't get spooked by tiebreakers. Keep your concentration and use the same type of play that got you to this point. Avoid the temptation to wrap it all up by trying low-percentage shots and taking unnecessary risks.

Gilbert and Jamison suggest that you, "separate the first two points of the tie break from the set you just played . . . isolate those first two points and play them with renewed alertness; get it in or get it back" (p. 133). Those first two points are like the first two games of a set. Your opponent may ease up a bit, especially if the last few points leading into the tiebreaker were pressure filled. But while your opponent is breathing easier, seize the advantage.

If you take a lead in a tiebreaker, such as 5-1, be aware that your opponent now has nothing to lose and will swing freely. Be on your guard or it could be 5-5 all before you know it. Pay attention to the setup point that puts you a point away from winning the set (or evening the match). Fight like crazy to keep the ball in play and don't take the complacent attitude of waiting for your opponent to lose the breaker. If your mind is looking for your opponent to double-fault or make unforced errors, it's time for you to refocus your attention on what you are trying to do—which is to *force* errors!

Set and Match Point Down

Players have come back from being down set point or even numerous match points to win the match. You never know when your opponents will doubt their abilities to close you out. You simply have to play one point at a time. Take your time but play your best shots. If you get a ball that you can attack, go for it. Show your opponent that you are willing to fight to the end.

Table 13.1—The Complete Player Strategy and Tactic Evaluation

Name: Date:

Location: Court:

Conditions:

Match Planning

Off court—prematch thinking (mental)
_____ Did you work through on-court scenarios?   _____ Did you scout out your opponent's style of play?

Off court—physical and getting the early break
_____ Did you warm up your body?   _____ Did you perform footwork drills?
_____ Did you do some practice swings?   _____ Did you stretch?

On court
___ Did you perform an on-court warm-up?
___ Did you scout for body type, grips, and SMARTS in your opponent?
___ What decision did you make on racquet spin?_____ Why? _____

The return game
_____ Return placement   _____ Aggressive with the return
_____ Picking your spot   _____ High-energy output

The first service
_____ The service warm-up   _____ First serve percentage
_____ Finding the weakness

Momentum Building

First two games—first set
Setup points: won _____ lost _____   Setup games: won _____ lost _____
Game points: won _____ lost _____   Break points: won _____ lost _____

First two games of the second set _____

Third set _____

Tiebreakers _____

Stretching Your Lead and Staying Mentally Sharp

Options	Serve				
		1	4	7	___
		2	5	8	
		3	6	9	
Serve deuce		1	Ad side 4		___
		2	5		
		3	6		
Return deuce/ad		1	4		___
		2	5		___
		3	6		___

Style of player: _____
Net attacker: _____

Pure striker: _____

Big forehand:____

Big forehand: _____(attacking baseliner)

Counterpuncher_____(Defensive)

Big server_____

Moonballer _____

Heavy attacking baseliner _____

Junkballer_____
Combination   11   12   21
Option   1   2   3   4   5

Managing Time and Energy

Double time (taking extra time)

Opponent is not concentrating

Feeling good

Breath control

Eating from start to finish

Relaxing

Using a towel

Going to your special place by the fence

Eating between changeovers

Losing A Lead

Game plan ___

Opponent is coming on

Playing From Behind

Keeping your energy up

Moving

Trying something new (three strikes)

Emergency Action

String breaks

Poor calls

No Feeling

Focusing on playing goal

Pumping up energy

Keeping the ball in play

Playing your best combinations

Using topspin cross

Higher net clearance

Changing racquets

Postmatch

Cooldown

Debriefing

Complete player evaluation

Getting the right nutrients

SMARTS
Worked on:
            Load and explode
            Low and punch

Postmatch Routine

Follow these guidelines after your match.

Step 1: Jog lightly or swim for 5 to 15 minutes just to help your muscles loosen up and get rid of lactic acid and toxins that may have built up during the match.

Step 2: Stretch for 10 to 15 minutes.

Step 3: Change to dry clothes.

Step 4: Rehydrate immediately.

Step 5: If you are playing another match on the same day, eat an adequate meal.

Step 6: Get a massage if you can to help you to recover for your next day's match. If massage isn't realistic, jump into a jacuzzi for no more than a few minutes.

Step 7: Fill out your evaluation form (table 13.1) to help you learn from the match, whether you've won or lost.

Postplay Stretching

Your postplay stretching is crucial in maintaining muscle consistency. I have found that the physical and mental discipline of yoga provides some fantastic coordination and stability exercises for the tennis player. It aids your concentration, stimulates your metabolism, and helps you breathe better. These exercises are especially helpful after your practice or set, but you can use them before playing or as a daily ritual before going to bed or just after rising.

Here's a suggested program of yoga exercises for tennis players. It's always a good idea to do your stretches on a mat that you easily can roll up and take with you wherever you go. This gives your knees a bit of padding and prevents you from slipping.

1. **Greeting.** Stand up straight with your feet together. Hold your hands, palms together, in front of your chest. Relax your whole body. This is the starting position, creating a state of rest in the body and mind. Inhale as you raise your arms and stretch them back over your head.

2. **Stretching the body.** With your arms stretched up behind your head, slightly parted, and your back slightly arched, experience openness and receptivity in your body, stretching in the sun's light. And now . . . breathe out while you bend forward and touch the floor next to your feet, if possible. Keep your legs straight. Your head should hang down, relaxed.

3. **Hands by your feet.** In this pose, with your legs straight, try to touch your knees with your head. Empty your lungs completely by drawing your stomach inward. Inhale as you move one leg back and let that knee touch the floor, while your hands and other foot stay put. You now have one leg forward, bent; the other leg kneeling behind it.

4. **The equestrian pose.** Extend the kneeling leg back as far as possible. Now your hands are touching the floor, as well as your forward foot and the toes and knee of the leg you moved back. Lean your head back and look upward toward the space between your eyebrows.

5. **The mountain pose.** When you exhale, move your forward leg back beside the other leg, push your buttocks up in the air, and draw your head down between your shoulders. You now form a triangle with the floor as the base and your butt as the apex. Now empty your lungs. Keep your heels on the floor. After exhaling, hold your breath and lower your body until only your chin, chest, knees, feet, and hands touch the floor. See that your buttocks, thighs, and abdomen are off the floor, and keep your lungs empty while you stay in this pose.

6. **The cobra pose.** Now drop your whole body to the floor. When you have to breathe again, inhale while lifting your head up and back, then push your upper body off the floor. Keep your hips on the floor, but feel a thorough stretch in your abdomen, chest, and neck.

7. **The mountain pose.** Return to the mountain pose by raising your buttocks again as you exhale, until you form a triangle with the floor.

8. **The equestrian pose.** Return to the equestrian pose by moving one leg forward until that foot rests on the floor between your hands. Remember to focus on the space between your eyebrows.

9. **Hands by your feet**. Return to pose 3 by exhaling and bending forward until your hands touch the floor by your feet.

10. **Stretching the body.** Return to pose 2 by rising and stretch your arms back over your head while inhaling.

11. **Greeting.** Return to position 1 by bringing your arms down in front of your chest, palms together, during a relaxed exhalation.

Rest at least three minutes in absolute calm. Then do the whole round once more, moving the opposite leg forward during each stretch.

14

Becoming a Complete Player

One of the first computer games was basically tennis. *Pong* had a ball going back and forth across a court, and you moved your racquet to intercept it. At the time, it was great fun, though now it seems pretty dull, compared to the intergalactic mutant warfare you can find on some screens.

After going through the strategies presented in chapter 13, you might think you need a computer to keep everything straight. Ball sent, ball received, combination 12, or was that 21? What do you do when . . .? There are a lot of details to master.

But you're more than a computer. And a great game of tennis goes far beyond calculating the proper response to every ball received. At the fine-tuning level, successful players develop a feel for the game. Yes, you need to do your analytical homework, but don't let the facts get in your way. Learn to trust your instincts once you step onto the court.

The game has an ebb and flow to it. Learn to bodysurf with each wave. I've discussed the importance of momentum. At every moment of a match, the tide is rolling toward you or away from you. There are nuances underlying every point. You can win something on a point you lose—maybe you learn something, or you tire your opponent, or you finally return that wicked serve. And you can lose some things even when you win a point—rhythm, form, energy, humility. Being able to read the direction of the tide and adjust your play to it spells the difference between winning and losing the match.

Playing to the Situation

Let's step back from our specific point-by-point strategy and try to get the feel for different stages of play. In the following scenarios I've identified 10 situations in which the game becomes more than the score. We might use some gambling terms to describe each of these stages—stakes and odds. Stakes are simply a question of, "What do I have to lose?" Odds are an indication of the high-percentage (favorable odds) or low-percentage (odds against) plays that are called for in these situations.

Raise the Stakes

You are far ahead; stakes are low. Try low-percentage winners.

You are well up in the score. Chances are good that you'll win the match. Now is the time to punish your opponent, making him pay for stepping on the court with you and trying to take what you have determined to be yours . . . victory! By "punish," I don't mean that you try to hit screaming winners on every shot. Yes, you should put easy balls away, but this is a time to sharpen up your attack. Aim a little closer to the lines, come in behind your first serve if you want, but keep applying pressure. You can afford to take some low-percentage shots. What you are looking to do is to make your opponent work extremely hard to hang on. Play on your opponent's weaknesses. Make him run like crazy.

Sharpen your attack if you are ahead. Aim a little closer to the lines, come in, and apply pressure with depth and consistency in your shots.

Play this way when you have nothing to lose—that is, when you are comfortably ahead and even a lost game or two won't kill you. If you're up 4-0 in the first set, having broken serve twice, punishment can demoralize and wear out your opponent. Or if you've won the first set and you've broken serve early in the second, this strategy can put your opponent away and make him think twice about the next time he has to play you. Even if your lead in the match is not great but you're up 40-0 in a game, you can afford to try some punishing combinations.

Note, however, that the tide of a game can turn quickly. If your punishing shots start going wide and you're losing momentum, give up that plan and go back to the strategies that gave you the lead in the first place. Don't wear yourself out with fancy shots. And practice good sportsmanship. If your punishing play is accompanied by taunts and hotdogging, you'll make an enemy for life. Next time you have to play that opponent, he will be fired up.

Stay With What Works

You are solidly ahead; stakes are low. Stay with high-percentage shots.

The situation may be similar to the punishment scenario ("Raise the Stakes"), but for some reason, you don't want to take chances. You're comfortably ahead, but maybe you're afraid of getting out of your own rhythm. Or maybe your opponent is known for a great kick and coming back late in matches. Either way, you're sticking with high-percentage play, using the same style of play that brought you this comfortable lead.

Start the points by making a high percentage of serves or returns. As Pete Sampras recommends, always look to get another break and not just rely on your serve to finish the match. Be prepared for your opponent to come after you on a mission of revenge to get back in the match. Brave his assault and play with a positive mindset to expand your lead. Play the setup points and games with discipline, as well as the game points. Keep on the pressure. Bobby Banck, coach of Mary Joe Fernandez, encourages Fernandez to play high-percentage, aggressive tennis when she is leading, trying to capitalize on her lead.

Close the Deal

You are up a break; stakes are high. Vary your percentages to keep control of the match.

In her competitive league matches, a player (in this example we'll call her Sandy) may get up a break against higher-seeded players, but the higher-seeded players always break her back and then go on to win three or four games until she comes back into her game. This is what I call the ahead-I'm-dead syndrome. When Sandy takes a lead, she starts to panic and tightens up. She forgets everything that brought her the lead and starts playing with the objective of not to lose.

Her self-talk might go something like this: "If I just hold serve two more times, I'll win the set, and then I have to break serve in the next set, which will be tough, because I'm really not supposed to win this match. My opponent is better than me, but if I'm really careful, she might make some mistakes and I could squeeze out a lucky victory." This kind of thinking is self-defeating. She's reminding herself that she *can't* win! And she's thinking three games ahead.

Sandy needs to keep her mind focused on the current point she's playing. She could do this by (a) focusing attention on hitting to certain spots on the court or (b) focusing on her own breathing or movement. She is doing something right, and she should stick with it. She should not pull back to only high-percentage, careful play. She should continue taking reasonable chances. Even though she's up a break, she really should play as if the score were even.

She also needs to anticipate that her opponent will fiercely try to break her serve and may try some risky, low-percentage shots to do so. Some of these shots may be winners (although good anticipation will enable Sandy to return some), but others will go into the net or out of play. The thing about low-percentage shots is that the percentages eventually catch up with you. Even if a winner goes whizzing past her, Sandy can shake it off and play her own game.

But Sandy can open up a bit when her opponent's serving. She's already broken serve once, and another break would be huge. So she can take some chances in trying to win this game. If she loses it, big deal. She's still up a break. And a more risky style when she's trying to break serve may keep her from being too careful when she's trying to hold serve.

Life Is Unfair

You are losing; stakes are high. Choose high-percentage shots to turn things around.

"I'm the better player, but why can't I win?" Sometimes you face a player you know you should beat, but you're struggling. In the prematch warm-up you can see that your opponent has poor strokes, runs slow, and has an iffy backhand. This person doesn't even look like a tennis player. "Piece of cake," you think.

That's your first mistake. You can't take anyone for granted. Let's say you try to blast your serve, just to put this player away quickly, but your serve's not working. After a few double faults, you find yourself down a break. And this opponent is scrappy; she can't hit a backhand to save her life, but she keeps you guessing with a variety of dinks and spins. You can't get into a rhythm. And if one more ball flicks the net and plops short onto your side, you'll scream. Before you know it, you've lost the first set 6-2 to this player, and you're upset. You know you're twice as good, so why aren't you winning?

Overconfidence, bad luck, and a serve that's not working for you are some culprits. And now you're playing mental games with yourself that make it worse. You're trying to punish this player with dazzling (but low-percentage) shots when you're in no position to punish. You've put yourself in a no-win situation. If you lose to this slouch, horrors! What kind of a slouch does that make you? But if you come back and beat this player, well, you should have beaten this player anyway. You work through a pretty vicious circle of thinking. You vacillate wildly between confidence and fear, trying to rip impossible winners and then tentatively pushing the ball.

What can you do? Start with your mind games. Forget what the player looks like and just play. Trust yourself and the game you're trying to play. You are the better player, and if you play your game the winning will take care of itself. Play high-percentage tennis. When you get a ball that you can challenge or attack, then go for it, but don't force matters. Play to your opponent's weaknesses and get into the rhythm of your own game. Be patient, willing to keep the ball in play rather than going for winners all the time. If a point goes long enough, chances are that your opponent will flub up first. Understand that your approach to this match has given you two opponents—the other player and your own mind. If you can emerge victorious after digging a hole for yourself, that's something to savor.

Mirror Ball

You are dead even with your opponent; stakes are high. Vary your percentages.

Sometimes you face a soul mate on the tennis court. Maybe your styles mirror each other, or maybe your abilities are just perfectly matched, but you always play each other to the wire. Whenever you two meet, you can win if you play well and lose if you're off. Some of the greatest rivalries in tennis have been McEnroe versus Borg, Connors versus anyone, Navratilova versus Evert, Agassi versus Sampras, and Graf versus Navratilova.

Forget about your opponent. You and the ball should be your main concern. Forget about liking or disliking the other player. Don't get frustrated by the way he keeps after you like a savage dog on your pant leg. Just stay positive about your game and play the percentages. That is, when the score is even, stick to high-percentage plays. When you're down or up two or three points, then you can be more aggressive. Work especially hard to win the first point of each game, the setup points, and game points.

Momentum makes a big difference in a match like this, so be sensitive to it. Learn quickly what's working for you and use it. Read your opponent's patterns of play and try to anticipate what you'll get. If you're feeling nervous or tired or you're losing your feel, push the game by creating opportunities to challenge or attack. If you feel you can outlast your opponent, choose high-percentage shots to keep the ball in play. A matchup like this is usually a tug-of-war. Sometimes breaks in concentration occur due to mental fatigue. Realize that point by point it's going to be a marathon. Unless your opponent has a meltdown, get ready to go the distance.

In some 16 years of coaching I have seen matches that have gone 7-6, 6-7, 7-6. In 1998, Yevgeny Kafelnikov (Russia) beat Slava Dosedel (Czechoslovakia) by this score at the Lipton Championships. The match lasted 178 minutes. Both players came from similar tennis conditioning backgrounds, growing up in Communist countries, and both play a pure striker style of tennis. It was like they were playing in a mirror.

Yevgeny Kafelnikov (pictured here) matches up well with Slava Dosedel.

The Shape of Things to Come

You are losing; stakes are high. Play high percentages for a delayed victory.

So you work out hard and take good care of yourself. From your observations before the match and in the early points, do you think your fitness is superior to your opponent's? If so, then take this into account in your game strategy. If you're down a game or two early in the first set, relax. You can come back, but you have to play your game.

Think like a boxer. Boxers throw body punches early in a match. Why? No one gets knocked out with a body punch. But this is the way boxers tire out their opponents, so they lower their hands, opening themselves for a later knockout punch to the head.

Maybe your opponent is throwing successful punches and you are constantly on defense. Maybe you're not on top of your game, missing shots you should handle easily. Don't give up. Just keep making your opponent work. Run your opponent up and back, side to side. Use lobs and drop shots to wear her out. Hit into the open court and play balls crosscourt. Wrong-foot your opponent and hit it right at her to keep her hopping. Above all, keep the ball in play. If you try to hit low-percentage winners, you'll probably miss and you'll make it easy on your opponent. Better to plan for long rallies to keep her moving.

If your fitness is substantially superior, you can expect two things to happen. First, your opponent will not get to some balls or will swing poorly after running a long way for some shots. Then, as this starts to occur, she will panic and try to quickly put you away, launching low-percentage shots (which are even lower percentage because she's so tired). Either way, the tide can turn in your favor.

Of course, you have to stay close enough in the second set to come back and win it. And you'd better be right about your opponent's fitness. Don't wait too long for the letdown to occur. It's no help if you first see your opponent gasping for breath while serving for the match at 5-1 in the second set.

Better When Behind

You are down a break; stakes are high. Play lower percentages to break back.

Some players play better when they are down a few games. They relax and swing with less inhibition. Their confidence in their ability to come back is commendable, but when they are even in the score, or ahead, they choke.

It makes some sense. If you're down a break, you have to break back. You can't be content to hold serve the rest of the way. And so you'll play a more aggressive game, taking chances with some low-percentage shots when your opponent is serving. Some players prefer this wide-open style. They're risk takers by nature, so they're comfortable coming back to break serve. On the other hand, they get tired of the high-percentage play that's appropriate when nursing a lead. They're apt to force a bad shot or lose concentration out of sheer boredom.

If this describes you, try to change your paradigm of how you need to play. If the score is tied, pretend you're behind. Or set a goal of winning each set by two breaks, so you feel as if you're always coming back.

Also work on your high-percentage game. Long rallies don't have to be boring, if you sense the nuances of court position and ball controls. Work on gaining position gradually and controlling the rhythm of the point. That will help you play well even when you're not losing.

Pick Your Spots

You are playing game by game; the stakes vary. Vary your percentages.

This is one of the game's dirty little secrets: you don't have to play all-out on every point. I know no one likes to see a player tank it on any point, but sometimes it's not worth the effort. Say you're up a break in the second set. You won the first set in a 7-5 thriller, and you're getting tired. Your opponent is serving and it's 40-0. Now your opponent starts toying with you, running you back and forth in the court.

Sure, it's possible for you to come back to break serve in this game, but you probably won't. So why keep running, just to lose the next point, or the next? It's really not so bad if you lose this game and throw your energy into holding serve a few more times. If it's late or hot and your energy is limited, it might be wise to conserve your resources. Win the games you have to win (holding serve), and ease up a bit on others. The first three points of your opponent's serve are crucial. If you get at least one of them, then it's well worth fighting to grab this game. If you lose all three, then you have to check your resources and ask yourself how important this game is.

A similar situation might occur when you've won the first set and trail badly—say, 5-1—in the second. A comeback is possible, but it's unlikely. It might be better to start fresh in set three.

I'm not talking about hitting the ball intentionally into the net or letting a returnable serve ace you. I'm talking about deciding not to run for a well-executed drop shot or letting a topspin lob drift overhead without running back for it. The extra effort you normally expend just isn't worth it in these situations. If that doesn't sound right to you, try this: Go for broke in those not-worth-it situations. Hit low-percentage shots that might be winners, or they might be losers. Either way, they get the point over with quickly, so you can keep the match moving. If you're lucky, those shots might get you back in the game. If not, no big deal. Every point is important; some are just more important than others.

Steffi Graf loading up to unleash her weapon.

New Game

You are trailing badly; stakes are low. Keep the intensity with varied percentages.

You're overmatched. Or maybe it's just a bad day. You lost the first set 6-1 and you're down 4-0 in the second. Your opponent shows no signs of flagging. What can you do? Not much. Face it, you're probably not going to win. Hope springs eternal, but you haven't been able to do much yet.

Reset your expectations. Can you win one game before your opponent wins two? Can you win six more points? Can you return 10 of your opponent's killer serves? Can you rally the ball 10 times, even if you eventually lose the point? Just for a moment, pretend that you can play at your opponent's level. Try it, and see how long you can keep it up.

You're going to lose the match. But if you can come out of this experience with some sort of victory—setting short-term goals and reaching them—you can redeem a bad situation.

Down, But All Out

You are trailing badly; stakes are low. Try low-percentage winners.

It's the same situation I just described: pretty hopeless. Or maybe there is a distant hope. You're serving, down 4-1 in the second set, having lost the first 6-1. You could possibly crawl back into this one, but you'd better get busy.

Look at the bright side: you've got nothing to lose. You can try anything at this point and it can't get much worse. So use this opportunity to work on your game. Experiment with some shots you'd never try if the game were on the line—maybe you can get them to work. Guess at where your opponent will hit the ball. If you're wrong, so what? Challenge or attack at every opportunity that presents itself. Chalk it all up to learning and improving your game. You might find some new shots or tactics that you can use in future games. You also might jolt your opponent into making some errors. It's possible you could steal a few games with your crazy style of play and get back into this one.

Overcoming Your Fears

As you fine-tune your game, you'll face a variety of foes. Some will be far better than you; they'll be tough to play. They may embarrass you. As you approach a match with a top-seeded player, you'll be tempted to be afraid. Don't be.

As a certified ski instructor, I commonly see people who are fearful—especially beginning skiers riding the chairlift for the first time. What scares them the most? The fear of the unknown. They're headed to the top of what appears to be Mount Everest and they don't know what will happen when they get there.

How can you handle fear? Focus your attention on something not so threatening. I get rookie skiers to look around at the beautiful scenery, gazing across the hill, not down. Tennis players can do the same, focusing on their own play rather than the unknown skill of a much-hyped opponent. Use imagery before and during the match to keep your attention on positive matters. Discipline your mind to focus on the present moment. Don't try to guess the score of the match; at this point the score is still tied at love.

Remember, you know how to play. You have practiced a multitude of shots and combinations. Just get out there and play your game, whatever your opponent throws at you. Try not to think of yourself as an underdog, no matter what anyone says. Maybe your opponent will underestimate you, but you mustn't underestimate yourself. "The underdog usually does not win," Chuck Kriese points out in *Total Tennis Training* (p. 92). "To win, a player must perform as if he were the favorite."

Of course you don't want to underestimate your opponent either. Overconfidence quickly can turn things around.

Making the Commitment

How serious are you about tennis? How good do you want to become? Are you committed to improving your game? Do you have the time and dedication to complete what you start?

The serious player is, first of all, committed. That doesn't mean you have to spend every waking moment on the tennis court. It doesn't mean you jeopardize your family life or your career to win the next club championship. It means that you do fully what you set out to do and you're not satisfied with a partial effort. You practice hard during the time you've set aside for practice. You work hard when you need to work. You enjoy your family thoroughly when you spend time with them. And on the court, you play the best tennis you possibly can.

Commit yourself to a training regimen you can follow. Eat good foods and get good exercise to keep your body fit and speed up the recovery process for this grueling sport.

Commit yourself to a practice schedule you can follow. Once a week? Twice a week? Every day? That depends on your level, your time, and whatever else is going on in your life. In any case, make sure you're getting the maximum advantage from every hour of practice.

Commit yourself to proper match preparation, mentally, emotionally, and physically. Whatever level—pro, amateur, school, club, or just with friends—make sure you're as ready as you can be.

Commit yourself to playing well. Summon all your abilities to perform well on the court. Set performance goals. Use your SMARTS, develop your tactics, plan your strategies, and do your best to win. Yes, you can play tennis just for fun. Hitting the ball around is a nice workout, but then why bother to keep score? Winning isn't everything, but it ultimately is your goal in a serious match.

Alex Corretja, 1998 World Champion, keeps the game in perspective with his life.

Commit yourself to good sportsmanship. If you cheat, berate your opponent, or quit in disgust, you're leaving a piece of your soul on the court. Then how can you be a complete player? Be honest, full of integrity, friendly but focused. Be the kind of player others love to play because it's good, hard work in an arena of mutual respect.

Achieving Balance

The complete player is also balanced. I've known some tennis players who totally were immersed in tennis. Nothing else mattered. Frankly, these people weren't much fun to be around. I firmly believe that most players become better when they seek balance in their lives, when they aspire to excel in all areas of life—physical, mental, spiritual, and emotional.

Physically, you want to develop strength, flexibility, agility, and endurance. Obviously, these qualities will help you on the tennis court, but they also will help you live a long and healthy life. Develop your own personal fitness program, and then add the tennis-specific training I've recommended in this book.

Mentally, you want to be focused, challenged, disciplined, knowledgeable, and tough. I've spent several chapters in this book already detailing the mental discipline of the complete player. But this not only will help you on the court, it will enhance every aspect of your life. The ability to focus on the task at hand will help you in your business, whatever that is. The ability to perform under pressure pays off in a variety of circumstances.

Spiritually, you want to be at peace with yourself and with your god. You want to go through life feeling grateful, fulfilled, aware, humane, understanding, loving, and giving. Some would say that these qualities are irrelevant to tennis, but I beg to differ. When people step on the court with gaping holes in their souls, it hurts the way they play. To be a truly complete player, you must be a complete person, and spirituality—in a personally meaningful way to you—is a key part of that.

I keep coming back to the often-overlooked spiritual dimension. Stress expert Dr. James Loehr says, "You have to have a very powerful core of values and beliefs, and somehow you anchor these things to something that is much bigger than yourself. It may take the form of a very strong religious belief or it might go in any number of directions. There has to be an all-encompassing understanding of your life having some meaning that you go beyond who and what you are at this moment. Somehow it fits into a bigger picture.

I believe that there is a very strong need in each one of us to get in touch with that. I encourage athletes to try and make sense of it, because if what they are doing does not make sense in the much larger context of their lives and is not consistent with their deepest values and beliefs, then it is a stress that cannot be properly balanced. It tears away at them constantly, and they never really understand it."

As a coach, I too personally encourage players to ask themselves what they would like to achieve with their tennis 10 years from now. If they are youths, they often say they would like to be professional or play for a college. Adults usually want to do well in their leagues and in club matches, stay in good shape, and so on. Whatever the end objective is, work backward from your desired outcome to the present (see chapter 8 on setting goals). This will give you some realistic goals to try to achieve. Give yourself something to shoot for, and allow a timeline that encourages your development without putting unreasonable pressure on yourself. Then talk to people who have been successful at obtaining the objectives they have set for themselves: not just in tennis, but in all of life. Ask them what they did to make it.

Emotionally, you want to be competitive but in a healthy way. You want to be fired up, but not burned out. You want to accept the stress of a challenging tennis match without becoming overstressed. You want to handle the ups and downs of tennis (and of life) with maturity. You want to feel the joy of a game well played and of a life well lived.

Staying Connected

The complete player also is connected. Tennis itself may be an individual sport with the exception of doubles, but it requires a team of support personnel. What would you do without your friends, your family, your coaches and instructors? The complete player knows that he or she is not alone.

Top professional players frequently have entourages that travel with them, including managers, stringers, coaches, fitness specialists, and even massage therapists. Your budget may not allow you the luxury of having such a team with you, but you can develop relationships with other local players, teaching pros, friends in other sports, and even family sometimes, to support you through the challenging times. Just having someone to relate to, to share what you are experiencing on the court, can help a great deal.

Continuing the Journey to Completion

The complete player is, finally, complete. There's a sense that you know who you are, and you know the place tennis has in your life. You know your goals, but you're honest about your expectations. You have various markers along the way that you are trying to reach, but you know your life will go on even if you don't reach them.

Prioritize what is important to you and build tennis around it. Develop routines around your priorities and create a support structure of love that encourages you to excel. Those who have done this are complete players. They can handle the stress of tennis—and the stress of life—because they can place it in the context of the bigger picture.

Bibliography

Chu, D. 1998. *Jumping into plyometrics, 2nd ed.* Champaign, IL: Human Kinetics.

—. 1994. *Power tennis training.* Champaign, IL: Human Kinetics.

Dintiman, G.B., Ward, B. and T. Tellez. 1997. *Sports speed.* Champaign, IL: Human Kinetics.

Gallwey, W.T. 1997. *The inner game of tennis.* New York: Random House.

Gilbert, B., and S. Jamison. 1994. *Winning ugly: Mental warfare in tennis.* New York: Simon and Schuster.

Hobden, B., Gonzalez, P. and N. Bollettieri. 1992. *Five keys of tennis.* Bradenton, FL: Manatee.

Jacobson. 1993. *Sport science for tennis.* White Plains, NY: USTA.

Kriese, C. 1997. *Coaching tennis.* Chicago: NTC Contemporary.

Loehr, J.E. 1995. *The new toughness training for sports: Mental, emotional, and physical conditioning from one of the world's premier sports psychologists.* New York: Putnum.

Loehr, J.E, and M. McCormack. 1998. *Stress for success.* New York: Random House.

Roetert, P. and Ellenbecker, eds. 1998. *Complete conditioning for tennis.* Champaign, IL: Human Kinetics.

Tantalo, V. 1986. *USA tennis course: 500 visual ways to better tennis.* Orlando, FL: USA Pub.

Index

Note: Page numbers in italic indicate photographs or illustrations; those in boldface indicate tables.